OECD Pensions Outlook 2016

OECD
BETTER POLICIES FOR BETTER LIVES

Please cite this publication as:
OECD (2016), *OECD Pensions Outlook 2016*, OECD Publishing, Paris.
http://dx.doi.org/10.1787/pens_outlook-2016-en

ISBN 978-92-64-26519-6 (print)
ISBN 978-92-64-26520-2 (PDF)
ISBN 978-92-64-26602-5 (epub)

Series:
ISSN 2313-7630 (print)
ISSN 2313-7649 (online)

Photo credits: Cover © Thinkstock – simoningate.

Corrigenda to OECD publications may be found on line at: *www.oecd.org/publishing/corrigenda*.

Foreword

This third edition of the OECD Pensions Outlook *provides an analysis of different pension policy issues in OECD countries covering both public and private pension systems.*

This report is the joint work of staff of the Financial Affairs Division of the OECD Directorate for Financial and Enterprise Affairs and the Social Policy Division of the OECD Directorate for Employment, Labour and Social Affairs. It has benefited from contributions from national government delegates, particularly delegates to the Committee for Financial Markets, the Insurance and Private Pensions Committee, the Working Party on Private Pensions and the Working Party on Social Policy. The views expressed here do not necessarily correspond to those of the national authorities concerned.

The editorial team for this report was led by Pablo Antolin. Chapter 1 was prepared by Romain Despalins and Pablo Antolin; Chapter 2 by Stéphanie Payet and Pablo Antolin; Chapters 3 and 4 by Jessica Mosher and Pablo Antolin; Chapter 5 by Chiara Monticone and Flore-Anne Messy; and Chapter 6 by Andrew Reilly and Hervé Boulhol. The editorial team would like to thank Ole Beier, Emmy Labovitch, and Dariusz Stanko for their insightful discussions and comments; and Sally Day-Hanotiaux for all her support. Editorial and communication support was provided by Pauline Arbel, Pamela Duffin, Kate Lancaster and Edward Smiley.

Financial help from various institutions is gratefully acknowledged. This publication has been produced with the financial assistance of the European Union. The view expressed herein can in no way be taken to reflect the official opinion of the European Union. The research on private pensions contained in this publication has also benefited from the financial support of Allianz Asset Management, International Pensions and Allianz Global Investors, Principal International Group, and Pruco Life Insurance Company.

Monika Queisser and Stefano Scarpetta of the Directorate for Employment, Labour and Social Affairs, and Adrian Blundell-Wignall, André Laboul, and Pierre Poret of the Directorate for Financial and Enterprise Affairs provided useful advice and feedback.

Table of contents

Tables

Figures

Follow OECD Publications on:

http://twitter.com/OECD_Pubs

http://www.facebook.com/OECDPublications

http://www.linkedin.com/groups/OECD-Publications-4645871

http://www.youtube.com/oecdilibrary

http://www.oecd.org/oecddirect/

This book has...

StatLinks

A service that delivers Excel® files from the printed page!

Look for the *StatLinks* at the bottom of the tables or graphs in this book. To download the matching Excel® spreadsheet, just type the link into your Internet browser, starting with the *http://dx.doi.org* prefix, or click on the link from the e-book edition.

Editorial
Pensions systems continue to adapt to the challenges they face

Population ageing, the financial and economic crisis as well as the current environment of low growth and low interest rates pose fundamental and far-reaching challenges to pension systems. They increase financial pressure on defined benefit (DB) pension arrangements, which translates into fiscal difficulties for pay-as-you-go (PAYG) financed public pension arrangements, and strains on solvency for funded DB pension arrangements. Defined contribution (DC) pension arrangements in which individuals bear many of the risks of saving for retirement will see reductions in the retirement income they are able to deliver.

Pension systems are responding to these challenges. After far-reaching reforms during past decades, PAYG financed public pensions in many countries are now on more financially sustainable ground. These reforms have also made some progress on adequacy, especially for low income socio-economic groups, but substantial gaps remain in several countries. Simultaneously, pension arrangements in which assets back pension benefits have grown in importance, contributing to diversification of sources to finance retirement and complementing public pensions. In particular, arrangements with a more direct and straightforward link between contributions and benefits (DC) are becoming more prominent. As a result, individuals now have to make retirement decisions and bear the risks associated with saving for retirement, such as investment and longevity, which could result in shortfalls in retirement income. This is in contrast with DB pension arrangements in which employers or the State, bear those risks.

These developments call for improving the regulatory framework governing funded private pensions. The OECD Council has recently approved the Core Principles of Private Pension Regulation, which have been endorsed by pension regulators across OECD countries. The Core Principles cover all types of funded pension arrangements and strengthen the regulatory framework to make sure that funded pension arrangements work in the best interest of members, both those saving for retirement and current retirees. Regulatory restrictions to pension funds' ability to diversify risks and improve returns by investing abroad are being further relaxed in a number of countries, consistent with long-standing advice by the OECD, including the Codes of Liberalisation of Capital Movements.

PAYG pensions reforms, coupled with the growth of DC pension arrangements, have led to concerns about whether pension systems will be able to deliver pension benefits that people would consider adequate to finance retirement. In this context, improving the design of DC pension arrangements would contribute to delivering better pension outcomes.

Most OECD countries have in place different tax treatments for retirement savings than for other savings in order to encourage people to save for retirement. This different tax treatment provides an immediate tax advantage to individuals as contributions are exempt from tax. Analysis in this Outlook goes further and shows that there is also an overall tax advantage for individuals over their life cycle, including both their working and retirement periods. Matching contributions and flat-rate subsidies will smooth out the tax advantage across the income scale.

Individuals in DC pension arrangements have to make essential decisions about managing their retirement. Those decisions include where and how to invest, when to retire, and how to allocate their retirement wealth to finance their years in retirement. In this context, integral components of a policy framework to improve retirement outcomes include: the quality, affordability and accessibility of retirement financial advice; the availability and sustainability of annuity products that protect individuals from longevity risk; and improvements in financial knowledge.

Policy makers need to ensure that people receive financial advice for retirement that is appropriate for their needs and that potential conflicts of interest of financial advisors are addressed. Working together, policy makers and the pension industry need to make sure that policies do not reduce the accessibility and affordability of financial advice – so called the advice gap –, particularly for people with low to moderate wealth. Technology-based advice has the potential to reduce any possible advice gap.

Life annuity products, i.e. insurance contracts that ensure lifelong benefit payments, protect people against the risk of outliving their financial resources in retirement. The OECD Roadmap for the Good Design of DC Pension Plans recommends partial annuitisation of accumulated assets, combining deferred life annuities that protect against the tail risk of longevity with drawdown programmes that provide flexibility and choice for individuals. However, this requires the sustainability of annuity products and their suitability for consumers. Both can be achieved by having a coherent pension framework to accommodate life annuities, comprehensive product disclosures, and a regulatory framework based on principles that allow for flexibility in capital requirements to adjust to changing product designs and that encourage appropriate risk management.

Policy makers also need to provide tools and mechanisms for individuals to make informed choices. National financial education strategies should ensure that people acquire at least basic financial skills. Financial education initiatives for retirement planning should take into account the extent of retirement planning challenges associated with different national pension systems and their structure, and with the financial environment. Governments and other stakeholders should ensure that information about pension systems, pension reforms, and private pension plans is available, clear and not overwhelming for individuals. Moreover, the information should be comparable and standardised.

Unifying pension schemes, covering private-sector and public-sector workers in a financially sustainable way, would also improve both equity and economic efficiency. Many of the original rationales for civil service pension arrangements are less relevant now, and recent reforms have brought the pension systems of many civil servants into line with those of the private sector. As a result, only a limited number of OECD countries maintain entirely separate schemes. Their implementation is often gradual though, which implies some legacy cost for the future.

In light of the challenges facing pension systems, the only long-term solution for achieving higher retirement income is to contribute more and for longer periods. Future work and policy discussions need to focus on how to achieve both.

Pierre Poret,
Director, OECD Directorate
for Financial and Enterprise Affairs

Stefano Scarpetta,
Director, OECD Directorate
for Employment, Labour and Social Affairs

Executive summary

Pension systems across OECD countries are still addressing the challenges posed by population ageing, the financial and economic crisis and the economic environment of low growth and low interest rates. This Outlook continues the OECD exploration of how pension systems are responding to these challenges.

The nature of funded private pension provision is changing, defined contribution (DC) and personal pension arrangements are growing in importance

The challenges facing pension systems have led to reforms that have increased the diversity of pension arrangements across OECD countries and the importance of arrangements in which assets back pension benefits, especially DC ones, in which pension benefits are linked to the value of assets accumulated. DC pension arrangements provide a clear, straightforward link between contributions and benefits, but put most risks (e.g. investment and longevity) onto individuals, and make them more responsible for managing their retirement.

To understand this changing landscape and distinguish among different pension arrangements, it is important to look at their characteristics: whether they are mandatory, how pension benefits are financed, who manages them, the role of the employer, the link between contributions and benefits, and who bears the risks.

The Outlook also considers the policy context of these changes, finding them to be in line with the main OECD messages about diversifying the sources to finance retirement, and the complementary role of funded pensions. The growing weight of DC arrangements makes it imperative to improve their design in line with the OECD Roadmap for the Good Design of DC Pension Plans. What follows discusses some of those policy guidelines.

In most OECD countries, the tax treatment of retirement savings provides a tax advantage when people save for retirement

Most countries have a preferential tax treatment of retirement savings to encourage people to save for retirement. Calculating the amount that an individual would save in taxes paid by contributing to a private pension plan instead of putting the same amount into an alternative savings vehicle suggests that the tax treatment of retirement savings does indeed provide a tax advantage. The size of the overall tax advantage varies, however. Flat-rate subsidies and matching contributions can be used to target tax advantages at low-income individuals or to smooth out the tax advantage across the income scale. Tax advantages can encourage people to save for longer periods, but not necessarily to save more. Straightforward and simple tax rules may increase people's confidence and help to increase participation in and contributions to private pension plans.

Policy makers need to ensure that consumers receive appropriate financial advice for retirement

Measures are needed to address financial advisers' conflicts of interest and to help to ensure that consumers receive financial advice for retirement that is appropriate for their needs. Such measures can potentially lead to an advice gap, however, reducing the availability and affordability of advice, particularly for consumers with low to moderate retirement wealth. Technology-based advice has the potential to increase the accessibility and affordability of advice and to overcome the behavioural biases of advisors. However, policy makers need to ensure that there is regulation in place so that the same level of consumer protection is provided.

Policy makers need to ensure the sustainability of annuity products and their suitability for consumers

Annuity products can play an important role in helping individuals mitigate investment and longevity risks. Nevertheless, these products and their associated guarantees present challenges. The lack of consistency with respect to what is meant by an annuity product and the terminology used to describe the different types of products calls for defining a common language. A coherent framework for retirement is needed to accommodate and encourage the use of annuity products. Increased product complexity, however, highlights the need for appropriate financial advice and comprehensible product disclosures to ensure that consumers purchase products suitable for their needs. The regulatory framework should put in place tools for managing risk and the incentives to do so, in order to encourage appropriate risk management by annuity providers. Approaches based on principles are better suited than static formulas, as they enable capital requirements to adapt to changing product designs, ensuring sufficient capital to back the annuity liabilities and to guarantee their sustainability.

Well-designed financial education can improve people's financial knowledge, attitudes and skills for retirement, and can help decision making

Low financial literacy poses serious challenges, as individuals are increasingly responsible for managing their own retirement wealth. Financial education initiatives for retirement planning should be implemented, taking into account national circumstances and the extent of retirement planning challenges due to the features of different national pension systems and of the financial environment. Governments and other stakeholders should ensure that information about pension systems, pension reforms, and private pension plans is available, clear and not overwhelming for individuals. Information about costs, performance, service quality, investment allocation and risk level should be comparable and standardised. Information regarding all of an individual's pension plans should be combined and pension statements should be complemented with calculators/ simulators in order to maximise the impact of information. There should be national financial education strategies to ensure people are able to acquire general financial skills. Additionally, practical tools for policy makers exist, such as a matrix of financial education needs and tools to support retirement decision making, and a checklist.

Most OECD countries have been aligning the pension systems for civil servants and private sector workers

In half of OECD countries, civil servants' future pension promises measured in terms of replacement rates are 20 percentage points higher for a full career than those of the private sector. This includes in Belgium, France, Germany and Korea, which maintain separate sector pension systems. Legacy costs exist in another quarter of those OECD countries that have aligned their pension systems since the 1990s. An integrated pension framework covering all workers identically might yield benefits in various dimensions. On the equity side, it is difficult to argue today that civil servants/public sector workers require higher income replacement in retirement than their private sector counterparts. On the efficiency side, there are significant economies of scale in managing unified pension systems, for example in contribution collection, recordkeeping and benefit payment. Moreover, restraining labour mobility across sectors (e.g. vested periods or limited portability) is inefficient, introducing rigidities in individual career management and restricting workers' capacity to adapt to sectorial shifts and new employment opportunities. A common pension scheme would make such choices easier and facilitate labour mobility.

Chapter 1

The changing pensions landscape: The growing importance of pension arrangements in which assets back pension benefits

The pensions landscape has changed in recent decades. All OECD countries have to varying degrees a combination of different pension arrangements to provide retirement income. This chapter first suggests a means for understanding and differentiating between the characteristics of different pension arrangements. Then, focusing on those pension arrangements in which assets back pension benefits, the chapter documents their growing importance over the last 15 years. The growth of pension arrangements in which pension benefits are linked to the amount of assets accumulated is also highlighted. Given these trends, the chapter discusses the advantages and disadvantages of defined benefit and defined contribution pension arrangements and ends with the main OECD policy messages.

The statistical data for Israel are supplied by and under the responsibility of the relevant Israeli authorities. The use of such data by the OECD is without prejudice to the status of the Golan Heights, East Jerusalem and Israeli settlements in the West Bank under the terms of international law.

The landscape of pension arrangements across OECD countries has changed substantially in recent decades. On the one hand, fiscal sustainability problems in public pension arrangements have led to a series of reforms that have reduced the benefits they provide.[1] On the other hand, pension arrangements in which contributions are used to build assets to finance future pension benefits have grown in importance. Simultaneously, there has been an increase in the importance of pension arrangements in which individuals bear most of the risks linked to saving for retirement (e.g. longevity, investment) as opposed to pension arrangements in which the employer or the State bear the risks associated with pension promises.

The purpose of this chapter is to assess this changing landscape and present the OECD's main pension policy messages. This first requires understanding the different types of pension arrangements and their distinguishing characteristics. Secondly, given the increased importance of pension arrangements in which assets back pension benefits, the chapter then focuses on those arrangements and documents its evolution over time.

The chapter first discusses several characteristics of the different types of pension arrangements that can be used to distinguish among them and understand them. It highlights that all countries have to varying degrees a combination of different arrangements to provide retirement income. The chapter then presents empirical evidence of the growing importance of pension arrangements in which assets back pension benefits over the last 15 years for OECD countries, including the split between defined benefit and defined contribution pension arrangements. It then discusses the advantages and disadvantages of DB and DC pension arrangements. The chapter ends with the main OECD pension policy messages.

1.1. Pension arrangements across OECD countries

This section discusses the characteristics that distinguish the different types of pension arrangements and that can be used to understand them. It also provides evidence on the growing importance of pension arrangements in which assets back pension benefits across OECD countries.

Characteristics to distinguish different types of pension arrangements

Different types of pension arrangements have different characteristics.[2] These characteristics allow one to understand and distinguish among them. Pension arrangements differ according to:

1. Whether they are mandatory or voluntary
2. How pension benefits are financed
3. Who manages the pension arrangement
4. The role of the employer in those pension arrangements
5. The link between pension contributions and pension benefits.
6. Who bears the risks

Whether the pension arrangement is mandatory or voluntary

Pension arrangements can be mandatory or voluntary for different parties: the provider, the employer and/or for members. They can be mandatory or voluntary with respect to participation, contributions, and setting up the plan. Pension arrangements provided by the State (e.g. public pensions, social security) are generally mandatory for workers. Pension plans in which employers automatically enrol their employees are generally mandatory for the employer but voluntary for employees (e.g. New Zealand, the United Kingdom). Arrangements based on individual accounts can also be mandatory for individuals (e.g. Chile, Sweden) or voluntary (e.g. Riester in Germany, KiwiSaver in New Zealand). Contributions can be voluntary for the individual but mandatory for the employer (e.g. Australia). Pension arrangements that people can contract out with insurance companies or banks are generally voluntary.

How pension benefits are financed

Pension arrangements also differ on whether pension benefits are financed using current contributions or assets accumulated. The former are referred to as pay-as-you-go (PAYG) pension arrangements, and the later as funded pension arrangements.

Who manages the pension arrangement

The public sector or the private sector can manage different types of pension arrangements. Those managed by the public sector (public pensions or social security) are generally PAYG and mandatory. Pension arrangements managed by the private sector are generally funded, and they may be either mandatory or voluntary. Pension arrangements for public sector employees sometimes have assets backing pension payments (e.g. the United Kingdom and the United States) or they are PAYG (e.g. most European countries).[3]

It is also important to consider the institutional framework. Private pension arrangements can be structured to leave more choice and decision-making to individuals or can be structured around large scale multi-employer platforms or schemes that may allow them to take advantage of economies of scale. Institutional frameworks structured around more individual choice can also rely on collective platforms.

The role of the employer

The role of the employer in setting up pension arrangements is a distinguishing feature, especially for pension arrangements managed by the private sector. Traditionally, pension arrangements are split between occupational and personal. Occupational pension arrangements are those in which the access point is through the employer, who sets up the pension plan and has an influence on its design. Occupational pension arrangements include employer-sponsored plans and plans where employers are responsible for making up any shortfall in the plan's ability to pay benefits. Personal plans are all other types of pension arrangements.[4]

Personal plans include pension arrangements which are linked to an employment or professional activity but the employer only plays an administrative role (e.g. record keeping, collection of contributions). Such arrangements can be the main source individuals have to finance retirement, and can be either mandatory (e.g. in Chile and Mexico) or voluntary (e.g. KiwiSaver in New Zealand). Personal pension arrangements also include all those arrangements in which the employer plays no role.

The link between pension contributions and pension benefits

Pension arrangements can also differ on how pension benefits are determined. Pension benefits can be determined according to a formula such as defined benefit (DB) pension arrangements in which benefits are calculated with respect to the number of contributing years and salary. Alternatively, there are pension arrangements in which there is a close link between pension contributions and pension benefits such as in defined contribution (DC) pension arrangements in which benefits depend on the level of assets accumulated.

The "hard" pension benefit guarantees involved in traditional final-salary DB pension arrangements have been changing into soft guarantees (e.g. defined ambition) in which risks (e.g. longevity, investment, benefit shortfalls) are shared between different stakeholders – members, employers, providers.

Who bears the risks

Finally, pension arrangements also differ on who bears the risks involved in saving for retirement – e.g. longevity, investment – and who has to make up for any pension benefit shortfall. The employer (the State when it is the employer) bears the risks in employer-sponsored DB plans. Pension providers bear the risks in pension arrangements in which benefits depend on assets accumulated and include guarantees. Individuals bear the risks in pure DC pension arrangements. Finally, the tax-payer bears those risks that affect financing retirement in PAYG public pensions or Social Security.

Pension arrangements across OECD countries

All OECD countries exhibit a combination of the different types of pension arrangements. They all have voluntary and mandatory pension arrangements; PAYG and funded pensions; public and private management; occupational and personal plans; DB and DC promises. What changes is the weight of each component in overall total retirement income.

All countries have non-contributory public pension arrangements as part of the old-age safety net – social assistance or universal pensions. These can be means-tested, universal, or targeted to certain groups. Contributions to public pension arrangements are sometimes used to finance non-contributory pensions. The OECD recommendation since the 1990s has been to finance non-contributory pensions fully out of general taxation (OECD, 1998).

Most countries have a contributory component PAYG-financed public pension, in which current pensions are financed with the current workers' contributions. In exchange people contributing today accumulate future pension rights. Some countries (e.g. France, Spain and the United States) have been accumulating surpluses in contributory pensions (current contributions are greater than current pension benefit disbursements) in an earmarked fund (e.g. Social Security or public pension reserve funds) in order to finance future needs when contributions will be lower than pension payments.

All OECD countries have funded pensions in which assets back pension benefits. They can be mandatory or voluntary, occupational or personal, DB or DC, and the employer may or may not guarantee, fully or partially, any shortfalls between promises and the value of assets backing those promises. Occupational defined benefit plans are either mandatory (e.g. Korea, the Netherlands) or voluntary (e.g. Canada, Germany, Japan, the United Kingdom and the United States). Occupational defined contribution plans are either mandatory (e.g. Australia;

Hong Kong, China, Korea, Singapore; Sweden and Turkey), voluntary (e.g. Canada, France, Germany, Japan, Poland, the Slovak Republic and the United States), or auto-enrolment (e.g. Italy, New Zealand, the United Kingdom and the United States). Personal plans can be mandatory (e.g. Chile, Mexico) or voluntary (e.g. Czech Republic, KiwiSaver in New Zealand and IRAs in the United States). All countries have voluntary funded personal pension plans.

While all countries have asset backed pension arrangements in one or another form, their coverage and their importance vary substantially from one jurisdiction to another.

Trends in funded pension arrangements

The role of funded private pension arrangements in which assets back pension benefits is quite significant in several OECD countries and has been growing over time. Figure 1.1 shows the importance of funded pension arrangements by looking at the ratio of total assets accumulated in private funded pension arrangements relative to the size of their respective economy.

Figure 1.1 **The growing importance of funded pension arrangements**

(Total assets as a % of GDP in OECD Countries, 2000-15)

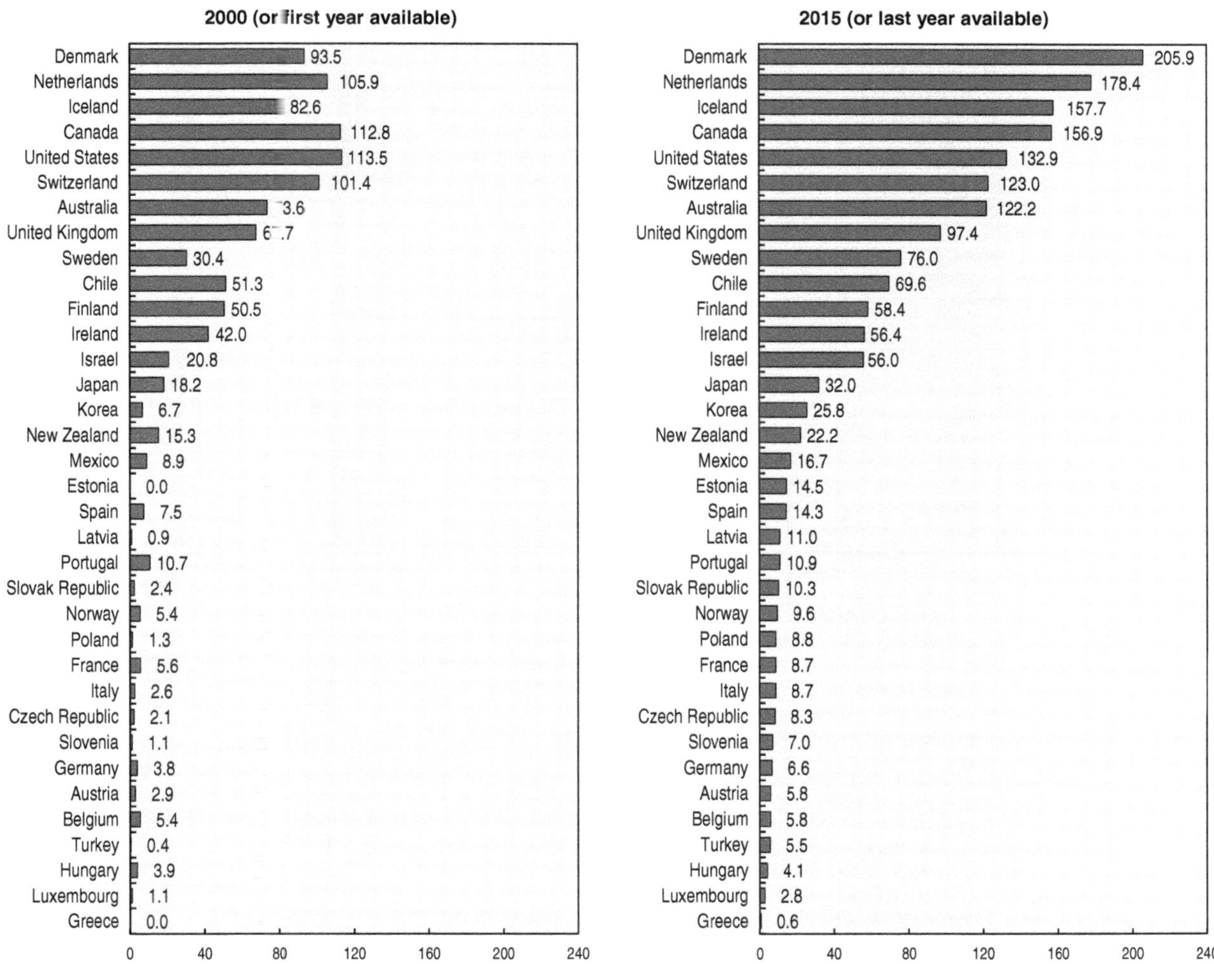

Notes: The data appendix in Annex 1.A2 provides specifics details on the data for each country. Please refer also to the *OECD Pension Markets in Focus 2016*.

Source: OECD Global Pension Statistics.

StatLink http://dx.doi.org/10.1787/888933426762

The ratio of assets to GDP in funded private pensions has increased in all OECD countries in the period from 2000 to 2015. Assets in funded pension arrangements were more than 50% of GDP in 10 OECD countries in the early 2000s and in 13 countries at the end of 2015. The number of countries where assets in funded private pension arrangements represent more than 100% of GDP has increased from 4 to 7 OECD countries over the last 15 years.

However, this is not a full picture of the potential role of funded pension arrangements. The current situation as regards accumulated pension savings is a function of past policies and it does not capture the long term effects of recent reforms and current policies. Some countries will experience further increases in pension savings over coming decades due to the maturation of relatively recent savings programs, increased coverage and/or increased contribution rates. Figure 1.2 supplements the information in Figure 1.1 by providing an assessment of the future retirement income mix in the first year of retirement for current workers aged 35 to 64 in 6 OECD countries. By doing so, the figure illustrates the potential role of funded private pensions in the retirement readiness of working-age individuals in these selected OECD countries (OECD, 2014a).

Figure 1.2. **Average composition of potential pension income at retirement**

As a % of total pension income

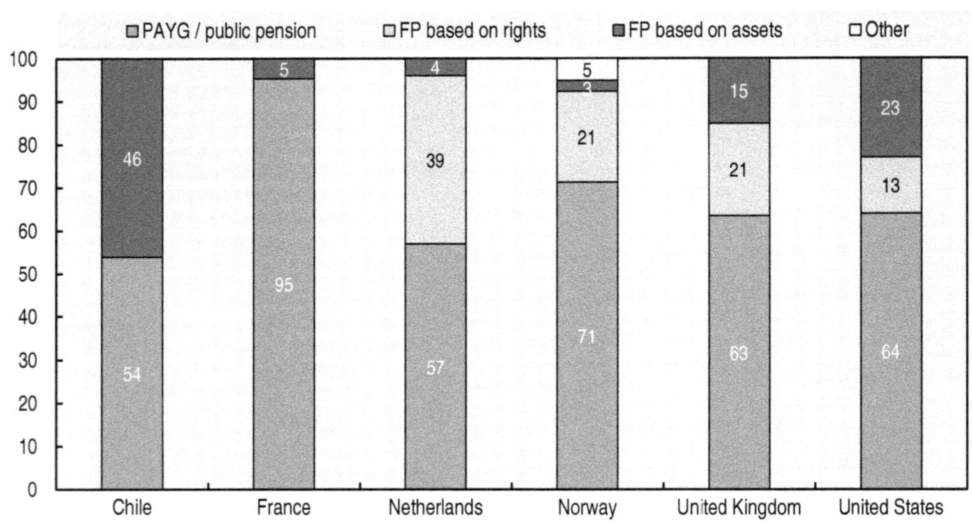

Notes: FP stands for funded pensions.

Source: *OECD Pensions Outlook 2014*, Chapter 3.

StatLink http://dx.doi.org/10.1787/888933426775

The importance of funded private pensions in the overall retirement income will also vary across different countries. In countries such as Chile, the Netherlands, the United Kingdom and the United States, funded private pension arrangements will be an important complementary component in the retirement income of individuals.

1.2. Defined benefit and defined contribution pension arrangements

The increasing importance of funded private pension arrangements across OECD countries has been accompanied by the growth of DC pension arrangements. This section looks at the evolution of DB and DC pension arrangements and discusses the potential advantages and disadvantages of each.

Evolution of DB and DC pension arrangements

Changes in the amount of assets and members in DB and DC pension arrangements provide evidence of their evolution and shifting relative importance. The analysis herein considers all types of pension plans (mandatory or voluntary, occupational or personal) irrespective of the pension plan provider (pension funds, insurance companies, employers or other providers). The analysis also covers plans for both public sector and private sector workers as long as they are funded. It uses the data contained in the OECD Global Pension Statistics to assess the evolution of DB and DC plans.[5] The definitions of occupational and personal, DB and DC plans used are those of the official OECD taxonomy (see the data appendix).[6] Finally, the analysis extends the coverage of previous studies on the subject to include more OECD countries and it uses data from 2000 to 2015.[7]

Data on assets and members in DB and DC plans from 2000 to 2015 confirm the increasing prominence of DC plans in many OECD countries. To the extent new schemes have been introduced in recent decades, they have almost entirely been DC schemes and in some countries the contribution rates applied in existing DC schemes (e.g. Australia and Denmark) have increased. In some countries where DB plans have been running for several decades (e.g. the Netherlands and the United States), the total value of assets in DB plans continues to grow but at a slower pace than assets in DC plans. This increasing importance of DC oriented pension arrangements follows different paths depending on the country. For instance, DB pension arrangements can sometimes be closed to all members and assets in DB plans can stop accruing; or they can just be closed to new members. Legislative reforms replacing DB with DC arrangements for new members have encouraged a rapid transformation of the pension system in some countries.

DB plans in 2015

Occupational DB arrangements still represented a significant part of the pensions landscape in the OECD in 2015, especially in terms of assets. Table 1.1 provides an overview of the aggregated values of assets and members in 2015 in occupational DB, occupational DC and personal plans.

DB plans were present in most OECD countries in 2015. In 2015, 26 OECD countries had assets and members in DB funded pension arrangements. Nine countries mostly from Eastern and Central Europe had no DB funded pension arrangements – Chile, the Czech Republic, Estonia, Greece, Hungary, Latvia, Poland, the Slovak Republic and Slovenia. Most of these countries introduced funded pension arrangements recently and DC only. In some other countries the coverage and overall importance of DB funded pension arrangements is limited (e.g. Denmark, France, Italy, New Zealand).

Assets in occupational DB plans still exceeded those of occupational DC plans in 2015 in most countries with DB plans. The split of assets in occupational pension plans between DB and DC plans was available for 22 of the 26 countries with DB plans in 2015 (Table 1). Assets in DB plans in these countries amounted to USD 13.1 trillion, while assets in occupational DC plans were worth USD 7.9 trillion. The difference is largely accounted for by the United States and the United Kingdom. Private pension funds, state and local government employee retirement funds and federal government retirement funds in the United States held more assets in DB plans than in DC plans which include the 401(k) plans. Occupational registered pension plans in Canada also recorded a bigger amount of DB assets than DC assets in 2015.

Table 1.1. **Private pension assets and members by type of pension plan in the OECD, in 2015**

	Assets (in USD m.)			Members (in thousands)		
	Occupational DB plans	Occupational DC plans	Personal plans	Occupational DB plans	Occupational DC plans	Personal plans
Australia	142 946	452 893	887 106	..	..	14 809
Austria	..	..	..	..	..	..
Belgium	23 554	4 735	..	568	909	..
Canada	1 338 469	105 092	804 983	5 160	1 097	5 974
Chile	x	..	154 711	x	..	10 811
Czech Republic	x	x	15 028	x	x	4 803
Denmark	8 759	523 632	66 184	15	4 783	812
Estonia	x	x	3 226	x	x	677
Finland	118 783	786	13 336	..	..	..
France	39 008	164 339	23 025	884	10 689	2 614
Germany	218 473	x	..	9 318	x	..
Greece	x	1 236	..	x	112	..
Hungary	x	..	4 819	x	..	1 209
Iceland	6 049	16 750	3 851	189	880	239
Ireland	78 169	47 903	5 674	126	282	..
Israel	108 906	x	56 322	790	x	4 475
Italy	10 236	101 606	43 145	160	3 448	4 090
Japan	..	..	..	..	..	..
Korea	74 703	34 170	234 443	3 735	2 467	17 355
Latvia	x	67	2 849	x	13	1 497
Luxembourg	1 275	215	..	11	4	..
Mexico	26 587	1 678	147 675	1 131	263	47 784
Netherlands	..	..	..	5 110	355	..
New Zealand	6 984	10 141	22 663	99	165	2 422
Norway	34 210	..	..	5 209	..	1 155
Poland	x	2 736	37 734	x	393	17 988
Portugal	16 295	2 984	2 009	187	149	297
Slovak Republic	x	x	8 750	x	x	2 079
Slovenia	x	..	..	x	..	..
Spain	69 923	9 795	88 327	8 440	1 662	9 249
Sweden	56 633	157 369	116 446	..	..	7 619
Switzerland	793 201	x	..	4 923	x	..
Turkey	19 431	1 880	15 886	1 081	550	5 568
United Kingdom	1 923 951	49 850	..	10 973	6 931	..
United States	7 985 785	6 263 961	9 604 933	72 577	95 379	52 392

Note: "x" means not applicable; ".." means not available. The table shows the aggregate amount of assets (in USD millions) and members (in thousands) of occupational DB, occupational DC and personal plans in 2015 (or the latest year available). In some countries, individuals may be members of several pension plans (e.g. in Australia, Canada, Iceland, Italy, Korea, or Norway). The aggregated number of members may therefore include the same individuals several times, and cannot be used to calculate a coverage ratio. For specific detail on the data for each country, please refer to the appendix in Annex 1.A2.
Source: OECD Global Pension Statistics and national sources.

StatLink http://dx.doi.org/10.1787/888933430319

However, assets in occupational DC plans together with those in personal plans exceeded assets in DB plans in most reporting countries. In the United States, assets in personal plans (mainly IRAs) were higher than those in DB plans. Only in Canada, Finland, Ireland, Israel, Portugal and Turkey DB plans represented more than 50% of the total reported assets of the funded pension system in 2015.

Occupational DB plans also have more members than occupational DC plans in several reporting countries. The number of members by type of plan is not available for as many countries as the breakdown of assets. However, available data show that there were more members in occupational DB plans than in occupational DC plans in at least nine OECD countries, namely Canada, Korea, Luxembourg, Mexico, the Netherlands, Portugal, Spain, Turkey and the United Kingdom.

The decline in the importance of DB plans, 2000-15

The amount of assets in DC pension arrangements and the number of people with DC accounts have grown by more than the amount of assets and the number of members in DB pensions in several OECD countries. Indeed, Figure 1.3 shows that assets and/or members in DC plans have grown in the period from 2000 to 2015 in 10 out of 16 OECD countries with assets representing more than 15% of GDP, for which the OECD GPS data are available.

The amount of assets in DB pension arrangements and the number of people in DB plans have evolved differently in different countries. Assets in DB plans either experienced a decline (Israel), remained broadly constant while assets increased in DC plans (Australia, Iceland, Mexico and Sweden); or increased but at a slower pace than assets in DC plans (e.g. the Netherlands, New Zealand and the United States).[8] Canada and Switzerland have both experienced an increase in assets in DB and in the case of Canada an increase that outpaced that of occupational DC pension arrangements.

The number of people with DB pension arrangements has decreased as well and this trend is more prevalent than the decrease in assets. Only Switzerland experienced a sizeable increase in members in DB pension arrangements over the period 2000-15, members in DB arrangements in Canada and the United States also increased but at a slower pace. All countries in Figure 1.3 but Canada experienced a larger increase in members of DC pension arrangements.

Potential reasons behind the different evolution of DB pension arrangements in OECD countries

The growing importance of DC pension arrangements and the relative decline in some countries of DB arrangements can be attributed to various factors. These include the challenges that DB plan sponsors face in partially or fully covering any shortfall between pension liabilities and pension assets, and the impact of legislative reforms in speeding up the closure of DB arrangements and encouraging savings in DC arrangements. Flexibility in adjusting sponsors' requirements regarding DB arrangements may explain why certain countries have not experienced a similar relative decline in DB arrangements (e.g. Canada, the Netherlands and Switzerland).

Challenges for DB plan sponsors that may lead to the closing of DB plans

Employers that sponsor DB plans are responsible for ensuring their funding. Therefore, employers are exposed to all the risks that can lead to either a reduction in the assets of the plan or an increase in its liabilities. These risks include investment risk, risks related to falling interest rates, and longevity risk.

Employers bear the investment or market risk in DB plans. If investments by DB plans perform poorly, as was the case of equities during the financial crisis, investment income may be lower than expected. A financial market downturn can therefore reduce the amount of assets held in DB plans. The 2008 financial crisis led to a decrease in the total amount of assets held in pension plans and deteriorated the funding of DB pension plans (OECD, 2015a).

Figure 1.3. **Evolution of DB and DC pension arrangements in OECD countries according to assets (millions national currency) and members (thousands)**

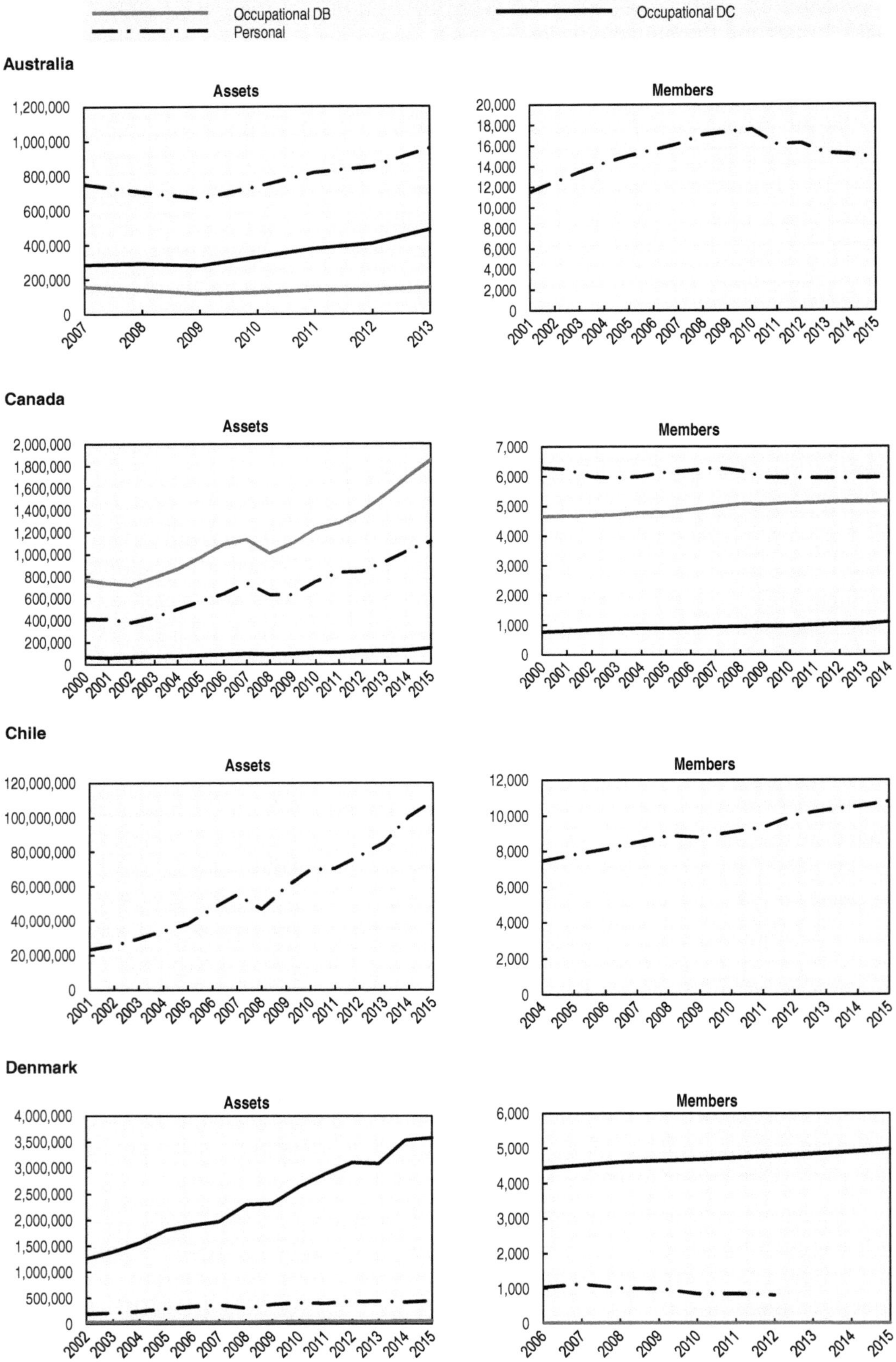

Figure 1.3. **Evolution of DB and DC pension arrangements in OECD countries according to assets (millions national currency) and members (thousands)** *(cont.)*

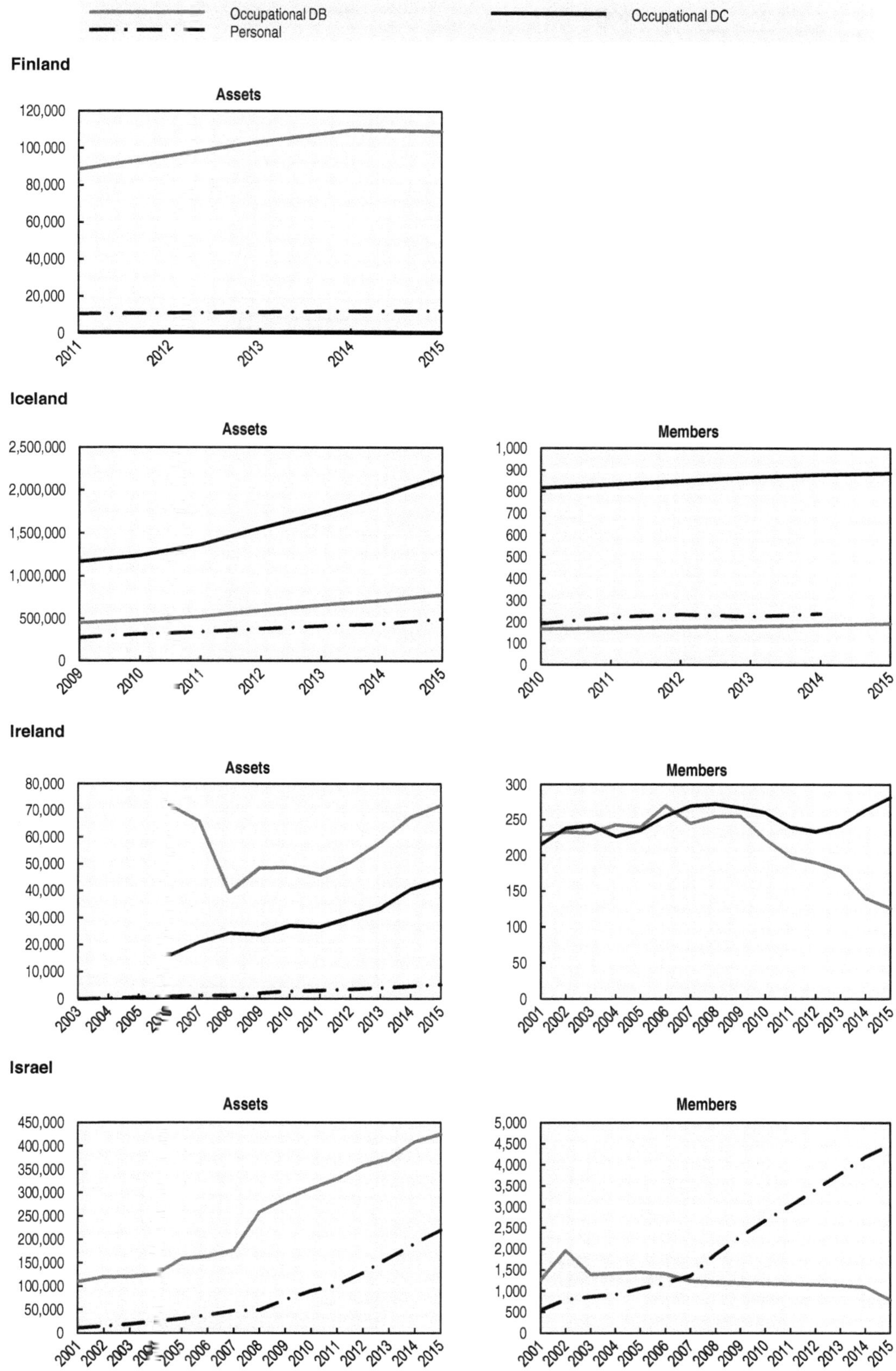

Figure 1.3. **Evolution of DB and DC pension arrangements in OECD countries according to assets (millions national currency) and members (thousands)** *(cont.)*

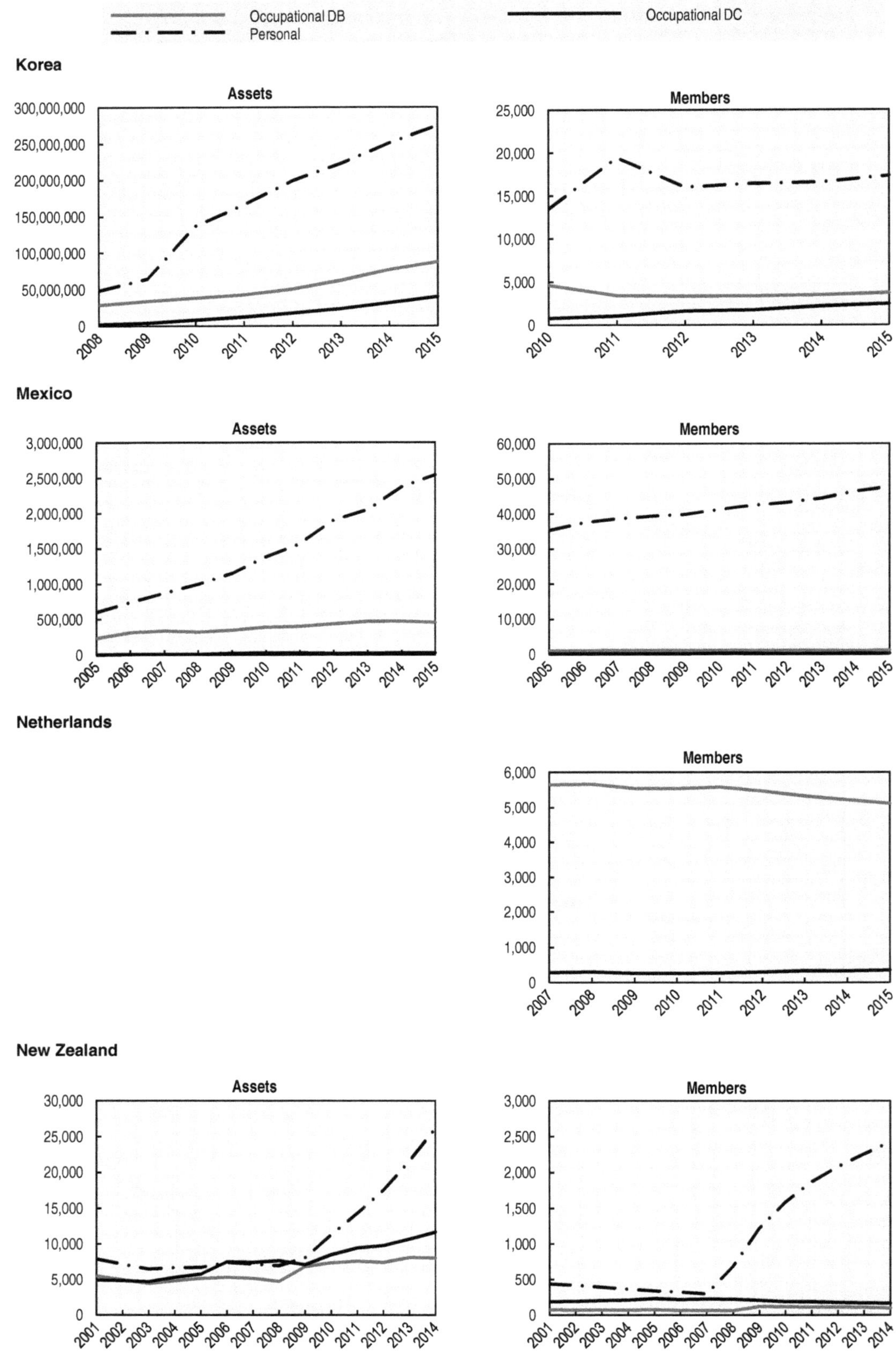

Figure 1.3. **Evolution of DB and DC pension arrangements in OECD countries according to assets (millions national currency) and members (thousands)** *(cont.)*

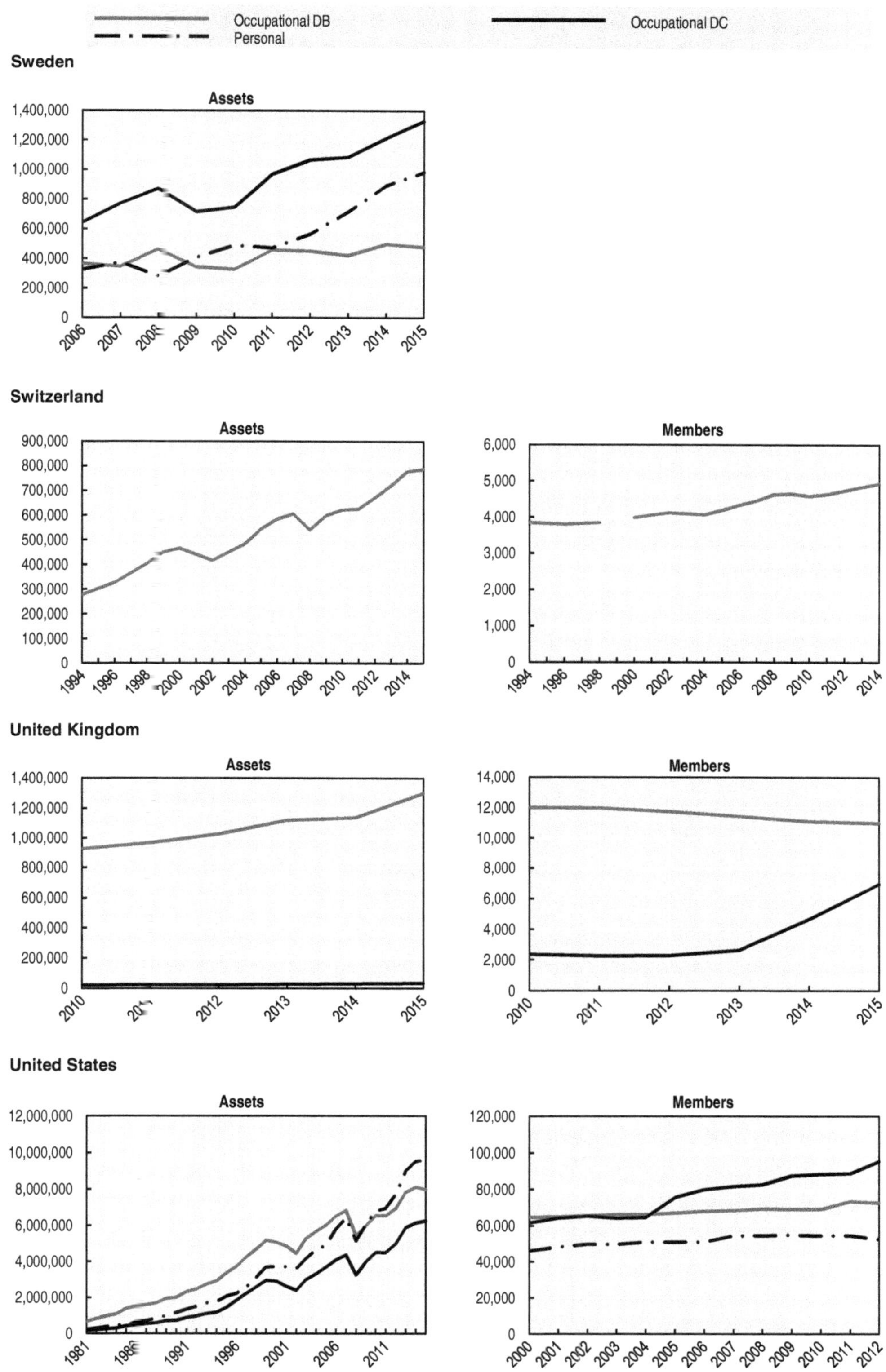

Note: This figure only covers countries with total pension assets above 15% of GDP in 2015. For specific detail on the data for each country, please refer to the data appendix in Annex 1.A2.

Source: OECD Global Pension Statistics and other national sources.

StatLink http://dx.doi.org/10.1787/888933426787

The low and falling level of interest rates is another risk for pension funds and DB plan sponsors. This risk can impact both the assets and the liabilities of pension plans. Interest rates have fallen over the recent years in several countries, such as the Netherlands, the United Kingdom and the United States (OECD, 2015a). Low and falling interest rates mean that the long-term yields of bonds are low and decreasing. This may lead in the long-run to a decrease in the returns of investments of pension funds holding newly issued government bonds. The problem is compounded by the fact that declining interest rates increase the actuarial valuation of the liabilities of DB pension plans (Antolin et al., 2011).

Sponsors of DB plans are also exposed to longevity risk that can result in an increase of the plan's liabilities. Populations in the OECD are ageing and living longer (OECD, 2014a). If the age at which members can benefit from these plans is not postponed accordingly, DB plan assets will have to cover benefit payments for longer than initially accounted and planned for. Furthermore, if the increase in the life expectancy of plan members is underestimated, DB pension plans will experience an unexpected increase of their liabilities that may not be covered by the plans' assets. Pension funds may not use mortality tables which provision for a future increase in life expectancy or may underestimate this increase (OECD, 2014b). Pension funds are exposed to the longevity risk to the extent that the increase of life expectancy of current and future retirees is underestimated in these mortality tables.[9]

Minimum funding requirements in place and the rules prescribing the method for calculating funding levels are important for the protection of pension rights accrued to members. They determine the amount of additional contributions that employers will have to make in the event of a shortfall. In the United States, minimum funding requirements are in place for U.S. employer-sponsored plans. Qualified defined benefit pension plans are subject to funding rules under the Employee Retirement Income Security Act of 1974 (ERISA) and the Pension Protection Act of 2006 (PPA). Single-employer DB pension plans must be fully funded, meaning the assets must cover liabilities. The liabilities for funding purposes are called the funding target. It is calculated as the present value of all benefit liabilities accrued to date using certain assumptions prescribed by regulation. If a plan is underfunded, then the employer can amortize the shortfall over seven years (Yermo and Severinson, 2010). In Ireland, the current funding standard requires DB plans to provide a recovery plan if they are in deficit (OECD, 2014c).

In order to deal with the solvency problems of DB plans, employers have been moving to offering DC plans instead. This move can follow different paths. The transition from DB to DC plans can be done by a hard freeze, a soft freeze or a partial freeze of existing DB plans (Broadbent et al., 2006). In the case of a hard freeze, DB plans are closed to new workers and existing members are no longer allowed to accrue additional benefits. A soft freeze consists of closing DB plans to new workers only, with existing members continuing to accumulate rights. A partial freeze is implemented when the plan is closed to new entrants, and the formula for calculating future benefits for a subset of active members is modified in order to limit future benefit accruals. All these types of freezes have been observed in the United States. According to a survey carried out by the US Government Accountability Office in 2008 based on a sample of 471 single-employer plan sponsors (GAO, 2008), 23% of DB plans froze the benefits accruals of existing members and were closed to new entrants (hard freeze) while an additional 12% and 6% reported a soft and partial plan freeze respectively. In Ireland, the financial and economic crisis led some employers to freeze and wind up DB schemes. The Pensions Board recorded that 164 DB plans were frozen and 58 in wind-up at the end of 2014 in Ireland (The Pensions Board, 2015). The Norwegian Financial Supervisory Authority also reports that employers tend to close down group DB occupational plans and convert them into DC.

Legislative reforms speed up the closure of DB pension arrangements and encourage savings in DC pension arrangements

The fastest decline in the share of DB pension arrangements has come from legislative reforms. At the same time that DB pension funds have been closed to new members, alternative DC pension arrangements have been created.[10]

Legislation has led to the closure of DB plans to new members in some OECD countries. Israel, Italy and Sweden have closed access to certain DB pension plans to new members. New members cannot join pre-existing pension funds in Israel since 1995, the pre-existing autonomous pension funds earmarked for specific sectors (e.g. the banking sector) in Italy since 1993, and the fund for white-collar workers (ITP) in Sweden since 2007. Old members of these DB plans continue to accumulate rights in Israel, Italy and Sweden.

Countries that have closed existing DB plans have generally created DC plans for new members. Israel, Italy and Sweden created new funds for new entrants at the same time as they prevented them from joining pre-existing DB funds. The whole population in Israel has been able to access DC plans in new pension funds since 1995. In Italy only some sectors offered DB pension arrangements before 1993. A legislative decree in 1993 introduced supplementary DC pension arrangements for all workers and closed existing DB plans to new members. Sweden split the ITP scheme for white-collar workers in 2007 into two schemes: a new scheme called ITP 1 (of DC type) and the old scheme called ITP 2 (of DB type). New entrants born before 1979 could not enter the DB fund for white-collar (ITP 2) after 2007, but they could join the new scheme ITP 1 of DC type.

Mandatory participation or automatic enrolment in DC plans can cause the number of members and the amount of assets increase faster in DC plans than in DB plans. Australia, Israel and Mexico chose to make participation in DC plans mandatory. Almost all the employees in Australia have had to be enrolled in a superannuation plan or a retirement savings account since 1992. All employers have to contribute on behalf of their employees older than 17 and earning more than AUD 450 a month. In Israel, in 2008, the pension reform made it mandatory to cover all workers that are not covered by collectively bargained pensions. In Mexico, the 1997 reform introduced a mandatory, funded individual account DC system for private sector workers in order to respond to demographic challenges and ensure the sustainability of pensions. In Italy and New Zealand, contribution to a pension plan is not mandatory but workers are automatically enrolled in a DC plan, with an opt-out option. Contributions of private sector workers to severance pay schemes (TFR) are automatically diverted to pension funds unless individuals opt out within a period of six months in the case of Italy (OECD, 2014a). The success of this reform was however limited. New Zealand also introduced automatic enrolment into a KiwiSaver scheme in July 2007. Employers must enrol new employees who then have 8 weeks to opt out. This may explain the increase in the significance of DC plans in New Zealand.

The decrease in the proportion of DB assets and members in the overall funded pension system can also be linked to the introduction of voluntary personal pension plans. Several countries created personal plans to increase private pension coverage or improve the replacement rate: Riester plans in Germany (2002), Personal Retirement Savings Accounts (PRSA) in Ireland (2002-03), individual pension insurance account (IKZE) in Poland (2012), Individual Pension System (IPS) in Turkey (2003).

In some countries, opening DB pension arrangements has been made harder or less attractive. In France, since November 2010, an employer can open a DB pension insurance "Article 39" for some employees only if other DC plans (such as PERCO or article 83) are offered to all the other employees.

Flexibility in DB pension arrangements in countries with a high or non-decreasing share of DB arrangements

Countries like the Netherlands and Switzerland introduced flexibility within their DB arrangements to address the risks faced by employers. As a result and despite the trend in most countries towards DC plans, occupational pension plans in these two countries were still mostly DB in 2015. In Iceland, occupational DB plans covering only public sector workers also remained strong.

Employers in the Netherlands and Switzerland no longer bear alone the investment market risk and the inflation risk. In the Netherlands, the pension rights that individuals accrue are revalued every year to take into account inflation and wage growth. When a pension plan is underfunded, employers, employees and pensioners contribute to the recovery of the pension plan. The contribution amount and the indexation depend on the funding ratio of the plan. In Switzerland, if a DB plan is underfunded plan sponsors may have to provide additional contributions, but the responsibility for guaranteeing the solvency of the plan is within the pension fund itself.

Some countries have reformed DB pension arrangements to limit the risk of insolvency. One of these reforms is to change the formula used to calculate the benefits, like in Iceland. In Iceland where DB plans covering public sector employees are not declining, a reformed pension system was established from 1997 for state employees and 1999 for those employed by the municipal authorities. The old DB funds based on final pay were closed to new entrants. The new system which was introduced is still a DB system but the calculations of benefits are based on average salary, indexed with the CPI, instead of the final wage, but old members' benefits are still calculated using final salary. This reform has led to an increase in funding rates for civil servant DB schemes; however, the funding ratio remains at only 58% in 2015.

In the Netherlands, there was a similar shift from final-pay DB pension arrangements to average-wage DB arrangements. DB pension arrangements were renegotiated, and many switched final-pay plans to average-wage plans (Bikker and Vlaar, 2006).

The Netherlands introduced a new financial assessment framework in 2015. Pension funds with a funding deficit must provide the pension supervisor with a ten-year recovery plan. However a transitional regime gives pension funds more time to reach a funding ratio that is at least equal to the required level in 2015 (12 years) and 2016 (11 years).[11]

Advantages and disadvantages of DB and DC pension arrangements

DB pension arrangements also have advantages. The previous section has presented one of the main disadvantages of DB arrangements: the responsibility placed on plan sponsors, generally employers, to partially or fully cover any shortfall between the value of assets backing pension promises and the cost of fulfilling those promises.

The disadvantage of DB pension arrangements from the perspective of the plan sponsor is a major advantage from the point of view of the pension member. They know with some degree of certainty the amount of pension benefits they will receive at retirement and they may not need to worry about the solvency of the plan, as the employer is responsible for making the promise full.[12] The main advantage and the main disadvantage of DB arrangements are the two sides of the same coin.

Other important advantages of DB pension arrangements put forward include that employers also contribute to asset accumulation, assets in DB pension arrangements are better managed because of asset pooling and economies of scale, and DB pension funds are professionally run by pension and long-term investment experts. Although these arguments are important, they are not inherent advantages of DB arrangements but more the result of pension design (e.g. employers make contributions), and adequate regulation and governance. There is no impediment to DC pension arrangements including employers' contributions, pooling assets to take advantage of economies of scale, or being run by professional experts. Finally, it is also argued that DB pension arrangements allow for risk sharing among members. Risk sharing is more difficult in DC pension arrangements, but not impossible.

The actuarial parameters used to determine the promise in DB arrangements may not always materialise. As a result, the resources (e.g. assets) behind the pension promise may fall short. In this sense, those original pension promises have become generous and affect the solvency of the plan sponsor. For example, if life expectancy was assumed to increase at age 65 by half a year per decade but it instead increased by one year per decade in the last four decades, the promised pension benefits will have to be paid for 2 more years, even though contributions and assets were not accumulated to cover for those 2 extra years. Similarly, if returns turn out to be 50 basis points lower than assumed, assets accumulated over a 40-year period will be around 10-11% lower than planned. Generous pensions – whereby pensions benefit promises based on forecasted parameters are higher than those that would result from using actual realisations of those parameters – may then bankrupt the plan sponsor or employer.

DC pension arrangements have an important advantage in this respect as they provide a transparent and straightforward link between pension benefits and contributions. They therefore avoid the problem of generous pension benefits that derives from the difference between actual and projected actuarial parameters. In DC pension arrangements assets accumulated at the end of one's working life directly determine the amount of retirement income. Those assets at retirement are used to generate a stream of income (e.g. buying a life annuity). An additional advantage of DC pension arrangements is that they make labour mobility easier than DB arrangements because it is more straightforward to determine the amounts accumulated in DC pension accounts than it is in DB arrangements. Finally, members of DC pension arrangements can have a say on how their assets are invested.

The main disadvantage of DC pension plans is that all the risks of saving for retirement (e.g. financial risk, employment and wage risks) as well as the risks in retirement (e.g. longevity risk) are borne by the individual. Most individuals may not be able or prepared to assume those risks. In addition, individuals, whether they are prepared or not, have to make many important decisions such as how much to save, where to invest, when to retire, how to allocate the assets accumulated when retiring, without having the necessary tools or knowledge.[13]

There are other concerns associated with DC pension arrangements, for example adequacy, that may put them in a negative light. For example, most DC pension arrangements may not be able to deliver the level of retirement income that people may have come to expect to finance their retirement. This is not an inherent negative feature of DC pension arrangements, but stems from the fact that DC contributions tend to be low by design. Contributions in DB pension arrangements tend to be higher than in DC plans. Indeed, whether PAYG financed DB public pension arrangements or funded DB private arrangements, contribution rates are above 20% of wages (e.g. Denmark 13.5%, France 21.3%, Italy 33%, and the Netherlands 20.9%).[14] Mandatory or default contribution rates in DC pension arrangements are much lower (e.g. 10% in Australia and Chile, 8.8% for private sector workers in Mexico, 6% in New Zealand). Nothing prevents DC pension arrangements from having higher contributions to increase the chances that they will deliver higher and more adequate pension benefits.[15]

The OECD, instead of prescribing specific pension arrangements, highlights the advantages and disadvantages of different pension arrangements to make sure that when policy makers make choices they are aware of the trade-offs they are incurring. The OECD has nevertheless a number of main pension policy messages.

1.3. Main OECD policy messages

The changes that have occurred in the pensions landscape are in line with the main pension policy messages that the OECD has put forward. The OECD has been working on pensions for more than two decades examining the different aspects of public and private, funded and PAYG financed pensions, as well as replacement rates, issues of coverage and pension policy in general (OECD 1998, OECD 2005b, OECD Pensions at a Glance, OECD Pensions Outlook). From this work, three main pension policy messages are:

1. Diversify the sources to finance retirement
2. Funded private pension arrangements are complementary to public pensions
3. Improve the design of DC pension plans

Diversify the sources to finance retirement

The OECD recommends combining PAYG financed pensions and pension arrangements in which assets back pension benefits, i.e. funded pensions. The analysis has shown that in the past decades there has been an increase in such pension arrangements. This increase has led to a greater diversification of the sources to finance retirement.

Diversification is important because the mechanisms through which shocks work into different pension arrangements vary. For example, population ageing has a different impact on PAYG and funded pension arrangements, or DB and DC pension arrangements. Population ageing may create fiscal sustainability problems for PAYG DB pension arrangements, solvency problems for funded DB arrangements, and adequacy problems for funded DC pension arrangements. Similarly, the environment of low interest rates and low economic growth affects funded private and PAYG public pension arrangements through different channels. Low interest rates increase the weight of pension liabilities in funded DB plans, it may lead to lower long-term accumulated assets in DC plans, and lower economic growth may affect the fiscal sustainability of public PAYG pension arrangements, especially if lower economic growth stems from lower employment.

The OECD also recommends separating the sources of financing for non-contributory and contributory public pensions. Countries should not use contributions to finance the safety net, social assistance, universal pensions or resident based basic pensions (i.e. non-contributory pensions). These should be fully financed through the budget, through taxes, while contributory public pensions should be financed with current contributions.

Regarding funded DB pension arrangements, the OECD has argued that in plans where the employer is fully or partially responsible for any gap between assets and pension promises, employers should cover this gap by for example increasing contributions, but some flexibility in applying funding and recovery plans should also exist to avoid bankrupting the employer (Antolin and Stewart, 2009).

Funded private pensions are complementary to public pensions

Funded private pension arrangements are complementary to public pensions and not a substitute. The growing importance of funded pension arrangements has been in general to complement PAYG-finance arrangements, becoming a component of overall retirement income.

They need to be designed taking into account the overall structure of the pension system in each jurisdiction. For example, retirement income and associated replacement rates in DC pensions should be higher in countries where they are the main source to finance retirement. In countries where PAYG-financed public pensions and DB funded pensions already provide high pension benefits, DC pension plans will only need to target a low replacement rate to achieve overall retirement income adequacy. Additionally, some degree of annuitization to provide protection from longevity risk should be in place in countries where DC pension arrangements are a main source to finance retirement.

Improve the design of DC pension plans

The growing importance of DC pension arrangements has led the OECD to assess their potential drawbacks and to incorporate these arrangements into the regulatory framework in order to protect members. As a result, the OECD has recently approved the new Core Principles of Private Pension Regulation, which extends the original Core Principles to all types of funded pension arrangements.[16]

In addition, the OECD Roadmap for the Good Design of DC Pension Plans, which has been endorsed and approved by pension regulators from OECD countries, in seeking to assist countries to strengthen retirement income adequacy in an environment of DC pension arrangements, makes the following recommendations:[17]

1. Ensure the design of DC pension plans is internally coherent between the accumulation and pay-out phases and with the overall pension system.
2. Encourage people to enrol, to contribute and contribute for long periods.
3. Improve the design of incentives to save for retirement, particularly where participation and contributions to DC pension plans are voluntary.
4. Promote low-cost retirement savings instruments.
5. Establish appropriate default investment strategies, while also providing choice between investment options with different risk profile and investment horizon.
6. Consider establishing default life-cycle investment strategies as a default option to protect people close to retirement against extreme negative outcomes.

7. For the pay-out phase, encourage annuitisation as a protection against longevity risk.
8. Promote the supply of annuities and cost-efficient competition in the annuity market.
9. Develop appropriate information and risk-hedging instruments to facilitate dealing with longevity risk.
10. Ensure effective communication and address financial illiteracy and lack of awareness.

This edition of the Pensions Outlook partially addresses some of the above recommendations. Chapter 2 examines the tax advantage provided by the tax treatment of retirement saving products relative to other saving vehicles. Chapter 3 focuses on financial advice and proposes several policy measures to address conflict of interest, minimise costs of providing financial advice in retirement and make sure that individuals receive quality financial advice for retirement that is appropriate for their needs (e.g. consumer protection). Chapter 4 examines the different types of annuity products that exist across OECD countries, and discusses their potential to play an important role in helping individuals to mitigate the investment and longevity risks they face in financing their retirement. Chapter 5 focuses on financial education and how to design it effectively for different types of pension arrangements. The final chapter of this volume will discuss the different pension arrangements that exist in some OECD countries between public sector and private sector workers.

Notes

1. Chapter 2 of the *OECD Pensions Outlook 2014* and various chapters in several editions of the OECD Pensions at a Glance publication document this.
2. This chapter uses the term "pension arrangements" to refer to both pension plans and pension schemes.
3. Chapter 6 of this volume discusses the differences in pension arrangements covering public and private sector employees across OECD countries.
4. Please see OECD (2005a). The OECD and its Working Party on Private Pensions where pension regulators from OECD and non-OECD countries sit, are currently discussing potential revisions to the OECD Classification of Private Pensions in recognition of the changing pensions landscape.
5. The OECD Global Pension Statistics collects harmonised data on funded private pensions in OECD, IOPS and non-OECD, non-IOPS World Bank countries. See *www.oecd.org/finance/financial-markets/globalpensionstatistics.htm* and *www.oecd.org/daf/pensions/gps*.
6. *www.oecd.org/finance/private-pensions/38356329.pdf*.
7. Annex 1.A1 provides a review of some of those studies.
8. Data on funded pensions are provided by the Central Bank of the Netherlands. They do not provide a split between DB and DC pension arrangements. However, Willis Towers Watson in its Global Pension Assets Study 2016 provides a split between DB and DC plans in terms of assets. The weight of DB assets in the total has declined from 99% in 2000 to 95% in 2015.
9. See OECD (2014b) for an extensive analysis of the mortality assumptions used by pension funds and insurance companies in selected OECD countries.
10. The development of DC plans may also come from incentives created to encourage people to save more for retirement in personal plans.
11. See DNB Bulletin of 1 September 2015: "More Room for recovery in new supervisory framework for pension funds".
12. In some countries there is also a Pension Protection Fund (e.g. the United Kingdom and the United States) that will partially fulfil the pension promise in case of bankruptcy of the plan sponsor.
13. Chapter 5 in this volume discuses some of these issues.
14. See tables 9.1 and 9.2 in OECD (2015b).

15. The OECD Roadmap for the Good Design of Defined Contribution Pension Plans recommends contributing more and for longer to address the adequacy problems that may arise in DC pension arrangements.

16. See *www.oecd.org/finance/principles-private-pension-regulation.htm.*

17. See *www.oecd.org/pensions/designingfundedpensionplans.htm.*

References

Antolin, P., S. Schich and J. Yermo (2011), "The Economic Impact of Protracted Low Interest Rates on Pension Funds and Insurance Companies", *OECD Journal: Financial Market Trends*, Vol. 2011/1, *http://dx.doi.org/10.1787/fmt-2011-5kg55qw0m56l.*

Antolin, P. and F. Stewart (2009), "Private Pensions and Policy Responses to the Financial and Economic Crisis", *OECD Journal: Financial Market Trends*, Vol. 2009/1, *http://dx.doi.org/10.1787/fmt-v2009-art5-en.*

Bikker, J.A. and P.J.G. Vlaar (2006), "Conditional Indexation in Defined Benefit Pension Plans", *Working Paper*, No. 86, De Nederlandsche Bank, Amsterdam.

Broadbent, J., M. Palumbo and E. Woodman (2006), "The shift from defined benefit to defined contribution pension plans – Implications for asset allocation and risk management".

FSA (2014), *Retirement Savings Adequacy in Iceland*, the Financial Supervisory Authority of Iceland.

GAO (2008), "Defined benefit pensions – Plan Freezes Affect Millions of Participants and May Pose Retirement Income Challenges".

Nakada, T. and M. Arimori (2008), "Recent Trend of the Shift from DB Plans to DC Plans in the Corporate Pension Plan Area".

OECD Pension Markets in Focus, several issues.

OECD (2015a), *OECD Business and Finance Outlook 2015*, OECD Publishing, Paris, *http://dx.doi.org/10.1787/9789264234291-en.*

OECD (2015b), *Pensions at a Glance 2015: OECD and G20 indicators*, OECD Publishing, Paris, *http://dx.doi.org/10.1787/pension_glance-2015-en.*

OECD (2014a), *OECD Pensions Outlook 2014*, OECD Publishing, Paris, *http://dx.doi.org/10.1787/9789264222687-en.*

OECD (2014b), *Mortality Assumptions and Longevity Risk: Implications for pension funds and annuity providers*, OECD Publishing, Paris, *http://dx.doi.org/10.1787/9789264222748-en.*

OECD (2014c), *OECD Reviews of Pensions Systems: Ireland*, OECD Publishing, Paris, *http://dx.doi.org/10.1787/9789264208834-en.*

OECD (2005a), *Private Pensions: OECD Classification and Glossary*, OECD Publishing, Paris, *http://dx.doi.org/10.1787/9789264017009-en-fr.*

OECD (2005b), *Financial Market Trends: Ageing and Pension System Reform: Implications for Financial Markets and Economic Policies*, OECD Publishing, Paris, *http://dx.doi.org/10.1787/fmt-v2005-sup1-en.*

OECD (1998), *Maintaining Prosperity in an Ageing Society*, OECD Publishing, Paris, *http://dx.doi.org/10.1787/9789264163133-en.*

The Pension Board (2015), *Annual Report and Accounts 2014*, Dublin.

Turner, J.A. and G. Hughes (2008), "Large Declines in Defined Benefit Plans Are Not Inevitable: The Experience of Canada, Ireland, the United Kingdom, and the United States", *Discussion Paper* PI-0821. Report prepared for the Ontario Pension Board. London: Pensions Institute, City University.

Willis Towers Watson (2016), *Global Pension Assets Study 2016.*

Yermo, J. and C. Severinson (2010), "The Impact of the Financial Crisis on Defined Benefit Plans and the Need for Counter-Cyclical Funding Regulations", *OECD Working Papers on Finance, Insurance and Private Pensions*, No. 3, OECD Publishing, Paris, *http://dx.doi.org/10.1787/5km91p3jszxw-en.*

ANNEX 1.A1

Research papers on the evolution of DB and DC plans

The research on the evolution of DB and DC plans concludes that DC plans have been expanding at the expense of DB plans in several large countries with long-dated DB plans such as the United Kingdom or the United States.

The conclusion draws on a selection of analytical work from various stakeholders. These stakeholders comprise central banks, academic research centres, and investment and consulting companies. Table 1.A1.1 lists the selected studies, the geographical coverage and scope of their analysis, the time period and the main results.

The four selected studies looked at similar indicators to analyse the evolution of DB and DC plans in some of the largest pension markets in terms of assets. Researchers have assessed this evolution in Australia, Canada, Ireland, Japan, the Netherlands, the United Kingdom and the United States. Depending on the data availability, they usually examined the evolution of assets, members or number of plans over a time period or at different points in time.

The type of plans considered in the different studies varies. Broadbent et al. (2006) only considered private sector pension plans covering private sector employees, excluding occupational funded DB plans covering public sector workers and personal plans. By contrast, Willis Towers Watson (2016) covered occupational pensions and individual savings, including Individual Retirement Accounts (IRAs) for the United States in their analysis.

Despite differences in scope, the studies reviewed found that the countries in their sample were experiencing a shift from DB to DC plans. All the studies examined the developments of the pension system in the United States and the United Kingdom. They all conclude that DC plan assets, members or schemes in the United States have been growing faster than those of DB plans since the 1980s. Three studies – Broadbent et al. (2006), Nakada and Arimori (2008), and Turner and Hughes (2008) – looked at the evolution of members in the United Kingdom and noticed a decrease in the number or in the proportion of members in occupational DB schemes. Willis Towers Watson (2016) showed the share of assets in DB plans in the funded pension system fell in Australia and the United Kingdom between 2010 and 2015 and in Canada, Japan, the Netherlands and the United States between 2005 and 2015.

Broadbent et al. (2006) compared the speed of the transition from DB to DC plans of Canada and the other countries. The authors considered that the shift towards DC plans in Canada was not as rapid in the United States. They concluded that a large transfer from DB to DC plans in Canada had not occurred yet at the time of their analysis in 2006.

Table 1.A1.1. Selection of studies analysing the shift from DB to DC plans

Study	Country	Scope	Indicators	Time period	Results
Broadbent et al. (2006)	Australia	Private sector plans	Assets	Mid-2005	The analysis provides the share of assets by type of plan as of mid-2005: 50% in DC, 4% in DB and 47% in combined DB/DC). The authors did not show the shift away from DB plans using numbers, but provided the factors accounting for the increasing prominence of DC plans
			Members	Mid-2005	The analysis provides the share of members by type of plan as of mid-2005: 66% in DC, 2% in DB and 32% in combined DB/DC) . The authors did not show the shift away from DB plans using numbers, but provided the factors accounting for the increasing prominence of DC plans
	Canada	Private sector trusteed pension plans, excluding occupational plans organised as insurance contracts	Members	1992, 2004	The share of DC plan members declined from 92.5% in 1992 to 77.1% in 2004, while the share of members of combined DB/DC plans increased from < 1% to 12% and the share of DC plan members from 6.8% to 7.6%.
			Companies providing a DB plan to new members	2000, 2003, 2006	Among 174 of Canadian companies sponsoring a DB plan, 49% provided a DB plan to new employees in 2000, 47% in 2003 and an expected 39% for 2006.
	United Kingdom	Private sector plans	Members	1995, 2005	Membership in private sector DB plans declined from 5.16 million in 1995 to 3.66 million in 2005, while numbers of DC plan members fell from 1.06 to 1.02 million in the same period of time.
	United States[1]	Private sector plans	Assets	1985-2005	The share of assets of DB plans decreased from 65% in 1985 to 40% in 2005.
			Active participants	Mid-1970s through the mid-1980s, 2004	The number of active participants in US DB plans remained flat from about the mid-1970s through the mid-1980s while DC participants grew rapidly.
Nakada and Arimori (2008)	Japan	Corporate pension plans	Number of plans	2006, 2007	The number of DC plans was 2 000 in September 2006, and reached 2 472 in September 2007.
		Corporate pension plans	Participants	2006, 2007	The number of DC members was more than 2 million in December 2006, and was about 2.5 million in September 2007.
	United Kingdom	Corporate pension plans	Members	1997-2005	The share of members of DB plans decreased from 46% in 1997 to 35% in 2005.
	United States	Corporate pension plans	Assets	1975-2004	The number of DC participants (excluding 401(k) plans) had been growing since 1975 and outstripped the number of DB participants in 1997.
		Corporate pension plans	Number of participants	1975-2004	The number of DC participants (excluding 401(k) plans) had been growing since 1975 and outstripped the number of DB participants in 1984.
Turner and Hughes (2008)	Canada	Private sector pension plans	Participants	1974-2004 (bi-annual data)	The percentage of private sector participants in DB plans in Canada decreased from 90.6% in 1974 to 74.2% in 2004.
	Ireland	Occupational pension schemes	Coverage	1992-2006	The percentage of those at work covered by DB plans declined from 33.1% in 1992 to 26.9% in 2006, while the percentage of those at work covered by DC plans increased from 4.5% to 12.6%.
			Number of schemes	1992, 2006	The number of DB schemes decreased from 2 560 in 1992 to 1 232 in 2006, while the number of DC schemes increased from 28 125 in 1992 to 92 075 in 2006.
			Number of members	1992, 2006	The number of DB members increased from 207 545 in 1992 to 269 529 in 2006, while the number of DC members increased from 52 786 in 1992 to 255 008 in 2006.

Table 1.A1.1. **Selection of studies analysing the shift from DB to DC plans** *(cont.)*

Study	Country	Scope	Indicators	Time period	Results
	United Kingdom	Occupational pension schemes	Active members	1987, 1991, 1995, 2000, 2005 and 2006	The number of DB active members amounted to 10.5 million in 1987, and 8.4 million in 2006. The number of DC active members amounted to 0.2 million in 1987, and 1.2 million in 2006.
		Occupational private sector schemes	Number of schemes	1991, 1995, 2005	The total number of DB private sector schemes was 37 285 in 1991, 37 980 in 1995 and 12 027 in 2005. The total number of DC private sector schemes was 90 715 in 1991, 113 020 in 1995 and 53 465 in 2005.
	United States	Occupational private pension plans	Number of plans	1975, 1980, 1985, 1990, 1995, 2000 and 2005	The number of DB plans reached a peak in 1985 (170 172 plans) and continuously declined down to 47 614 plans in 2005. The number of DC plans increased from 207 748 in 1975 to 631 481 in 2005.
		Occupational private pension plans	Participants	1975, 1980, 1985, 1990, 1995, 2000 and 2005	The number of DB plans members peaked at 30 100 thousand in 1980 and declined down to 20 310 thousand in 2005. The number of DC plan members increased from 11 217 thousand in 1975 to 62 355 thousand in 2005.
Willis Towers Watson (2016)	Australia	Occupational pension and individual savings	Assets	2000, 2005, 2015	The share of assets in DB plans was: 12% in 2005, 20% in 2010 and 13% in 2015.
	Canada	Occupational pension and individual savings	Assets	2000, 2005, 2015	The share of assets in DB plans was: 97% in 2005, 96% in 2010 and 95% in 2015.
	Japan	Occupational pension and individual savings	Assets	2000, 2005, 2015	The share of assets in DB plans was: 99% in 2005, 98% in 2010 and 96% in 2015.
	Netherlands	Occupational pension and individual savings	Assets	2000, 2005, 2015	The share of assets in DB plans was: 99% in 2005, 93% in 2010 and 95% in 2015.
	United Kingdom	Occupational pension and individual savings	Assets	2000, 2005, 2015	The share of assets in DB plans was: 67% in 2005, 74% in 2010 and 68% in 2015.
	United States	Occupational pension and individual savings	Assets	2000, 2005, 2015	The share of assets in DB plans was: 47% in 2005, 44% in 2010 and 40% in 2015.

1. The publication provides the amount of assets in individual retirement accounts (personal plans) in 1985 and 2004.

Source: OECD staff's selection of studies.

ANNEX 1.A2

Data appendix

Definitions

The OECD Classification and Glossary on Private Pensions (*www.oecd.org/finance/private-pensions/38356329.pdf*) first splits pension plans between occupational and personal, and then distinguishes between DB and DC plans within occupational plans.

The OECD taxonomy sets two criteria to consider a pension plan as occupational: access to the plan is linked to an employment relationship, and the employer is the one establishing the plan, in other words, the employer is the plan sponsor. Pension plans that individuals can join without any involvement of employers are considered personal.

Among occupational plans, DC plans are those in which the employer has no obligation to pay further contributions to an ongoing plan in the case of unfavourable plan experience. By contrast, in occupational DB plans, the employer has to pay further contributions if needed to ensure plan members will receive the promised benefits.

The OECD taxonomy identifies three types of DB plan. First, in traditional DB plans, benefits are linked through a formula to the members' wages or salaries, length of employment, or other factors. Secondly, hybrid plans are plans where benefits depend on a rate of return credited to contributions, where this rate of return is either specified in the plan rules, independently of the actual return on any supporting assets, or is calculated with reference to the actual return of any supporting assets and a minimum return guarantee specified in the plan rules. Finally, mixed DB plans are plans that have two separate DB and DC components but which are treated as part of the same plan.

The OECD taxonomy also breaks down occupational DC plans and personal plans into protected and unprotected. An unprotected DC plan is a plan where the pension plan/fund itself or the pension provider does not offer any investment return or benefit guarantees or promises covering the whole plan/fund. A protected pension plan is a plan other than an unprotected one.

Data

Data for personal plans in **Australia** do not include Retirement Savings Accounts. Data for assets refer to June 2001 instead of 2000, and to June 2013 instead of 2015.

Data on assets in 2000 for **Austria** refer to 2001 instead of 2000.

Data on assets in 2000 for **Belgium** refer to 2001 instead of 2000. The breakdown of assets and members between DB and DC plans comes from the website of the FSMA, and refer to institutions for occupational retirement provision only. The numbers for assets and members by type of plans refer to 2014 instead of 2015.

Data on members for ***Canada*** come from Statistics Canada's website, and refer to active members.

Data on assets in 2000 for **Chile** refer to 2001 instead of 2000. Assets held in Collective Voluntary Pension Savings managed by the AFPs are classified together with personal plans, although these schemes are occupational.

Data on assets in 2000 for the **Czech Republic** refer to 2001 instead of 2000. The number of members refers to 2014 instead of 2015.

Data on assets in 2000 for ***Denmark*** refer to 2001 instead of 2000. Members of occupational DC plans in Denmark only refer to ATP members. The numbers of members refer to 2012 instead of 2015.

Data on assets in 2000 for **Estonia** refer to 2001 instead of 2000. Data on members refer to the mandatory funded pension system only.

Data on assets in 2000 for **Finland** refer to 2011 instead of 2000. The amount of pension-related assets in employers' book reserves is not available and consequently not reported under "Occupational DB plans".

Data on assets in 2000 for ***France*** refer to 2005 instead of 2000. Data on assets and members refer to 2014 instead of 2015.

Data for ***Germany*** refer only to Pensionskassen and Pensionsfonds.

Data on assets in 2000 for **Greece** refer to 2007 instead of 2000.

Data for ***Hungary*** refer to voluntary privately-managed pension funds and voluntary private pension funds only. Data on assets in 2000 refer to 2001 instead of 2000.

Data on assets in 2000 for **Iceland** refer to 2001 instead of 2000. The numbers of members refer to 2014 instead of 2015.

Data on assets in 2000 for ***Ireland*** refer to 2001 instead of 2000. Assets reported for personal pension plans do not include assets held in Retirement Annuity Contracts. Data on members only refer to active members.

Data for ***Israel*** refer to old, new and general pension funds only.

Data on assets in 2000 for ***Italy*** refer to 2001 instead of 2000.

Data on assets in 2000 for ***Korea*** refer to 2002 instead of 2000. Data do not include personal pension funds with no guaranteed yield.

Data on assets in 2000 for ***Latvia*** refer to 2004 instead of 2000.

Data on assets in 2000 for ***Luxembourg*** refer to 2005 instead of 2000. The breakdown of assets and members between DB and DC plans refers to pension plans under the supervision of Luxembourg Financial Supervisory Authority (CSSF) only.

Data on assets in 2000 for **Mexico** refer to 2005 instead of 2000.

Data on members for the ***Netherlands*** come from DNB and refer to actively contributing members in pension funds only.

Data on assets in 2000 for ***New Zealand*** refer to 2001 instead of 2000. Data on assets and members refer to 2014 instead of 2015.

Data on assets in 2000 for ***Norway*** refer to 2001 instead of 2000. Data on assets only refer to municipal and private pension funds. Data on members of occupational DB plans refer to members of municipal pension funds, private pension funds and members having DB pension contracts held in life insurance companies.

Data for ***Portugal*** do not include collective and individual pension insurance contracts.

Data on assets in 2000 for the ***Slovak Republic*** refer to 2006 instead of 2000.

Data on assets in 2000 for ***Slovenia*** refer to 2003 instead of 2000.

Data on assets in 2000 for ***Spain*** refer to 2001 instead of 2000.

Data on assets in 2000 for ***Sweden*** refer to 2001 instead of 2000. The breakdown of assets and members between DB and DC plans does not include benevolent societies and pension foundations. Data for members refer to active members only and refer to 2014 instead of 2015

The amount of assets for ***Switzerland*** is a preliminary estimate based on first trend calculations for the year 2015. Data for members refer to 2014 instead of 2015.

Data on assets in 2000 for ***Turkey*** refer to 2004 instead of 2000.

Data on assets in 2000 for the ***United Kingdom*** refer to 2001 instead of 2000. Data for occupational DB plans refer to PPF-eligible DB schemes and do not include funded public sector schemes, while data for occupational DC plans come from the Pensions Regulator and only refer to DC schemes with 12 or more members.

The number of members for the ***United States*** refers to 2012 instead of 2015.

Chapter 2

Does the tax treatment of retirement savings provide an advantage when people save for retirement?*

This chapter assesses whether the tax treatment of retirement savings vehicles in different OECD countries provides an advantage when people save for retirement. It then calculates the tax advantage that individuals saving into private pension plans may enjoy over their lifetime. This overall tax advantage is the amount that an individual would save in taxes paid by contributing to a private pension plan instead of putting the same amount into an alternative, benchmark savings vehicle. It also includes the effect of state financial incentives, such as flat-rate subsidies and matching contributions, and it is calculated for different types of private pension plans across all OECD countries.

*The statistical data for Israel are supplied by and under the responsibility of the relevant Israeli authorities. The use of such data by the OECD is without prejudice to the status of the Golan Heights, East Jerusalem and Israeli settlements in the West Bank under the terms of international law.

Policy makers may wish to promote retirement savings through tax advantages and other financial incentives in order to increase national savings, reallocate savings into retirement products and reinforce the role of private pensions in the provision of retirement income.

Some countries have low national savings relative to their investment needs and may wish to increase overall savings. This could be achieved by introducing incentives with the goal of encouraging new savings. These incentives could focus on retirement savings products, as a way to help people accumulate enough financial resources by the time they retire, thus preventing them from relying on the public safety net, which would increase budgetary expenditures.

Retirement saving is for the long haul. Therefore, increasing saving for retirement could increase long-term investment and eventually bring higher long-term growth. Thus, even a country that has enough overall savings may still want to promote private pensions: reallocating other types of savings into retirement vehicles will not increase overall national savings but will earmark a greater share for retirement.

Recent reforms to pay-as-you-go public pension systems have increased the need to develop the complementary role of private pensions in the provision of retirement income in some countries. OECD governments have been active in reforming pension systems over the last decade (OECD, 2015a), often reducing public pension benefits and increasing the role of private pensions, in particular defined contribution plans. Providing financial incentives intends to make retirement savings more attractive in order to complement public provision and increase overall pension adequacy.

OECD countries encourage saving for retirement through private pensions by taxing retirement savings differently than alternative savings vehicles or offering other financial incentives. Historically, tax breaks (through tax exemption, tax deductions and tax credits) have been the main type of financial incentive provided by governments to promote private pensions. A more recent trend is to provide other types of financial incentives, for example, flat-rate subsidies or matching contributions. The OECD has recently performed a stocktaking exercise, collecting information on the tax treatment of retirement savings for all OECD and EU countries (OECD, 2015b). This report assesses the differences across various tax regimes that exist for private pension plans, and compiles country profiles, validated by national officials, giving detailed information on the tax treatment of funded private pension plans. The analysis shows that many countries apply a variant of the "Exempt-Exempt-Taxed" ("EET") regime, where both contributions and returns on investment are exempted from taxation while benefits are treated as taxable income upon withdrawal. A wide range of other tax regimes can also be found, from the "Exempt-Exempt-Exempt" ("EEE") regime where contributions, returns on investment and pension income are all tax-exempt, to regimes where two out of three flows of income are taxed.

This chapter assesses whether the tax treatment of retirement savings vehicles in different OECD countries provides an advantage when people save for retirement. It calculates the tax advantage that individuals saving in private pension plans may enjoy over their lifetime. It calculates this overall tax advantage for different types of private pension plans across all OECD countries. The approach used consists in comparing the tax treatment of a private pension plan to that of a benchmark savings vehicle, i.e. comparing how contributions, returns on investment and withdrawals are taxed in each savings vehicle. This includes the effect of state financial incentives, such as flat-rate subsidies and matching contributions, which are considered as tax credits paid into the pension accounts of entitled individuals. The overall tax advantage is defined as the amount that an individual would save in taxes paid during their working and retirement years by contributing the same pre-tax amount to a private pension plan instead of to a benchmark savings vehicle.

In most OECD countries, the tax treatment of retirement savings does indeed provide a tax advantage when people save for retirement instead of saving into other traditional savings vehicles. The size of the overall tax advantage varies however, and depends on the tax regime applied to pension plans and savings vehicles, as well as on the characteristics of the personal income tax system (i.e. the tax brackets and the tax rates), the income level, the amount saved, the length of the contribution period, the type of pay-out option, the benchmark savings vehicle chosen as a comparator and other financial and economic parameters.

Before providing country-specific results in Section 2.2, Section 2.1 first explores the mechanisms through which different tax regimes may provide a tax advantage to individuals contributing to private pension plans. This section introduces the approach used to calculate the overall tax advantage and uses illustrative examples to help explain which tax regimes may be more favourable to individuals and how different factors may influence the results. As the section abstracts from country-specific parameters, the comparison between tax regimes is possible. Section 2.2 then calculates the amount of tax saved by individuals in different OECD countries when contributing to various types of private pension plans instead of to a benchmark savings vehicle. The overall tax advantage is calculated for all types of private pension plans existing in OECD countries, as long as a different tax regime applies. The analysis considers mandatory and voluntary plans, occupational and personal plans, defined benefit (DB) and defined contribution (DC) plans. Section 2.3 concludes. Finally, Annex 2.A1 provides the full description of the framework and assumptions.

2.1. How different tax regimes may provide a tax advantage when individuals save for retirement

This section first introduces the approach used to calculate the overall tax advantage when people save for retirement. It calculates the overall tax advantage for illustrative tax regimes built to show the mechanisms through which these tax regimes may provide a tax advantage. The section then looks at the effect on the tax advantage of different levels of income, lengths of the contribution period, contribution rates, pay-out options and financial and economic parameters (inflation, productivity growth, rate of return and discount rate). It ends with a summary of the main findings.

How to assess the tax advantage

This sub-section introduces the approach used to calculate the overall tax advantage that different tax regimes may offer to individuals saving in private pension plans. The calculation consists in comparing the tax treatment of a private pension plan to that of a benchmark savings vehicle, i.e. comparing how contributions, returns on investment and withdrawals are taxed in each case.[1]

In principle, all income is taxed either when earned or at some point in the future. Saving, including for retirement, involves three income flows that can be taxed. These incomes flows are contributions, returns on investment and withdrawals. In general, savings are made out of taxed earnings and the returns on investment are also subject to income tax. In return, the income received from such savings vehicles is fully exempt from taxation. Such arrangements are known as "Taxed-Taxed-Exempt" or "TTE" schemes. Table 2.1 illustrates how much tax would be paid under different tax regimes by an individual contributing EUR 100 before tax to a savings or pension vehicle in the first year and withdrawing a lump sum three years later. The calculations assume that the individual is subject to a 25% marginal income tax rate and that investments earn a 3% rate of return annually. The discount rate is set equal to the rate of return to calculate the present value of tax paid. Under the "TTE" regime, the individual pays EUR 25 in tax when the contribution is made, so that only EUR 75 is actually invested after tax. At the end of each investment year, the individual also pays taxes on investment income amounting to EUR 0.6. In present value terms, the total tax paid is equivalent to EUR 26.6.

Table 2.1. **Tax paid for different tax regimes: illustrative example**

			TTE				EET			
		Discount factor (A)	Pre-tax balance (B)	Tax paid (C)	Post-tax balance (D=B-C)	Present value of tax paid (E=C×A)	Pre-tax balance (B)	Tax paid (C)	Post-tax balance (D=B-C)	Present value of tax paid (E=C×A)
Contribution	Year 0	1.00	100.0	25.0	75.0	25.0	100.0	0.0	100.0	0.0
Accumulation of assets	Year 1	0.97	77.3	0.6	76.7	0.5	103.0	0.0	103.0	0.0
	Year 2	0.94	79.0	0.6	78.4	0.5	106.1	0.0	106.1	0.0
	Year 3	0.92	80.8	0.6	80.2	0.5	109.3	0.0	109.3	0.0
Withdrawal	Year 3	0.92	80.2	0.0	80.2	0.0	109.3	27.3	82.0	25.0
			Present value of total tax paid:			26.6	Present value of total tax paid:			25.0

			ETT				TEE			
		Discount factor (A)	Pre-tax balance (B)	Tax paid (C)	Post-tax balance (D=B-C)	Present value of tax paid (E=C×A)	Pre-tax balance (B)	Tax paid (C)	Post-tax balance (D=B-C)	Present value of tax paid (E=C×A)
Contribution	Year 0	1.00	100.0	0.0	100.0	0.0	100.0	25.0	75.0	25.0
Accumulation of assets	Year 1	0.97	103.0	0.8	102.3	0.7	77.3	0.0	77.3	0.0
	Year 2	0.94	105.3	0.8	104.6	0.7	79.6	0.0	79.6	0.0
	Year 3	0.92	107.7	0.8	106.9	0.7	82.0	0.0	82.0	0.0
Withdrawal	Year 3	0.92	106.9	26.7	80.2	24.5	82.0	0.0	82.0	0.0
			Present value of total tax paid:			26.6	Present value of total tax paid:			25.0

Note: E stands for exempt and T for taxed.

The most popular tax regime for private pension plans is the one in which contributions and returns on investment are exempt, while withdrawals are taxed. Such arrangements are known as "Exempt-Exempt-Taxed" or "EET" schemes (OECD, 2015b). Table 2.1 shows that at the end of the third year, the accumulated assets are larger under the "EET" regime (EUR 109.3) than under the "TTE" regime (EUR 80.2) because contributions and returns on investment are exempt from taxation. Under the "EET" regime, taxes are only paid on withdrawals and are equal to EUR 25 in present value terms. The individual therefore saves EUR 1.6 in taxes in present value terms when contributing to an "EET" scheme rather than to a "TTE" one.

The "EET" and "TEE" regimes deliver the same tax advantage when the discount rate is equal to the rate of return, and contributions and withdrawals are subject to the same income tax rate. Table 2.1 shows that "EET" and "TEE" generate the same present value of tax paid. Conversely, the "ETT" regime is identical to the "TTE" regime in terms of the present value of total tax paid. The "EET" and "TEE" regimes therefore confer a tax advantage relative to the "TTE" and "ETT" regimes, which comes from the exemption from taxation of the returns on investment.

Building on the above example, the analysis herein calculates the overall tax advantage by extending it to the entire lifetime of the individual and considering the particularities of different tax regimes, as well as different pension and economic parameters.[2] This overall tax advantage is defined as the difference in the present value of total tax paid on contributions, returns on investment and withdrawals between a benchmark savings vehicle and a private pension plan, assuming a flow of contributions made yearly over the entire career, given a constant contribution rate of 10%, a constant real rate of return on assets of 3%, and annuity pension payments calculated with a discount rate equal to the rate of return and a fixed life expectancy. The overall tax advantage therefore represents the amount saved in taxes by the individual over their working and retirement years when contributing the same amount (before tax) to a private pension plan instead of a benchmark savings vehicle. It is expressed as a percentage of the present value of pre-tax contributions.

There are several ways to provide preferential tax treatment to contributions to private pension plans. It can be done through tax exemptions/deductions, tax credits or state financial incentives. A tax exemption or a tax deduction reduces an individual's taxable income, as contributions are excluded/deducted (either fully or partially) from income before calculating the tax due. Tax credits depend on the amount contributed and directly reduce the amount of tax due. A tax credit is non-refundable when the amount of the credit cannot exceed the amount of tax due. State subsidies and state matching contributions can be interpreted as refundable tax credits paid into the pension account. In the case of flat-rate state subsidies, the amount paid into the account is fixed across the income scale. In the case of state matching contributions, the amount paid into the account depends on the amount contributed. For all these tax treatments, caps can be introduced to limit the tax advantage. The analysis considers tax credits and state financial incentives as a negative tax on contributions to private pension plans, which makes it possible to include their impact on the overall tax advantage.

The analysis assumes that wage income is the only source of income during working life. Marginal tax rates are derived by determining the income tax bracket in which the individual's wage falls every year. Wages are assumed to grow in line with inflation and productivity (both assumed to be constant at 2% and 1.5% respectively), while the income limits for all income tax brackets are assumed to grow in line with inflation.[3] When contributions or returns on investment are subject to personal income tax (for the private pension plan or the benchmark savings vehicle), the tax rate that implicitly applies to them is the marginal tax rate, i.e. the tax rate that an individual would pay on the latest unit of income earned.

During retirement, the analysis assumes that the only sources of income are pensions, both mandatory public pensions and the pension payments/withdrawals from the private pension plan. The comparison made with respect to the benchmark savings vehicle substitutes the income from the private pension plan with the income from this alternative savings vehicle. When withdrawals are subject to personal income tax, the tax due is therefore calculated by applying the corresponding rates to each income tax bracket up to the individual's total taxable pension income.

Comparing different tax regimes

The analysis in this section uses stylised tax regimes in order to abstract from the effect of country-specific parameters and assess just the impact of observed differences between tax regimes on the overall tax advantage. Before calculating the overall tax advantage for different types of private pension plans across all OECD countries in Section 2.2, the analysis focuses on selected tax regimes, assuming a common hypothetical personal income tax system to assess their impact on the overall tax advantage. These selected tax regimes are stylised versions of tax regimes that actually exist in different countries for private pension plans, maintaining the main features. Comparing the actual tax regimes applied to different pension plans across all OECD countries is less revealing, as it becomes impossible to disentangle the effect of the tax regimes themselves from the country-specific parameters. For example, when contributions are deductible from taxable income, the tax-deductibility limits that apply vary across and within countries and may also vary across pension plans (OECD, 2015b). In addition, the characteristics of the personal income tax system (i.e. the tax brackets and the tax rates) have an impact on the calculation of the overall tax advantage. In Canada and Greece for example, the average earner faces a different marginal tax rate (31.15% and 22% respectively). Everything being equal, this will lead to differences in the overall tax advantage.

The analysis focuses on 16 selected stylised tax regimes based on their relevance and importance in different OECD countries.[4] Table 2.2 presents the different stylised tax regimes used, which result from the combination of different tax treatments for contributions, returns on investment and pension payments/withdrawals.[5] Each stylised tax regime is symbolised by the combination of three letters representing the tax treatment for contributions, returns on investment and withdrawals respectively. For example, the "EET" stylised tax regime assumes that contributions are tax deductible up to EUR 7 300 a year (the first "E" in "EET"), returns on investment are tax-exempt (the second "E" in "EET") and withdrawals are subject to personal income tax (the "T" in "EET"). Partial tax relief on contributions can be given in two ways, either by reducing taxable income (partial tax deductibility of contributions) or by reducing the tax liability (tax credit calculated based on the amount contributed). This is denoted by a "t". Some of the stylised tax regimes are also combined with state financial incentives, either flat-rate subsidies or matching contributions. Obviously, the choice of the different parameters defining the stylised tax regimes has an important impact on the results. For example, the overall tax advantage for the "tEE" stylised tax regime will be lower when assuming that 20% of the contributions are tax deductible instead of 25%.

These stylised tax regimes are compared to the "TTE" tax regime that usually applies to traditional savings accounts to calculate the overall tax advantage when saving for retirement. As a baseline, the analysis assumes that the average earner enters the labour market at age 20 in 2015 and contributes 10% of wages yearly until age 65. The total amount of assets accumulated at 65 is converted into an annuity certain with fixed nominal payments.[6] Inflation is set at 2%, productivity growth at 1.5%, the real rate of return on investment at 3% and the real discount rate at 3%.

For all the selected stylised tax regimes, average earners can expect to pay less tax when contributing during a full career to a private pension plan rather than to a traditional savings account. For the 16 selected stylised tax regimes, Figure 2.1 shows the size of the overall tax

Table 2.2. **Selected stylised tax regimes**

Stylised tax regimes	Contributions (1)	Returns on investment	Withdrawals	Financial incentive (2,3)
"EEE"	Tax deductible up to EUR 7 300 a year	Tax-exempt	Tax-exempt	
"EET"	Tax deductible up to EUR 7 300 a year	Tax-exempt	Subject to income tax	
"EEt"	Tax deductible up to EUR 7 300 a year	Tax-exempt	Subject to income tax after a 10% deduction	
"EET + subsidy"	Tax deductible up to EUR 7 300 a year	Tax-exempt	Subject to income tax	Flat-rate subsidy of EUR 365
"EET + matching"	Tax deductible up to EUR 7 300 a year	Tax-exempt	Subject to income tax	20% matching contribution up to EUR 1 825
"TEE"	Subject to income tax	Tax-exempt	Tax-exempt	
"tEE + matching"	20% of the contributions are tax deductible up to EUR 7 300 a year	Tax-exempt	Tax-exempt	20% matching contribution up to EUR 1 825
"tEE (tax credit)"	Tax credit equal to 10% of the contributions up to EUR 7 300 a year	Tax-exempt	Tax-exempt	
"ETE"	Tax deductible up to EUR 7 300 a year	Subject to income tax	Tax-exempt	
"tEt"	20% of the contributions are tax deductible up to EUR 7 300 a year	Tax-exempt	Subject to income tax after a 10% deduction	
"tEt (tax credit)"	Tax credit equal to 10% of the contributions up to EUR 7 300 a year	Tax-exempt	Subject to income tax after a 10% deduction	
"TEt"	Subject to income tax	Tax-exempt	Subject to income tax after a 10% deduction	
"ttE"	20% of the contributions are tax deductible up to EUR 7 300 a year	Taxed at a flat rate of 15%	Tax-exempt	
"TtE + matching"	Subject to income tax	Taxed at a flat rate of 15%	Tax-exempt	20% matching contribution up to EUR 1 825
"Ett"	Tax deductible up to EUR 7 300 a year	Taxed at a flat rate of 15%	Subject to income tax after a 10% deduction	
"EtT"	Tax deductible up to EUR 7 300 a year	Taxed at a flat rate of 15%	Subject to income tax	

Note: E stands for exempt and T for taxed. 1. The limit for the tax deductibility of contributions and for the tax credit (EUR 7 300) is equivalent to 20% of wages for the average earner in 2015 and is assumed to be inflation-indexed. 2. The analysis assumes that a maximum flat-rate subsidy of EUR 365 is paid into the pension account if the individual contributes at least 5% of wages. The flat-rate subsidy, which represents 1% of wages for the average earner in 2015 and grows in line with inflation, is proportionately reduced to zero for lower contribution rates. 3. The analysis assumes that 20% of individual contributions are matched by the state and paid into the pension account, up to a maximum state contribution of EUR 1 825 (this limit represents 5% of wages for the average earner in 2015 and grows in line with inflation).

advantage for the average earner, measured as the difference between the present value of total tax paid in a traditional savings account and in a private pension plan, expressed as a percentage of the present value of contributions. The overall tax advantage (solid line) is broken down into three components: tax advantage on contributions, tax advantage on returns and tax advantage on withdrawals. Each selected stylised tax regime would promote private pensions for average earners, with a positive overall tax advantage. Indeed, for most of the selected stylised tax regimes, private pension plans enjoy a preferential tax treatment on contributions and returns on investment as compared to traditional savings accounts (in which contributions and returns on investment are subject to personal income tax), as illustrated by the blue and grey bars on the positive side of the y-axis. This preferential tax treatment outweighs the potential taxation of pension payments (light-blue bars on the negative side). The preferential tax treatment on contributions and returns may come in the form of a tax exemption (full or partial), a tax credit or a lower tax rate. In addition, state financial incentives may increase the tax advantage.

Among the stylised tax regimes, the one where none of the flows is taxed ("EEE") provides the largest overall tax advantage to an average earner. It is followed by tax regimes where only one of the flows is taxed ("EET"/"EEt", "ETE" and "TEE"/"tEE") and finally tax regimes where two of the flows are taxed ("ttE"/"TtE", "Ett"/"EtT" and "tEt"/"TEt").

Figure 2.1. **Overall tax advantage provided through stylised tax regimes by component, average earner**

As a percentage of the present value of contributions

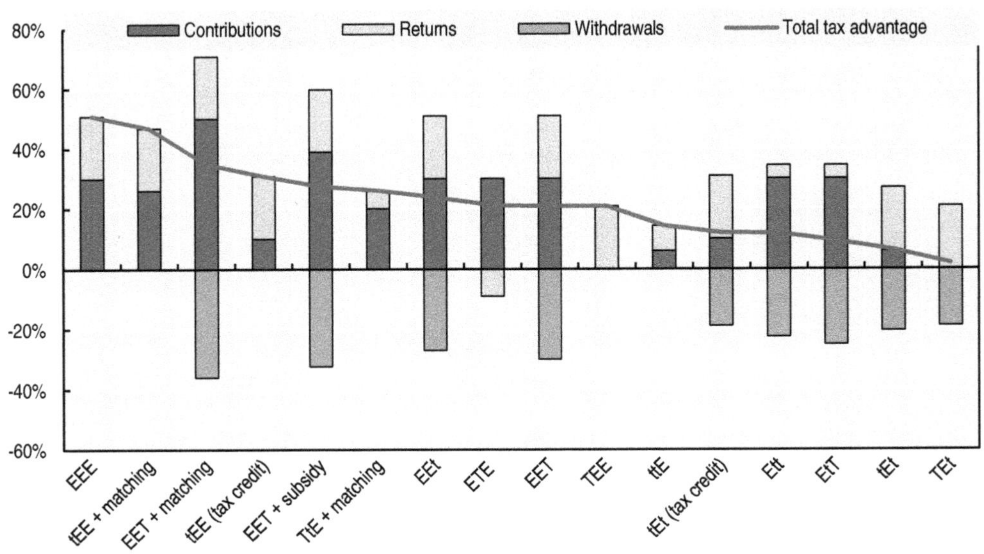

Note: E stands for exempt and T for taxed.

StatLink http://dx.doi.org/10.1787/888933430320

State subsidies and state matching contributions increase the overall tax advantage. For example, the "EET" stylised tax regime provides a larger overall tax advantage to the average earner when combined with a state matching contribution (35% of the present value of contributions) or with a state subsidy (27%) than on its own (21%). When combining state subsidies or state matching contributions with the "EET" stylised tax regime, the increase in the tax advantage on contributions outweighs the additional tax due on withdrawals.

In regimes where only one flow is subject to personal income tax, the overall tax advantage for an average earner contributing to a private pension plan is the same whether the tax is collected on contributions, returns on investment or withdrawals. With each of the "EET", "ETE" and "TEE" stylised tax regimes, the average earner would save in taxes an amount equivalent to 21% of the present value of contributions.[7]

A tax credit on contributions brings in more tax savings than a partial tax deduction of contributions as long as the tax rate applying to contributions is lower than the ratio of the tax credit rate to the deduction rate. The "tEt" stylised tax regime is designed either with a partial tax deduction of contributions (20% of contributions are tax deductible) or with a tax credit on personal income tax (corresponding to 10% of the contributions). For an average earner, the tax credit on personal income tax leads to a larger overall tax advantage on contributions (10% of the present value of contributions) than the partial tax deduction of contributions (6% of the present value of contributions). Indeed, as long as the marginal tax rate is lower or equal to 50% (10% divided by 20%), the effective tax rate that applies to contributions will be lower with the tax credit (marginal tax rate minus 10 percentage points) than with the partial tax deduction (80% of the marginal tax rate).

Impact of the level of income

The overall tax advantage varies with the level of income for all the selected stylised tax regimes. Figure 2.2 illustrates how the overall tax advantage (solid line) and its different

Figure 2.2. **Overall tax advantage provided though stylised tax regimes, by income level and component**

As a percentage of the present value of contributions

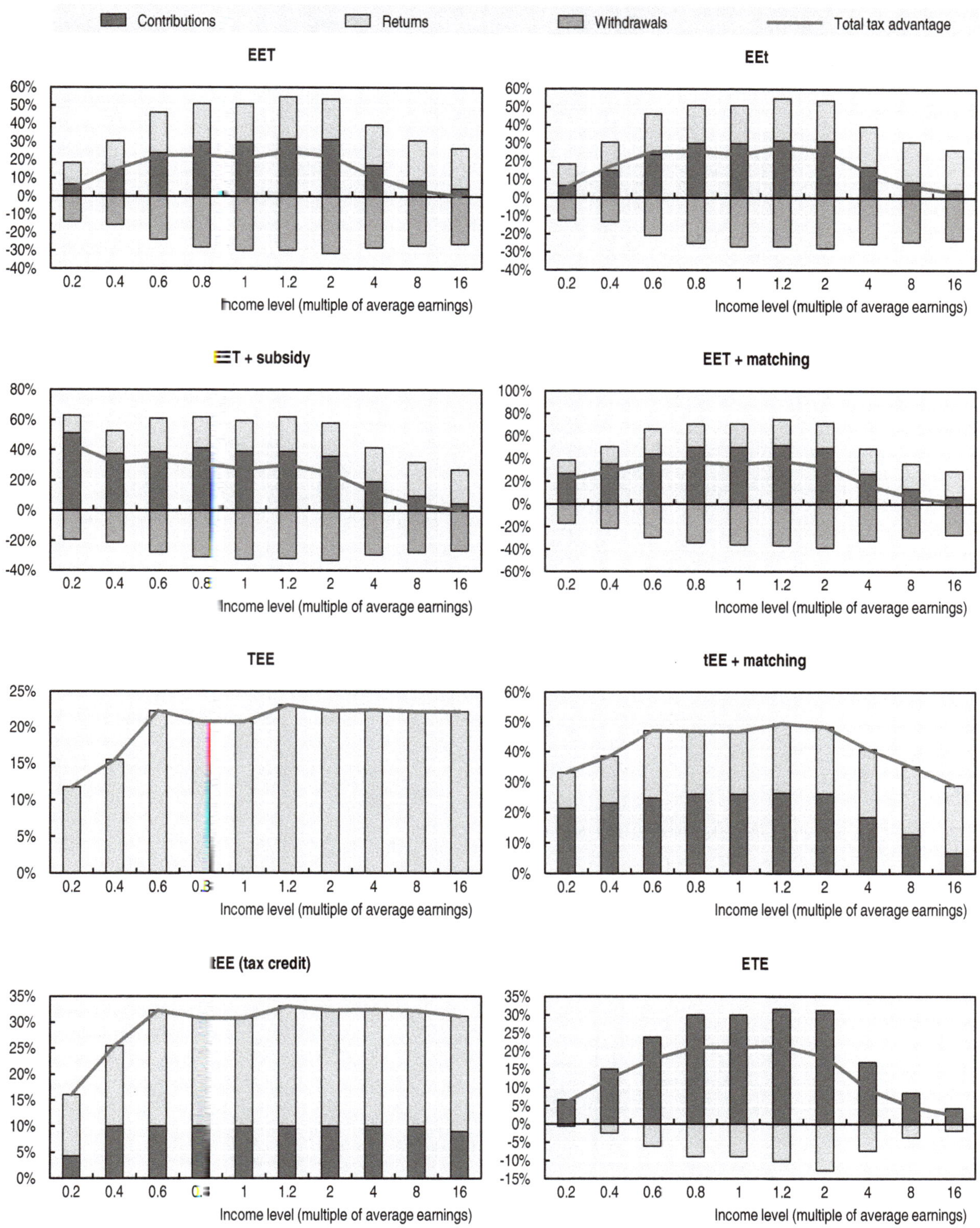

Figure 2.2. **Overall tax advantage provided though stylised tax regimes, by income level and component** *(cont.)*

As a percentage of the present value of contributions

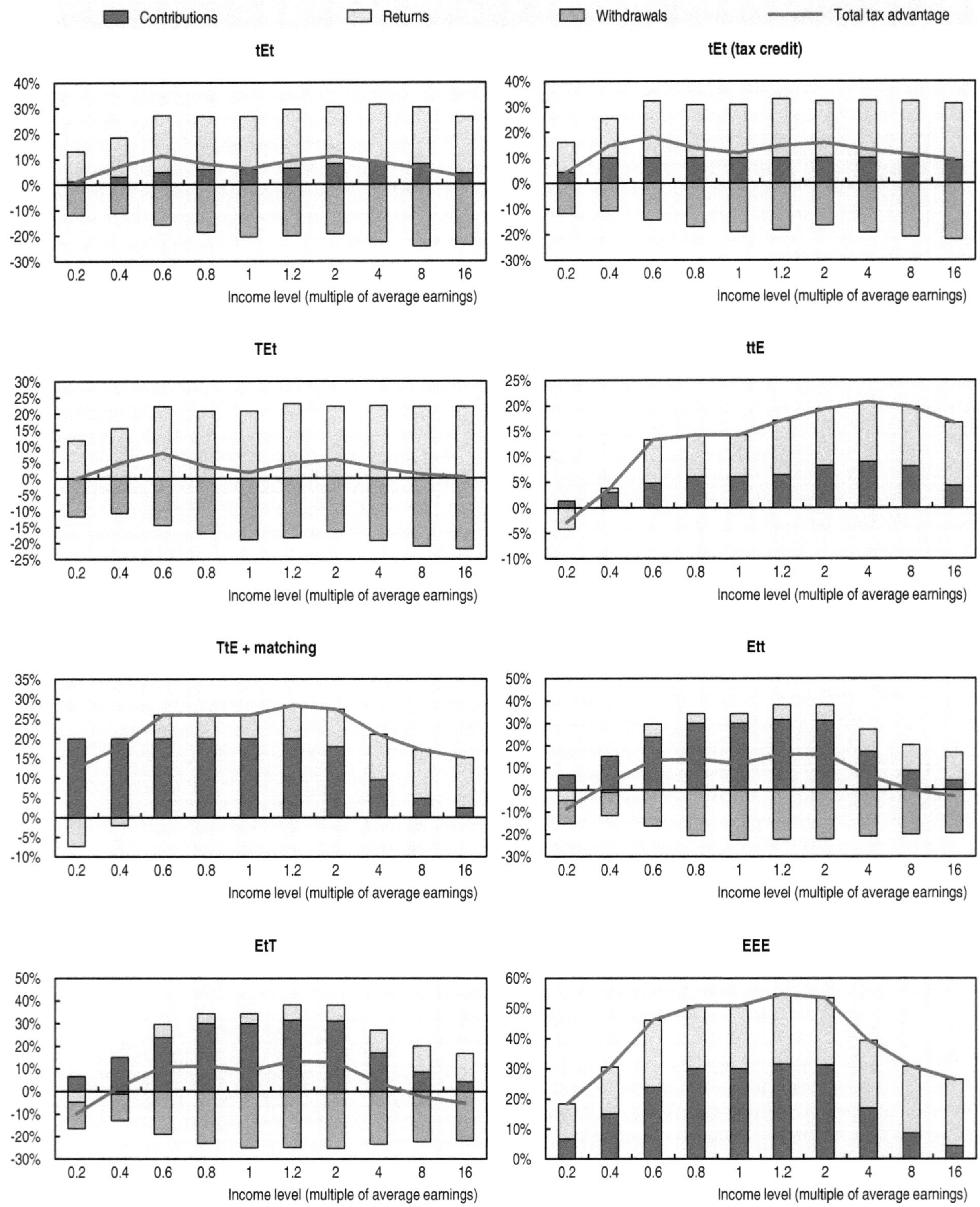

Note: E stands for exempt and T for taxed.

StatLink http://dx.doi.org/10.1787/888933430331

components (tax advantage on contributions, tax advantage on returns and tax advantage on withdrawals) change with the level of income for the 16 selected stylised tax regimes. Depending on the tax regime, different groups of individuals can expect to get a larger overall tax advantage. The analysis considers three income groups: low-income individuals (earning less than 60% of the average earnings), medium-income individuals (earning between 0.6 and 2 times the average earnings) and high-income individuals (earning more than 2 times the average earnings).

Individuals of all income levels can expect to pay less in taxes when contributing to a private pension plan rather than to a traditional savings account for all the selected stylised tax regimes, except for three cases relevant to very low-income individuals. Very low-income individuals, earning only 20% of average earnings, would pay more tax on private pensions than on traditional savings accounts if the "ttE", "Ett" or "EtT" stylised regimes applied to private pension plans. These individuals have a null marginal tax rate during part of their career, meaning that returns in the traditional savings account are not taxed, while returns in the private pension plan are taxed at the flat rate of 15%.

Of the 16 selected stylised tax regimes, 10 provide a larger tax saving to medium-income individuals as compared to low and high-income individuals when they contribute to a private pension plan rather than to a traditional savings account. The overall tax advantage increases with income and then falls for the following stylised tax regimes: "EEE", "EET", "EEt", "tEE + matching", "tEE (tax credit)", "ETE", "ttE", "TtE + matching", "Ett" and "EtT". The main driving force is the tax treatment of contributions (the tax treatment of returns on investment and withdrawals have a lesser impact on the change in the overall tax advantage by income). When contributions are deductible from income ("E××"), the tax advantage on contributions increases with income, because the tax paid on contributions to a traditional savings account increases as the individual reaches higher income tax brackets. However, the analysis assumes a limit on the tax deductibility of contributions. This means that contributions to the private pension plan above EUR 7 300 are subject to personal income tax. The higher the income, the higher the likelihood that contributions will exceed the limit (with a 10% contribution rate). Consequently, individuals earning more than the average wage will pay tax on part of their contributions to private pension plans, thereby reducing their overall tax advantage on contributions.[8] The same mechanism is engaged when contributions are partially deductible from income ("t××"). The overall tax advantage on contributions initially increases with income, but then declines for high-income individuals because of the limit on the tax deductibility of contributions.

Medium and high-income individuals can expect to save more in taxes paid than low-income individuals when only contributions to private pension plans are taxed ("TEE" stylised tax regime). This tax regime only differs from that of traditional savings accounts ("TTE") in the tax treatment of returns on investment. As returns in the pension plan are exempt from income tax, the overall tax advantage on returns increases with income, because the tax paid on returns in a traditional savings account increases as the individual reaches higher income tax brackets. As long as there are no limits on the tax exemption of returns, the overall tax advantage does not diminish for high-income individuals.

Flat-rate state subsidies paid into the private pension plan can help target tax advantages at low-income individuals. As the value of the subsidy is fixed across the income scale, its value in relative terms is higher for low-income individuals. Therefore, the state subsidy significantly increases the overall tax advantage for low-income individuals only when comparing the "EET + subsidy" stylised tax regime with the "EET" stylised tax regime.

Tax credits on personal income tax and state matching contributions paid into the private pension plan can be used to smooth out the tax advantage across income groups. The "TtE + matching" stylised tax regime illustrates perfectly the impact of the matching contribution on the tax advantage on contributions. The tax advantage on contributions is income neutral for low and medium-income individuals (the tax advantage corresponds to 20% of the present value of contributions – same as the match rate) and falls with income after reaching the contribution cap. As for the tax credit, the tax advantage on contributions is equal to 10% of the present value of contributions for most income levels (see "tEE (tax credit)" and "tEt (tax credit)" stylised tax regimes). However tax credits are less valuable for low-income individuals who pay little or no income tax, because they are non-refundable, and for high-income individuals, because of the cap on the amount of the tax credit.

As a result of the different effects of income on the overall tax advantage, the ranking of the 16 selected stylised tax regimes as shown in Figure 2.1 for the average earner varies according to income. Thus, while medium-income individuals are better off with the "EEE" stylised tax regime, low-income individuals would save more tax with the "EET + subsidy" and with the "tEE + matching" stylised tax regimes. For high-income individuals, the "tEE (tax credit)" and "tEE + matching" stylised tax regimes are more interesting in terms of tax saved.

Impact of the length of the contribution period

The overall tax advantage of contributing to a private pension plan rather than to a traditional savings account increases with the length of the contribution period. For each of the selected stylised tax regimes, Table 2.3 shows the overall tax advantage for three different lengths of the contribution period: 45 years (baseline, from age 20 to 65), 40 years (late entry at age 25 or early retirement at age 60) and 50 years (delayed retirement to age 70). The longer the contribution period, the larger the overall tax advantage.[9] For example,

Table 2.3. **Overall tax advantage provided through stylised tax regimes, according to the length of the contribution period, average earner**

As a percentage of the present value of contributions

Stylised tax regime	Baseline (20-65)	Late entry (25-65)	Early retirement (20-60)	Delayed retirement (20-70)
EEE	51	49	49	54
tEE + matching	47	45	45	50
EET + matching	35	33	33	36
tEE (tax credit)	31	29	29	34
EET + subsidy	27	27	27	29
TtE + matching	26	26	26	27
EEt	24	22	22	27
ETE	21	22	22	20
EET	21	19	19	24
TEE	21	19	19	24
ttE	14	14	14	16
tEt (tax credit)	12	10	10	15
Ett	12	11	12	14
EtT	9	8	9	12
tEt	6	4	5	9
TEt	2	0	0	5

Note: E stands for exempt and T for taxed.

StatLink http://dx.doi.org/10.1787/888933430370

for an average earner contributing to an "EET" private pension plan, the present value of tax saved represents 19% of the present value of contributions after 40 years of contributions, 21% after 45 years and 24% after 50 years.[10]

The main driver of this result is the compound interest. When returns on investment in private pension plans are tax-exempt (×E×) or taxed at a preferential rate (15% as opposed to the individual's marginal rate of personal income tax, ×t×), the tax advantage on returns on investment is positive. The longer is the contribution period, the longer the investment income can accumulate and the larger is the tax advantage on returns. The tax advantages on contributions and on withdrawals also vary with the length of the contribution period, but the variations are not significant when expressed as a percentage of the present value of contributions. Because of the compound interest, returns on investment increase in a larger proportion than contributions and withdrawals when the contribution period is longer. Therefore, the variation in the tax advantage on returns is the main driver of the variation in the overall tax advantage when the length of the contribution period changes.

Impact of the contribution rate

The overall tax advantage varies with changes in the contribution rate. The comparison of the overall tax advantage when contributing 5% or 10% to a private pension plan rather than to a traditional savings account produces interesting results.

A lower contribution rate translates into a larger overall tax advantage for high-income individuals in tax regimes in which contributions are tax-deductible, either fully (E××) or partially (t××). As illustrated in Figure 2.3, with a 5% contribution rate the overall tax advantage does not decline for the last two income groups for the "ttE" stylised tax regime, while it does with a 10% contribution rate. This is because the tax deductibility limit on contributions is harder to reach when the contribution rate is halved. The same explanation applies in the case of state matching contributions and tax credits (see "tEE + matching" and "tEE (tax credit)" stylised tax regimes).

For tax regimes in which pension payments and withdrawals are taxed, either fully (××T) or partially (××t), a lower contribution rate may translate into a larger overall tax advantage for individuals earning between 60% and 80% of the average wage. Indeed, a lower contribution rate leads to lower pension payments during retirement, potentially moving individuals into lower income tax brackets. If a lower marginal tax rate applies, then the individual pays less tax on withdrawals. For example, for the "EET" stylised tax regime, individuals earning between 60% and 80% of the average wage pay less in taxes on pension withdrawals (as a proportion of the present value of their contributions) when they contribute 5% instead of 10%.

An individual entitled to a state subsidy will not get any additional tax advantage when saving above the amount laid down in the plan rules that prompts the maximum subsidy. In the stylised "EET + subsidy" tax regime, the maximum subsidy is obtained with a 5% contribution rate. When contributing more than 5%, the subsidy does not increase, but the present value of contributions does. Therefore, the tax advantage on contributions (ratio between the difference in the present value of tax paid on contributions and the present value of contributions) gets smaller for higher contribution rates, reducing the overall tax advantage. As the value of the subsidy is proportionally reduced for contribution rates below 5%, the tax advantage on contributions remains constant for lower contribution rates.

Figure 2.3. **Overall tax advantage provided through stylised tax regimes, according to the contribution rate, by income level**

As a percentage of the present value of contributions

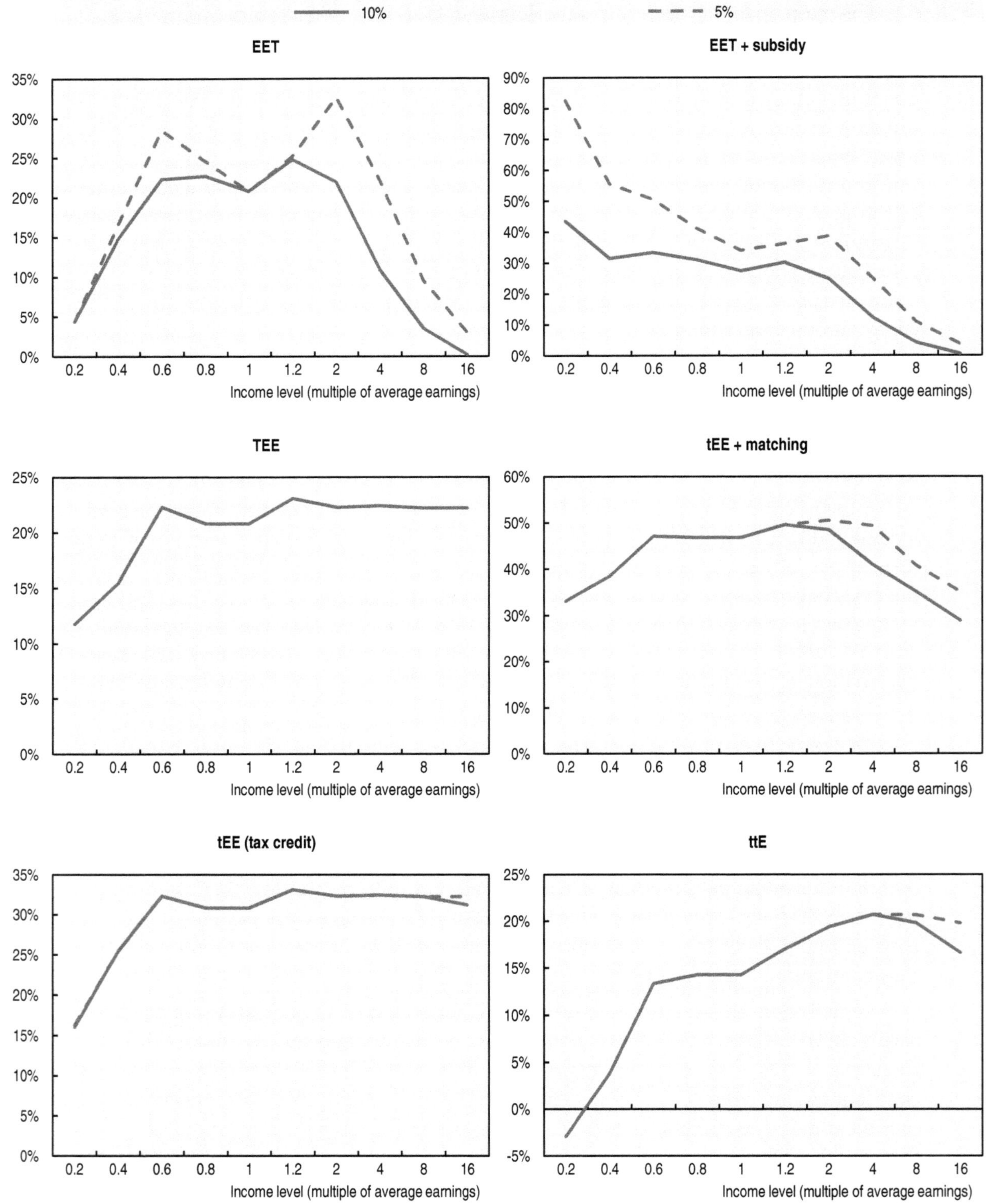

Note: E stands for exempt and T for taxed.

StatLink http://dx.doi.org/10.1787/888933430349

Finally, the overall tax advantage is not sensitive to the contribution rate in the case of the "TEE" stylised tax regime. Indeed, the overall tax advantage provided through this tax regime is only derived from the preferential tax treatment of returns on investment. As long as there are no limits to the tax exemption of returns in the private pension plan, and the returns in the traditional savings account are subject to personal income tax, the amount contributed has no impact on the tax advantage on returns.

Impact of the type of pay-out option

This sub-section considers five types of pay-out options and explores how sensitive the overall tax advantage under different tax regimes is to them. The types considered are: annuity certain with fixed nominal payments, annuity certain with inflation-indexed payments, life-long annuity with fixed nominal payments, programmed withdrawals and single lump-sum payment.[11] For certain stylised tax regimes, the type of pay-out option can have an impact on the tax paid on returns on investment and the tax paid on withdrawals. The tax paid on contributions is never sensitive to the type of pay-out option.

Individuals withdrawing their savings all at once as a lump sum receive a lower overall tax advantage than individuals getting regular income during retirement (annuities and programmed withdrawals) for stylised tax regimes in which pension payments and withdrawals are taxed (either fully or partially). As illustrated in Figure 2.4, which shows only a subset of the stylised tax regimes, the tax due on withdrawals is larger in the case of a lump-sum payment for the "EET", "TEt" and "Ett" stylised tax regimes. When the whole amount of assets accumulated at retirement is taken as a lump sum, the individual may move to a higher income tax bracket (with a bigger tax rate), therefore paying more tax than when the assets are spread over retirement to get a regular income. As a consequence, the overall tax advantage is lower with the lump-sum option, and even negative in the case of the "TEt" stylised tax regime.

Programmed withdrawals provide a larger overall tax advantage than annuities for most stylised tax regimes. With programmed withdrawals, assets remain invested during the retirement phase and continue to be taxed in the traditional savings account. Therefore, the overall tax advantage is larger with programmed withdrawals than with annuities for stylised tax regime in which returns are tax-exempt (e.g. "EET", "TEE" and "TEt" stylised tax regimes) or taxed at a lower rate than in the traditional savings account (e.g. "ttE" and "Ett" stylised tax regimes). It is the other way around for the "ETE" stylised tax regime because, even though returns are subject to personal income tax for both the private pension plan and the traditional savings account, the tax due on returns in the case of the "ETE" private pension plan is larger (because after-tax contributions are bigger).

Differences are smaller between different types of annuity products. For all stylised tax regimes, the overall tax advantage is exactly the same when comparing an annuity certain with fixed nominal payments to an annuity certain with inflation-indexed payments. Although the payments in each year are different, the sum of the present value of payments over the retirement period is identical for both types of annuities. Individuals getting a life-long annuity receive a slightly lower overall tax advantage than individuals getting an annuity certain for stylised tax regimes in which pension payments and withdrawals are taxed (either fully or partially). The main difference between a life-long annuity and an annuity certain is that the number of payments is not known in advance for the life-long annuity.[12] In the calculation of the annuity factor, the probability of still being alive at each age is taken into account. The consequence is that the payments are

Figure 2.4. **Overall tax advantage provided through stylised tax regimes, by type of pay-out option and component, average earner**

As a percentage of the present value of contributions

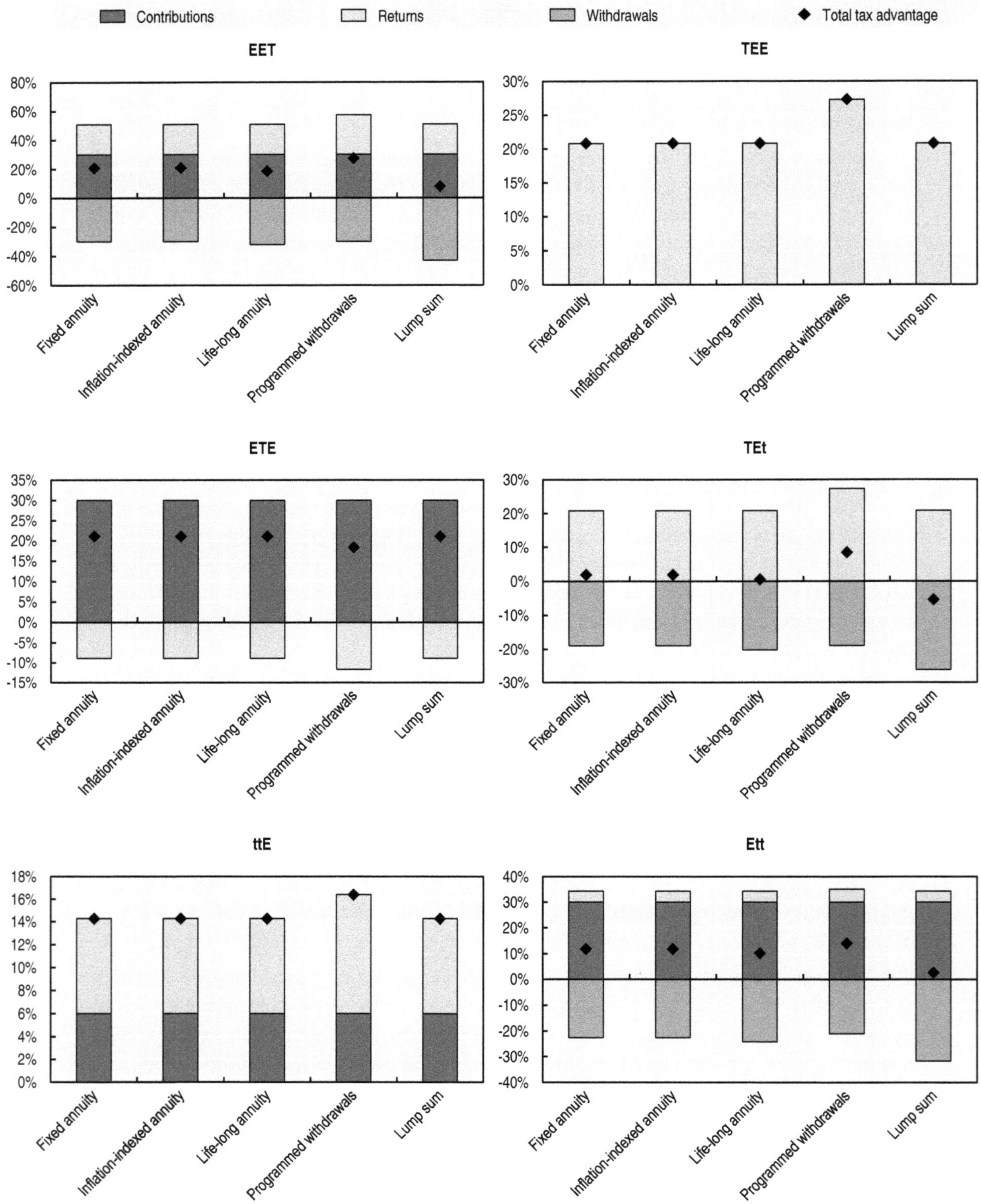

Note: E stands for exempt and T for taxed.

StatLink http://dx.doi.org/10.1787/888933430353

bigger with a life-long annuity than with an annuity certain because the annuity provider considers that there is a positive probability for the individual to die before reaching the average life expectancy of their cohort. When pension benefits are taxed, this translates into a higher tax due and a lower overall tax advantage.

Impact of financial and economic parameters

The overall tax advantage can also change when parameters such as returns, discount rates, inflation and productivity growth change. The baseline has inflation at 2%, productivity growth at 1.5%, and the real rate of return on investment and the real discount rate equal to 3%.

The overall tax advantage increases with inflation and real returns for all the stylised tax regimes except one (Table 2.4). Higher inflation (from 2% to 3%) or higher real rates of return (from 3% to 4%) lead to higher nominal rates of return. Therefore, for all the tax regimes offering a preferential tax treatment on returns on investment, the tax advantage on returns is larger in a higher inflation and return scenario, because the tax paid on returns in the traditional savings account is higher. A higher inflation or return has no impact on the tax advantages on contributions and withdrawals. For the "ETE" stylised tax regime, even though returns are subject to personal income tax in both the private pension plan and the traditional savings account, the tax due on returns in the case of the "ETE" private pension plan is larger (because after-tax contributions are bigger).

Table 2.4. **Overall tax advantage provided through stylised tax regimes, according to different economic parameters, average earner**

As a percentage of the present value of contributions

Stylised tax regime	Baseline	Higher inflation (+1pp)	Higher real return (+1pp)*	Lower real discount rate (-1pp)
EEE	51	54	55	53
tEE + matching	47	50	51	49
EET + matching	35	38	38	27
tEE (tax credit)	31	34	35	33
EET + subsidy	27	30	31	21
TtE + matching	26	27	27	26
EEt	24	27	28	18
ETE	21	20	19	20
EET	21	24	25	15
TEE	21	24	25	23
ttE	14	15	16	15
tEt (tax credit)	12	15	16	9
Ett	12	13	13	6
EtT	9	10	11	3
tEt	6	9	11	3
TEt	2	5	6	-1

* In this scenario, the discount rate is still equal to the rate of return.

Note: E stands for exempt and T for taxed.

StatLink http://dx.doi.org/10.1787/888933430389

The impact on the overall tax advantage differs according to the tax regime when the discount rate is lower than the rate of return. A lower discount rate gives a higher weight to future flows. The overall tax advantage therefore declines significantly for tax regimes in which withdrawals are taxed (××T or ××t) because any future differences are amplified by the lower discount rate.

The impact of productivity growth on the overall tax advantage varies according to both the stylised tax regime and the income level.

- An increase in productivity growth translates into higher contributions through higher wages. For stylised tax regimes with a preferential tax treatment on contributions (E×× and t××), this leads to an increase in the tax advantage on contributions for low-income individuals and a decrease in the tax advantage on contributions for high-income individuals because:
  - the tax paid on contributions is larger in the traditional savings account;
  - but the tax-deductibility limit for contributions is reached by more wage-earners, as this limit is assumed to be indexed to inflation only.
- Inflation-indexed state subsidies have a lower weight on the tax advantage on contributions when productivity growth increases.
- State matching contributions still provide the same tax advantage on contributions when productivity growth increases, except that the maximum state contribution, which is assumed to be indexed to inflation only, is reached by more wage-earners.
- An increase in productivity growth translates eventually into higher pension payments and withdrawals. For stylised tax regimes with taxable withdrawals (××T and ××t), this leads to an increase in tax due on withdrawals, potentially at higher marginal tax rates as income limits for all tax brackets are assumed to be inflation-indexed only.

Main findings

The comparison of the stylised tax regimes allows for a better understanding of the mechanisms through which they may provide an overall tax advantage to individuals contributing to private pension plans rather than to traditional savings accounts. The main findings are:

- For all stylised tax regimes and most income levels, individuals can expect to pay less in taxes when contributing to a private pension plan rather than to a traditional savings account. Usually, the positive overall tax advantage derives from a preferential tax treatment for private pension contributions and returns on investment that is not offset by the potential taxation of benefits. The preferential tax treatment for contributions and returns comes in the form of tax exemptions/deductions, tax credits, lower tax rates and state financial incentives.
- State subsidies and state matching contributions increase the overall tax advantage.
- A tax credit on contributions will provide higher tax savings than a partial tax deduction of contributions as long as the tax rate on contributions is lower than the ratio of the tax credit rate to the deduction rate.
- The overall tax advantage increases with income for tax regimes in which contributions are deductible from income, either fully or partially. It then falls after a certain level of income because of the tax-deductibility limits.
- Flat-rate state subsidies paid into the private pension plan change the profile of the tax advantage with respect to income as they target the tax advantage at low-income individuals. Low-income individuals may even be better off in terms of tax paid with the "EET + subsidy" stylised tax regime than with the "EEE" stylised tax regime, as long as the subsidy represents a significant share of their income.

- Tax credits on personal income tax and state matching contributions paid into the private pension plan can be used to smooth out the tax advantage across income groups. However, low-income individuals, who pay little or no income tax, benefit less from non-refundable tax credits. Caps can be introduced to lower the tax advantage for high-income individuals.
- The overall tax advantage increases with the length of the contribution period because of the compound interest.
- A higher contribution rate translates into a lower overall tax advantage for high-income individuals in tax regimes where contributions are tax deductible up to a limit as they are more likely to reach this limit.
- An individual entitled to a state subsidy will not get any additional tax advantage when saving above the amount laid down in the plan rules that prompts the maximum subsidy.
- Lump sums provide a lower overall tax advantage than pay-out options offering regular payments in stylised tax regimes in which pension payments and withdrawals are taxed, because they may move individuals into a higher income-tax bracket.
- Programmed withdrawals provide a larger overall tax advantage than annuities for most stylised tax regimes because assets remain invested during the retirement phase and continue to be tax-exempt in the retirement vehicle, while they are taxed in the traditional savings account.
- A higher nominal rate of return translates into a larger overall tax advantage when returns on investment receive preferential tax treatment in the private pension plan. This remains true when higher nominal returns are just the result of higher inflation.
- A lower discount rate translates into a lower overall tax advantage for tax regimes in which withdrawals are taxed because any future differences are amplified.

2.2. Does the tax treatment of retirement savings in different OECD countries provide an advantage when people save for retirement?

This section sets out the overall tax advantage in different OECD countries. The overall tax advantage is the amount of tax saved by individuals when contributing to different types of private pension plans instead of to a benchmark savings vehicle. It is calculated for all types of private pension plans that exist in OECD countries, as long as a different tax regime applies.

The methodology is the same as that described in Section 2.1, but in addition:

- The analysis considers all mandatory and voluntary plans, occupational and personal plans, DB and DC plans.[13]
- All the country-specific parameters that apply for each type of plan are taken into account (e.g. specific tax-deductibility limits, ceiling on the lifetime value of pension assets, state financial incentives).
- The personal income tax system (i.e. the tax brackets and the marginal tax rates) is also country-specific.
- The private pension plans are compared to different benchmark savings vehicles: a traditional savings account, a mutual fund (or collective investment scheme) and any other country-specific popular savings vehicles (e.g. life insurance contracts, special

savings accounts). The analysis accounts for the country-specific tax treatment that applies to each benchmark savings vehicle.

- Minimum and mandatory contribution rates fixed by regulation are applied whenever they exist. For voluntary contributions, the analysis assumes a 10% contribution rate.
- The age of retirement assumed in the analysis is the official age of retirement in each country.

The section first presents the results when the benchmark savings vehicle is a traditional savings account. It then looks at the impact of changing the benchmark.

Average earners in all OECD countries enjoy an advantage when saving for retirement in a private pension plan rather than in a traditional savings account in terms of tax paid. This is because the preferential tax treatment that contributions and returns on investment usually enjoy in a private pension plan (as compared to a traditional savings account) outweighs the potential taxation of benefits. Table 2.5 provides for the average earner the overall tax advantage and its three components (tax advantage on contributions, tax advantage on returns and tax advantage on withdrawals), for all OECD countries and selected types of private pension plans. It shows that the overall tax advantage is positive for all types of plans except two: personal pension insurance plans in Austria (-14% of the present value of contributions) and personal pension plans in Norway (-2%). In the case of Austria, contributions are not tax deductible and an extra 4% insurance tax is levied on individual contributions. In the case of Norway, contributions to voluntary personal plans are partially deductible from income, but this is not sufficient to compensate for the tax paid on withdrawals. For the other countries, the amount of tax saved varies from 1% of the present value of contributions in Luxembourg (personal plans) and Slovenia, up to 51% in Israel and Mexico (mandatory contributions), with a maximum overall tax advantage corresponding to 281% of the present value of contributions in Mexico for solidarity savings (voluntary scheme for public sector employees).[14]

Table 2.5. **Overall tax advantage in OECD countries by component and type of plan, average earner**

As a percentage of the present value of contributions

	Type of plan/contribution	Tax regime	Overall tax advantage			
			Contributions %	Returns %	Withdrawals %	Total %
Australia[1]	Concessional contributions	ttE	22	15	0	37
	Non-concessional contributions	TtE + matching	0	18	0	18
Austria	Pension companies	tEt	19	15	-23	11
	Direct commitments	EET	42	15	-49	8
	Direct insurance	tEt + matching	0	15	-7	8
	Personal pension insurance	TET	-2	15	-27	-14
	State-sponsored retirement provision plans	TEE + matching	0	15	0	15
Belgium	Occupational plans	tEt (tax credit)	62	2	-62	3
	Pension savings accounts	tEt (tax credit)	5	2	-3	5
Canada	All	EET	37	25	-39	24
Chile	Mandatory contributions	EET + matching	5	7	-1	11
	Type A voluntary contributions	TTE + matching	15	1	0	16
	Type B voluntary contributions	EET	5	7	-1	11
Czech Republic	Supplementary plans	tEE + matching	11	15	0	26
Denmark	ATP	EtT	37	7	-30	13
	Quasi-mandatory occupational	EtT	37	7	-17	27
	"Age savings" plans	TtE	-10	15	-3	2

Table 2.5. **Overall tax advantage in OECD countries by component and type of plan, average earner** *(cont.)*

As a percentage of the present value of contributions

	Type of plan/contribution	Tax regime	Overall tax advantage			
			Contributions %	Returns %	Withdrawals %	Total %
Estonia	Mandatory contributions	EEt	20	17	-14	23
	Voluntary contributions	tEE (tax credit)	20	17	0	37
Finland	Voluntary occupational plans	EET	34	17	-46	5
	Voluntary personal plans set up by employers	EET	42	17	-49	11
	Voluntary personal plans set up by individuals	tET (tax credit)	27	17	-17	27
France	"Article 83" plans	tEt	30	24	-29	25
	"Article 39" plans	EEt	33	24	-30	27
	"PERCO" plans	ttt	15	19	-12	21
	"PERP" plans	tEt	30	24	-29	25
Germany	Pension funds	EET	26	14	-20	20
	Direct commitments	EET	40	14	-39	15
	"Riester" plans	EET + subsidy	14	14	-9	19
	Private pension insurance	TEt	0	14	-3	11
Greece	All	EET	26	13	-25	14
Hungary	Voluntary private pension funds	tEE + matching	26	19	0	46
	Individual retirement accounts	TEE + matching	20	19	0	39
Iceland[2]	Occupational DB plans	EET	43	12	-18	37
	Occupational DC plans	EET	43	12	-12	44
	Personal plans	EET	22	16	-31	7
Ireland	All	EET	40	24	-29	35
Israel	All	tEt (tax credit)	31	20	0	51
Italy	All	Ett	38	-1	-5	32
Japan	Corporate DB plans	EEt	31	15	-21	24
	Corporate DC plans	EEt	31	15	-19	26
	Individual DC plans	EEt	31	16	-16	31
Korea	Occupational DB plans	EEt	18	17	-17	17
	Occupational DC plans	tEt (tax credit)	16	17	-18	14
Latvia	Mandatory scheme	EET	23	9	-23	9
	Voluntary scheme	EtE	23	-3	0	20
Luxembourg	Occupational DB plans	tEE	22	6	0	28
	Occupational DC plans	tEE	17	5	0	23
	Personal plans	EEt	10	5	-14	1
Mexico[3]	Mandatory contributions	tEt + matching + subsidy	33	18	0	51
	Short-term voluntary contributions	tTE	2	6	0	8
	Complementary contributions	ETt	22	3	0	24
	Long-term voluntary contributions	EEt	22	18	0	40
	Special accounts	EET	22	18	-30	10
	Solidarity savings	TTt + matching	325	-44	0	281
	Occupational plans	EEt	22	18	0	40
Netherlands	Occupational DB plans	EET	48	26	-42	32
	Occupational DC plans	EET	49	24	-41	32
	Personal plan	EET	48	26	-46	29
New Zealand	Occupational plans	ttE	1	2	0	3
	"KiwiSaver" plans	ttE + matching	12	-1	0	11
Norway	Occupational plans	EET	35	18	-33	20
	Personal plans	tET	5	18	-25	-2
Poland	"OFE" plans	EET	19	17	-18	18
	"IKZE" plans	EEt	19	17	-10	26
	"PPE" and "IKE" plans	TEE	0	17	0	17
Portugal	Occupational plans	EET	32	20	-36	15
	Personal plans	tEt	5	20	-4	21

Table 2.5. **Overall tax advantage in OECD countries by component and type of plan, average earner** *(cont.)*

As a percentage of the present value of contributions

	Type of plan/contribution	Tax regime	Overall tax advantage			
			Contributions %	Returns %	Withdrawals %	Total %
Slovak Republic	"Pillar 2" plans	EEE	19	17	0	36
	"Pillar 3" plans	tTE	2	7	0	9
Slovenia	All	EET	24	8	-31	1
Spain	All	EET	33	15	-38	9
Sweden	Quasi-mandatory occupational	EtT	44	4	-35	13
	Individual pension savings	EtT	39	6	-34	12
Switzerland	Mandatory occupational plans	EET	31	18	-18	31
	Personal plans	EET	30	22	-22	30
Turkey	Personal plans	TtE + matching	25	5	0	30
	Employer-sponsored group contracts	TtE	0	6	0	6
United Kingdom	Occupational DB plans	EET	31	26	-28	30
	Occupational DC plans	EET	31	26	-23	34
	Auto-enrolment plans	EET + matching	46	25	-23	48
United States	401(k) plans	EET + tax credit	25	21	-22	24
	Individual retirement accounts	EET + tax credit	25	22	-21	26
	"Roth" contributions	TEE + tax credit	0	22	0	22

1. The calculations do not include the Medicare Levy nor the policy changes to superannuation announced in the 2014-17 Budget.
2. The analysis assumes that benefits are taken as an inflation-indexed annuity in the case of occupational plans and as programmed withdrawals in the case of personal plans instead of an annuity certain.
3. The analysis assumes that benefits are taken as a lump sum for short-term contributions and contributions into special saving for retirement accounts instead of an annuity certain.

Note: E stands for exempt and T for taxed. Minimum and mandatory contribution rates apply whenever they exist. For voluntary contributions, the analysis assumes a 10% contribution rate. When the accrual rate for an occupational DB plan is not known, the analysis assumes 1.5%.

StatLink http://dx.doi.org/10.1787/888933430393

The differences observed across countries are due not only to the characteristics of the tax regimes applied to pension plans and savings vehicles, but also to the characteristics of the personal income tax system in each country (i.e. the tax brackets and the tax rates). In Canada and Greece for example, the overall tax advantage of contributing to a private pension plan is different (24% and 14% of the present value of contributions respectively), even though an "EET" tax regime applies to pension plans in both countries. However, an average earner in Canada has a 31.15% marginal tax rate, while an average earner in Greece has a 22% marginal tax rate.[15]

In many OECD countries, the overall tax advantage varies according to the type of plan to which individuals contribute. Indeed, many countries apply different tax treatments to different types of plans. For example, in Mexico, individuals can choose between six different vehicles for their voluntary pension contributions. However, because the tax treatment of these voluntary contributions varies according to the vehicle, the overall tax advantage changes from 8% of the present value of contributions for short-term voluntary contributions to 40% for long-term voluntary contributions and occupational pension plans, or even 281% for solidarity savings, which is a scheme exclusively for public sector workers.

When employee and employer contributions to occupational pension plans receive a different tax treatment, the overall tax advantage depends on the relative importance of each type of contribution in the total. For instance, in Hungary, employer contributions are not considered as taxable income for individuals, while employees' contributions are made out of taxed earnings. As the analysis assumes that employer contributions represent 40% of the total contributions in occupational plans and 0% in individual retirement accounts, the tax advantage on contributions is larger for occupational plans because part of the contributions is tax-exempt.

Introducing financial incentives like state subsidies or state matching contributions increases the overall tax advantage. For example, in New Zealand, the same tax regime applies to occupational pension plans and to KiwiSaver plans (contributions and returns on investment are taxed, but at a lower rate than for a traditional savings account, and withdrawals are tax-free). Adding the state matching contribution for KiwiSaver plans boosts the overall tax advantage from 3% to 11% of the present value of contributions.

In some countries, the overall tax advantage is larger for mandatory pension savings than for voluntary pension savings. This is the case in Australia, where the amount of tax saved by the average earner represents 37% of the present value of contributions when making mandatory contributions, but only 18% when making voluntary contributions. This trend is also found in Iceland (44% for occupational DC plans as opposed to 7% for personal plans), Mexico (51% for mandatory contributions as opposed to 40% for long-term voluntary contributions), the Netherlands (32% for occupational plans as opposed to 29% for personal plans), Norway (20% for occupational plans as opposed to -2% for personal plans) and the Slovak Republic (36% for pillar 2 plans as opposed to 9% for pillar 3 plans).

However, some other countries encourage more voluntary savings. This is the case in Chile (the amount of tax saved represents 16% of the present value of contributions for type A voluntary contributions as opposed to 11% for mandatory contributions), Denmark (27% for quasi-mandatory occupational plans as opposed to 13% for the ATP plan), Estonia (37% for voluntary contributions as opposed to 23% for mandatory contributions), and Latvia (20% for the voluntary scheme as opposed to 9% for the mandatory scheme).

In 20 OECD countries, there is at least one type of pension plan for which the overall tax advantage increases with income and it decreases after certain level of income. Table 2.6 identifies 12 groups of pension plans according to the way the overall tax advantage varies with the income level. The variation of the overall tax advantage with income is the result of the different tax regimes, the plan-specific limits on the amount of contributions attracting tax relief and the characteristics of the personal income tax system in each country. The group with most countries in it is that in which medium-income individuals get the largest tax savings when contributing to a private pension plan rather than to a traditional savings account, because the overall tax advantage first increases with income but then decreases once caps or limits on tax relief are reached.

Low-income individuals get the largest tax savings in 19 countries, for selected pension plans. For most of these pension plans, there is a financial incentive from the state in the form of a matching contribution or of a subsidy. However, there are other ways to achieve the same result. Personal pension plans in Portugal can be used as an illustration. A "tEt" tax regime applies to them: 20% of contributions are tax deductible, up to a limit which varies with age; returns on investment are tax-exempt; and 15% of the annuity is subject to taxation at the marginal rate of income tax. When compared against a traditional savings account, where contributions are subject to personal income tax and returns are taxed at the fixed rate of 28%, the overall tax advantage obtained with a personal pension plan decreases with income. This is mainly because the tax advantage on returns decreases with income (the tax paid on returns in the traditional savings account

Table 2.6. **Variation of the overall tax advantage with income in OECD countries, by type of plan**

Variation of the overall tax advantage with income	Country – Pension plan
Increase	LUX – Occupational DB; MEX – Short-term voluntary contributions
Increase/Flat/Increase	SVK – Pillar 2
Increase/Flat	BEL – Occupational; CHL – Mandatory; ISR – All; JPN – Corporate DC/Individual DC; CHE – All
Flat/Increase/Flat	DNK – ATP/Quasi-mandatory occupational; POL – IKZE
Increase/Decrease	AUS – Concessional contributions; AUT – Pension companies/Direct commitments; CHL – Agreed deposits/Voluntary B; DNK – Age savings; FIN – Personal set-up by employee; FRA – All; DEU – Pension funds; GRC – All; ISL – Personal; IRL – All; ITA – All; JPN – Corporate DB; KOR – All; LUX – Occupational DC/Personal; MEX – Complementary/ Long-term/Special accounts/Occupational; NLD – All; NZL – Occupational; NOR – Occupational; SVN – All; GBR – All
Flat/Increase/Decrease	POL – OFE
Decrease/Increase/Flat	CAN – All; ESP – All; USA – All
Decrease	AUT – Direct insurance/State-sponsored retirement provision; CZE – All; FIN – Voluntary occupational/Personal set-up by employer; DEU – Riester; MEX – Solidarity savings; NZL – KiwiSaver; NOR – Personal; PRT – All; SVK – Pillar 3; TUR – All
Decrease/Flat	AUS – Non-concessional contributions; AUT – Personal pension insurance; BEL – Personal; EST – Mandatory contributions; LVA – Mandatory scheme; MEX – Mandatory contributions
Flat/Decrease	CHL – Voluntary A; EST – Voluntary contributions; DEU – Basisrente; HUN – All; ISL – Occupational; SWE – All
Flat/Decrease/Flat	POL – PPE/IKE
Flat	DEU – Direct commitments/Private pension insurance; LVA – Voluntary scheme

represents a lower share of the present value of contributions for higher-income individuals because of the fixed tax rate).

Conversely, high-income individuals enjoy the largest tax savings in 10 countries, for selected plans. This is usually because there is no limit on the tax-deductibility of contributions (e.g. mandatory contributions in the Slovak Republic).

Figure 2.5 shows that the choice of the benchmark savings vehicle is also important. For 23 OECD countries, the overall tax advantage that individuals get when contributing to a private pension plan changes when the benchmark changes; for the other 12 countries, the benchmark savings vehicle does not matter. In most cases, the overall tax advantage is lower when the benchmark is a mutual fund rather than a traditional savings account (e.g. those in Figure 2.5 except Luxemburg, Spain and Turkey).[16] This stems from the fact that some forms of investment income attract a more favourable tax treatment in a mutual fund than in a traditional savings account, thus lowering the tax advantage on returns derived from the non-taxation or lower taxation of returns in private pension plans. For example, in Canada, returns on investment are taxed at the individual's marginal rate of income tax in traditional savings accounts. However, for mutual funds, 50% of capital gains from shares and bonds are tax-exempt, with the rest being taxed at the individual's marginal rate of income tax. Conversely, the overall tax advantage increases in the case of

Figure 2.5 **Overall tax advantage in selected OECD countries by type of benchmark savings vehicle, average earner**

As a percentage of the present value of contributions

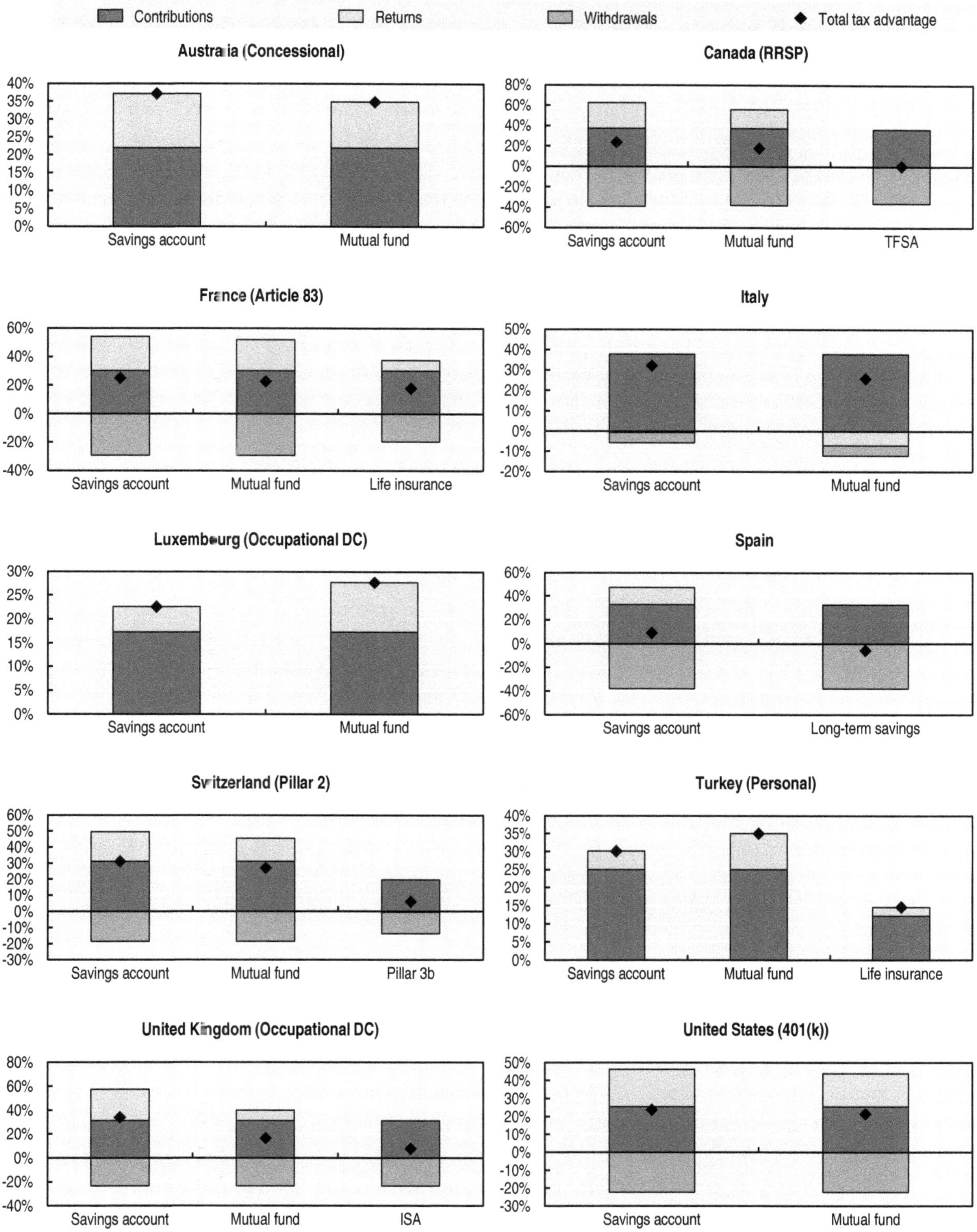

StatLink http://dx.doi.org/10.1787/888933430368

a mutual fund benchmark in Belgium, Korea, Luxembourg, Slovenia and Turkey. Again, the taxation of returns on investment is the cause for the change.

Finally, in some countries, there exist other commonly used savings vehicles with attractive tax treatments that may lower the overall tax advantage of saving for retirement in private pension plans. This is the case in Canada with Tax-Free Savings Accounts (TFSAs), in France with life insurance contracts, in Spain with long-term savings plans, in Switzerland with pillar 3b plans, in Turkey with life insurance contracts and in the United Kingdom with Individual Savings Accounts (ISAs). In these countries, the overall tax advantage when saving in a private pension plan is lower when choosing those special savings accounts as comparators. In Canada, Spain and the United Kingdom, a "TEE" tax regime applies to TFSAs, long-term savings plans and ISAs respectively. Contributing to a private pension plan as compared to one of these savings vehicles therefore does not bring any tax advantage on returns on investment. In the case of Switzerland, an "EET" tax regime applies to pillar 3b plans, just as for private pension plans (the tax relief on contributions is however more limited for pillar 3b plans). Regarding life insurance contracts, a "Ttt" tax regime applies in France and a "ttE" tax regime applies in Turkey.

2.3. Conclusions

This chapter has assessed whether the tax treatment of retirement savings vehicles in different OECD countries provides an advantage for people to save for retirement. The analysis has calculated the overall tax advantage that the tax treatment of saving for retirement provides in different types of pension plans compared to a benchmark savings vehicle. This indicator represents the amount saved in taxes paid by an individual over their lifetime when contributing the same pre-tax amount to a private pension plan instead of a benchmark savings vehicle. It includes the effect of state financial incentives, such as flat-rate subsidies and matching contributions, which can be considered as tax credits paid into the pension account of eligible individuals.

In most OECD countries, the tax treatment of retirement savings provides a tax advantage when people save for retirement instead of saving in other traditional savings vehicles. The size of the overall tax advantage however varies and depends on the tax regime applied to pension plans and savings vehicles, as well as on the characteristics of the personal income tax system (i.e. the tax brackets and the tax rates), the income level, the amount saved, the length of the contribution period, the type of pay-out option, the benchmark savings vehicle chosen as a comparator and other financial and economic parameters.

The amount of tax saved by an average earner when contributing to a private pension plan rather than to a traditional savings account varies greatly across countries. Usually, the positive overall tax advantage derives from a preferential tax treatment for private pension contributions and returns on investment (as compared to a traditional savings account) which is not offset by the potential taxation of benefits.

While many types of pension plans in different OECD countries offer the largest overall tax advantage to medium-income individuals, there are ways to target tax advantages at low-income individuals or to smooth out the tax advantage across the income scale. Flat-rate state subsidies for example significantly increase the overall tax advantage for low-income individuals, as the value of the subsidy is higher for low-income individuals in relative terms. In addition, tax credits on personal income tax and state matching contributions paid into the private pension plan can be used to smooth out the tax advantage across income groups. A state matching contribution provides the same tax advantage on contributions to all income groups, until the contribution cap is reached. It is the same for the tax credit, except that low-income individuals, who pay little or no income tax, benefit less from tax credits.

Tax advantages can encourage people to save for longer periods, but not necessarily to save more in private pension plans. Indeed, individuals contributing longer can expect a larger overall tax advantage, independently of the tax regime applied to their private pension plan. This is due to the effect of compound interest. The longer the contribution period, the longer the investment income can accumulate and the larger is the tax advantage on returns on investment. On the other hand, higher contribution rates may translate into lower tax advantages for high-income individuals, in particular when tax reliefs are provided up to certain limits. Moreover, an individual entitled to a state subsidy will not get any additional tax advantage when saving above the amount laid down in the plan rules that prompts the maximum subsidy.

Straightforward and simple tax rules applying to the private pension system as a whole may increase people's confidence and help to increase participation in and contributions to private pension plans. In a majority of countries, different tax regimes apply to different types of pension plans and savings vehicles at the national level. In addition, the progressivity of income tax systems and the limits that apply to certain tax reliefs modify the tax advantage by income level. This may create confusion for people who may not have the ability to understand the differences, assess the different options and choose the best one for them.

This chapter has measured the overall tax advantage that individuals may enjoy when saving for retirement. However, whether people actually increase retirement savings as a result of these tax advantages is an empirical question that needs to be investigated. In addition, it is important to assess the convenience of tax advantages and financial incentives from the point of view of the state, considering situations where national savings increase or remain constant. These issues will be addressed in future OECD work.

Notes

1. Contributions to private pension plans and savings vehicles, as well as benefits paid by these plans, can be subject to social contributions. These social contributions are usually levied on gross income to finance, among others, health care insurance, unemployment insurance, public pensions and disability pensions. They are not taken into account for the calculation of the overall tax advantage.
2. Annex 2.A1 provides the full description of the framework and assumptions to calculate the overall tax advantage.
3. As a consequence, the individual's wage may move to a higher income tax bracket over time, therefore increasing the marginal tax rate.
4. Table 2.5 in Section 2.2 shows the tax regimes applying to different types of plans in OECD countries. Thirty-one different potential stylised tax regimes could have been selected from the regimes that exist in OECD countries. Only the most relevant ones have been selected for the analysis.
5. Section 2.A1.3 in the annex provides a full description of the assumptions used to build the stylised tax regimes.
6. With an annuity certain, individuals receive a fixed number of payments, determined according to a fixed and equal for all life expectancy defined at the age of retirement. This is different from a life-long annuity, with which individuals receive payments until death.

7. In the case of the "EET" stylised tax regime, the overall tax advantage is actually equal to the tax advantage on returns on investment, as the tax advantage on contributions is compensated by the tax due on withdrawals (the same average tax rate applies during the working life and during retirement for the average earner).
8. The overall tax advantage even ends up negative for individuals earning eight times the average wage or more in the case of the "Ett" and "EtT" stylised tax regimes. The preferential tax treatment on contributions (reduced because of the limit on tax deductibility) and on returns on investment does not compensate for the tax paid on withdrawals.
9. The seemingly opposite result for the "ETE" stylised tax regime is only due to the construction of the indicator. The present value of tax saved (the numerator of the indicator) actually increases with longer contribution periods, as for the other stylised tax regimes. However, the present value of contributions (the denominator of the indicator) also increases with longer contribution periods, leading to a smaller indicator.
10. Early retirement and late entry for the same length of the contribution period provide similar results.
11. With an annuity certain, individuals receive a fixed number of payments, defined according to life expectancy at the age of retirement. This is different from a life-long annuity, with which individuals receive payments until death. With programmed withdrawals, assets remain invested during retirement and the analysis assumes that individuals receive a fixed number of payments, defined according to life expectancy at the age of retirement.
12. The analysis however still considers a fixed time horizon for the calculations, corresponding to the remaining life expectancy at the age of retirement.
13. OECD (2015b) describes the tax treatment of private pension plans in all member countries.
14. Solidarity savings enjoy a very generous state matching programme, as the federal government contributes 3.25 pesos for each peso contributed by the individual.
15. In Canada, tax rates vary according to the province or territory. The calculations assume that the individual lives in Ontario.
16. Also other countries not shown in Figure 2.5, such as the Czech Republic, Denmark, Finland, Greece, Hungary, Iceland, Ireland, Latvia, Mexico, and the Slovak Republic.

References

OECD (2015a), *Pensions at a Glance 2015: OECD and G20 indicators*, OECD Publishing, Paris, *http://dx.doi.org/10.1787/pension_glance-2015-en*.

OECD (2015b), "Stocktaking of the Tax Treatment of Funded Private Pension Plans in OECD and EU Countries", *www.oecd.org/pensions/financial-incentives-retirement-savings.htm*.

ANNEX 2.A1

Framework and assumptions

This annex describes the framework and assumptions used for the stylised tax regimes and the different pension plans that exist in OECD countries to assess the tax advantage provided to individuals saving for retirement in a funded private pension plan. The assessment of the tax advantages is done by comparing the tax treatment of saving in a funded private pension plan instead of a benchmark savings vehicle.

2.A1.1. Definition of the indicator

The overall tax advantage is defined as the difference in the present value of tax paid on contributions, returns on investment and withdrawals between a benchmark savings vehicle and a private pension plan. It represents the amount saved in taxes by the individual over their working and retirement years when contributing to a private pension plan instead of to a benchmark savings vehicle. This indicator is calculated for a flow of contributions made yearly over the career between an initial age, e.g. 20, and the age at which the individual retires, e.g. 65, given a constant contribution rate. It is expressed as a percentage of the present value of contributions.

The overall tax advantage allows assessing the tax advantage over the entire career of an individual by summing-up the effects of the tax treatment of private pension plans induced by a yearly flow of contributions. In addition, it can be calculated for all types of pension plans, including DB plans, and can appropriately account for caps or limits on the amount of contributions attracting tax relief and ceilings on the lifetime value of pension assets, when relevant.

The indicator is calculated for individuals on different levels of income. The level of income is expressed as a multiple of the annual average wage, from 0.2 to 16 times. The annual average wage in 2015 is taken from the OECD Average annual wages database for each country. During the contribution period, wages are assumed to grow in line with inflation and productivity. The analysis assumes constant values for inflation, the growth rate of productivity, the real rate of return on assets and the real discount rate for the entire simulation (Table 2.A1.1).

Table 2.A1.1. **Baseline values of parameters**

Parameter	Value
Age of entry in the labour market	20
Age of retirement	Official age in each country
Inflation	2.0%
Productivity growth	1.5%
Real rate of return	3.0%
Real discount rate	3.0%

2.A1.2. Benchmark savings vehicles

Each type of private pension plan in a given country is compared against different benchmark savings vehicles. The analysis considers at least two benchmark savings vehicles for each country: a traditional savings account and a mutual fund (or collective investment scheme). When other savings vehicles are commonly used in a given country (e.g. special savings accounts, life insurance contracts), they are also considered.

For comparability purposes, the portfolio of the benchmark savings vehicle is assumed to be the same as the one for the private pension plan. Funds are assumed to be invested in only two asset classes: fixed income and shares. Other asset classes, such as real estate or cash and deposits, are not considered.

In addition, the same pay-out option as for the private pension plan is also assumed for the benchmark. All pay-out options available in a country are considered. These are usually lump sum payments, life annuities (inflation-indexed or not) and programmed withdrawals.[1] Payments from annuities and programmed withdrawals are calculated according to the life expectancy at retirement given by the most recent life tables for both sexes in the Human Mortality Database (the expected age of death is therefore assumed to be fixed).[2]

2.A1.3. Personal income tax system

The analysis uses the tax schedule and tax brackets in place in each country in 2015 to calculate income tax and derive marginal tax rates. Both national (respectively federal) and local (respectively state) personal income tax systems are taken into account. Personal allowances and tax credits are also taken into account when they are available to all taxpayers. The income limits for all tax brackets, the allowances and the credit amounts are assumed to be indexed to inflation going forward, unless country-specific rules indicate otherwise.

2.A1.4. The calculation of contributions and their taxation

The analysis assumes the same amount of pre-tax contributions for both the private pension plan and the benchmark savings vehicle. The amount of money saved in a private pension plan can comprise employee, employer and government contributions, while the amount saved in a benchmark savings vehicle generally only comprises the individual contribution. Assuming different levels of contributions to both plans would prevent distinguishing between the impact of different contribution levels and the impact of the tax treatment of private pension plans on the overall tax advantage. The analysis therefore assumes that the individual pays the full equivalent total employee and employer contribution in the savings vehicle.[3]

State contributions only accumulate in the relevant plan for eligible individuals. State matching contributions and state subsidies are increasingly common ways to promote savings for retirement in private pension plans. These amounts are deposited in the private pension plan for eligible individuals. As this type of contribution is not part of the wage bill, there is no reason to count them as well for the benchmark savings vehicle. In addition, the analysis considers state contributions as a negative tax on contributions to private pension plans, which allows identifying their impact on the overall tax advantage.

Funded private pension plans based on accumulated rights (occupational DB plans)

Contribution rates in occupational DB pension plans at the national level are not easily available. In a DB plan pension benefits are defined according to a formula based on an accrual rate, the salary and the length of employment. The level of benefits obtained for a given contribution is not known. However, the analysis calculates the contribution rate that would be needed in a plan with asset accumulation to reach the same level of benefits than the DB pension plan. To that end, the analysis proceeds with the following steps:

1. Calculate the pension income received from a DB plan according to the country-specific formula;[4]
2. Calculate the equivalent amount of assets accumulated at retirement to get this annual payment by reversing the annuity formula;
3. Calculate the after-tax contribution rate needed to provide the same amount of assets at retirement with a plan with asset accumulation (e.g. DC plan or a savings vehicle) by dividing the amount of assets calculated under step 2 by the amount of assets that would have been accumulated in a plan with asset accumulation had the whole salary been invested over the career;
4. Taking into account the tax treatment of contributions for the DB pension plan, calculate back the tax due on contributions to the DB pension plan and the pre-tax contribution rate;
5. Use this pre-tax contribution rate for the benchmark savings vehicle. The benchmark savings vehicle and the private pension plan therefore receive the same pre-tax contribution.[5]

Even though actual contributions made to the DB pension plan are not known for certain (because there is no direct link in DB plans between contributions and benefits), step 4 uses the contribution rate calculated under step 3 to estimate how much may have been contributed to the DB plan and to approximate the tax due on these contributions, when relevant.

Funded private pension plans based on assets accumulated (DC, hybrid and personal plans)

The analysis assumes a constant contribution rate during the career for occupational DC plans, personal pension plans and occupational hybrid DB plans (in which benefits depend on a rate of return credited to contributions). A 10% contribution rate is assumed, except for private pension plans in which mandatory contribution rates and minimum contributions rates apply. Caps on contributions are applied when relevant.

Taxation of contributions

The analysis applies the specific tax treatment in place in each country for contributions to the private pension plan and the benchmark savings vehicle respectively. When contributions are made from income that has already been taxed, as is usually the case for savings vehicles, the analysis multiplies the pre-tax contribution by the appropriate tax rate to calculate the tax already paid. The appropriate tax rate can be the individual's marginal rate of income tax (which varies depending on the level of income) or any flat tax rate defined by regulation. When contributions are tax-exempt up to a limit (expressed either as a percentage of the salary or as an absolute amount), any excess contributions, when allowed, are taxed at the appropriate tax rate. Tax credits are calculated as a proportion of the pre-tax contributions and considered as a negative tax on contributions.

2.A1.5. The taxation of returns on investment

The amount of assets accumulated at the end of each year is the sum of the amount of assets accumulated at the beginning of that year, the new after-tax contributions and the investment income earned. This amount is reduced by the tax due on returns on investment earned when they are taxed.

The tax treatment of returns on investment may depend on the portfolio composition. The analysis assumes a portfolio composed of 60% government bonds and 40% equities. When capital gains and dividends attract a different tax treatment, the analysis assumes that investment income derives one-third from dividends and two-thirds from capital gains. The analysis assumes a holding period of securities of 6.7 years when this criteria matters for the tax treatment of investment income.[6]

2.A1.6. The calculation of withdrawals and their taxation

For DB plans, only life annuities are considered, as such plans usually promise a regular payment for life. The life annuity payment is calculated according to the country-specific formula when available. Otherwise, expected benefits from the DB pension plan are calculated as the product between the career length, a 1.5% accrual rate and the final salary.

For DC plans, personal plans and savings vehicles, the analysis calculates the annuity payment by transforming the estimated assets accumulated at retirement into a stream of annual payments. It calculates the benefit payment of an annuity certain priced using the annuity formula, based on the life expectancy at the age of retirement and a constant discount rate. The annuity payments can either be fixed in nominal terms or inflation-indexed.[7]

In the case of programmed withdrawals, the expected age of death is assumed to be fixed and is defined by adding the remaining life expectancy at retirement to the age of retirement. The rate of return on investment remains constant, at the same level as during the accumulation phase. The same tax treatment than the one applied during the accumulation phase is assumed to continue applying during the pay-out phase, unless country-specific rules indicate otherwise.

After-tax withdrawals are calculated as before-tax withdrawals minus the tax due on withdrawals, calculated by applying the appropriate tax rate. The analysis takes into account the impact of public provision when calculating the tax due on withdrawals. This means that it accounts for the fact that retired individuals may also receive a public pension. To that end, the analysis first estimates the level of the public pension that the individual may receive, according to the level of income while working. The OECD pension models provide the gross replacement rates from mandatory public pension schemes, taking into account potential coverage by private schemes (cf. Table 6.4 in the 2015 edition of the *OECD Pensions at a Glance* for three income levels). The analysis applies the different replacement rates to final earnings depending on the individual's level of income. Public pension payments are indexed according to country-specific rules. The derived public pension income is added to withdrawals from the private pension plan and from the benchmark savings vehicle. The total taxable income is then run through the personal income tax brackets to determine the tax due on that income.

2.A1.7. The taxation of funds accumulated

Some countries also tax the total amount of funds accumulated in private pension plans. This tax can take several forms. In some countries (e.g. Belgium), funds accumulated (returns on investment and past contributions) are taxed at a given age. In some other countries (e.g. the United Kingdom), the total amount of funds accumulated at retirement is taxed upon withdrawal when it exceeds a certain limit. In all cases, the analysis adds this tax to any tax due on withdrawals.

2.A1.8. Stylised tax regimes

Coverage of the analysis

The analysis considers a funded private pension plan in which benefits are calculated based on assets accumulated (e.g. occupational DC plans and personal plans). The stylised tax regimes are the results of the combination of different tax treatments for contributions, returns on investment and withdrawals for that private pension plan.

The benchmark savings vehicle is a traditional savings account for which the "TTE" tax regime applies, i.e. contributions and returns on investment are subject to personal income tax, and withdrawals are tax-exempt.

Personal income tax system

The analysis assumes a common hypothetical personal income tax system to compare the stylised tax regimes. It uses the tax rates and income tax brackets in force in France in 2015 (see Table 2.A1.2), although some specificities of the French system are not taken into account.[8] The income limits for all brackets are assumed to be indexed to inflation. The average earner in the hypothetical personal income tax system is the average earner in France (earning EUR 36 491 in 2015 according to the OECD Average annual wages database).

Table 2.A1.2. **Income tax brackets and marginal tax rates for the stylised tax regimes**

Taxable income (EUR)		Tax rate
Lower band	Higher band	%
0	9 700	0
9 700	26 791	14
26 791	71 826	30
71 826	152 108	41
152 108	over	45

Construction of the stylised tax regimes

The different stylised tax regimes result from the combination of different tax treatments for contributions, returns on investment and pension payments/withdrawals, as presented in Table 2.A1.3. Each stylised tax regime is symbolised by the combination of three

Table 2.A1.3. **Options for the tax treatment of contributions, returns on investment and withdrawals to build stylised tax regimes**

Symbol	Contributions[1]	Returns on investment[2]	Withdrawals
E	Contributions are tax-deductible up to EUR 7 300 a year (excess contributions are subject to personal income tax)	Returns are tax-exempt	Withdrawals are tax-exempt
t	Contributions are subject to personal income tax but 20% of the contributions are tax-deductible up to EUR 7 300 a year Contributions are subject to personal income tax but the individual receives a tax credit on personal income tax, corresponding to 10% of the contributions up to EUR 7 300 a year	Returns are taxed at a flat rate of 15%	Withdrawals are subject to personal income tax after a 10% deduction
T	Contributions are subject to personal income tax	Returns are subject to personal income tax	Withdrawals are subject to personal income tax

1. The limit for the tax deductibility of contributions and for the tax credit (EUR 7 300) is equivalent to 20% of wages for the average earner in 2015 and is assumed to be inflation-indexed.
2. During the pay-out phase, when payments are done in the form of programmed withdrawals, the analysis assumes that returns on investment are taxed in the same way as during the accumulation phase.

letters representing the tax treatment for contributions, returns on investment and withdrawals. For example, the "EET" stylised tax regime assumes that contributions are tax-deductible up to EUR 7 300 a year, returns on investment are tax-exempt and withdrawals are subject to personal income tax. Partial tax relief on contributions can be given in two ways, either assuming that only part of the contributions is tax-deductible or that a tax credit is calculated based on the amount contributed. For example, the "tEE" stylised tax regime assumes that 20% of the contributions are tax-deductible up to EUR 7 300 a year, while the "tEE (tax credit)" stylised tax regime assumes that contributions are subject to personal income tax with a tax credit equivalent to 10% of the contributions up to EUR 7 300 a year. In both cases, returns on investment and withdrawals are tax-exempt.

In addition, the analysis considers that individuals may be entitled to state financial incentives, either subsidies or matching contributions. In the case of state subsidies, the analysis assumes that a maximum flat-rate subsidy of EUR 365 is paid into the pension account if the individual contributes at least 5% of wages. The flat-rate subsidy, which represents 1% of wages for the average earner in 2015 and grows in line with inflation, is proportionately reduced to zero for lower contribution rates. In the case of state matching contributions, the analysis assumes that 20% of individual contributions are matched by the state and paid into the pension account, up to a maximum state contribution of EUR 1 825 (this limit represents 5% of wages for the average earner in 2015 and grows in line with inflation).

The analysis focuses on 16 selected stylised tax regimes based on their relevance and importance in different OECD countries, as described in Table 2.2. Combining all the possible options for the tax treatments of contributions, returns on investment and pension payments/withdrawals and the type of state financial incentive would lead to 108 stylised tax regimes. Most of those combinations have no counterpart in the real world.

Payments from annuities and programmed withdrawals are calculated according to the life expectancy at retirement given by the 2013 French life table for both sexes from the Human Mortality Database. The level of mandatory public pension that the individual may be entitled to is calculated using the OECD pension models for the OECD average. The analysis assumes that public pensions grow in line with inflation and are fully subject to personal income tax.

Notes

1. The model does not consider lump sum payments and programmed withdrawals for DB pension plans.
2. More information on the Human Mortality Database can be found at *www.mortality.org/*.
3. In addition, the same cap on contribution applies to both plans if excess contributions are not permitted in one of them.
4. When the formula is not available, expected benefits from the DB pension plan are calculated as the product between the career length, a 1.5% accrual rate and the final salary.
5. The resulting benefit at retirement may however differ as the tax treatment of the benchmark savings vehicle most likely varies from the one for the DB pension plan.
6. This is equivalent to assuming that 15% of the securities held in the portfolio are sold every year. Admittedly, this is based exclusively on US observations for shares (see Burman, L.E. and P.D. Ricoy (1997), "Capital gains and the people who realize them", *National Tax Journal* Vol. 50, No. 3).
7. The annuity formula is given by $P = Total\ assets\ at\ retirement \times \frac{1 - \frac{1+indexation}{1+dr}}{1-(\frac{1+indexation}{1+dr})^{LE}}$ where P is the periodic payment, *indexation* is equal to 0 in the case of fixed nominal payments and is equal to inflation in the case of inflation-indexed payments, *dr* is the discount rate and *LE* is the life expectancy at retirement.
8. The standard allowance for work-related expenses (10% of net pay), the tax credit for low-income individuals and the exceptional contribution for high-income individuals are not taken into account. Social taxes (CSG and CRDS) are disregarded as well for the stylised tax regimes.

Chapter 3

Policy measures to improve the quality of financial advice for retirement

This chapter looks at policy measures which can be taken to help ensure that consumers receive appropriate financial advice for retirement. The measures include duty of care standards, disclosure requirements, and remuneration limits in order to mitigate conflicts of interest, qualification standards to ensure that advisors are competent to provide advice, and ensuring that mechanisms are in place to facilitate dispute resolution for consumers. The chapter discusses the objectives and potential effectiveness of each of these measures, along with their potential impact on the affordability and availability of advice. Finally, it proposes approaches to improve the effectiveness of these measures and reduce the impact on the accessibility of advice.

Individuals are bearing increasing responsibility for planning how they will finance their retirement. This planning involves the decision to save, the selection of investments and the determination of the best strategy for drawing down assets in retirement. Yet much evidence shows that individuals are ill-equipped to make such complex decisions on their own. Savings gaps are persistent, levels of financial literacy are low, and retirement planning in particular includes numerous variables that are uncertain, including future inflation, returns and longevity, which most individuals simply do not have the knowledge to assess. Furthermore, retirement products can be particularly complex and present features which may be difficult for the average consumer to easily understand.

Given the complexity of retirement planning, individuals need support or assistance to make the right financial decisions for retirement. Financial literacy and financial advice for retirement play a complementary role in guiding individuals to make better retirement decisions (Calcagno and Monticone, 2015; Debbich, 2015). Chapter 5 looks at how policy makers can support this process through financial education and initiatives to empower individuals themselves to take charge of their retirement planning. This chapter focuses on financial advice for retirement.

In light of the potentially important the role that financial advice can play in retirement planning, there has been an increased focus on the regulation of financial advice in recent years. Many jurisdictions have adopted, or are in the process of adopting, new regulations that aim to improve the quality of financial advice received. Measures implemented to improve consumer outcomes from financial advice revolve around ensuring the appropriateness of advice, the competency of the advisor, and consumer access to redress in the event of a complaint.

Measures implemented to address the appropriateness of advice focus on mitigating the conflicts of interest of financial advisors. Conflicts of interest can result in a bias in the advice to be more in the interest of the advisor than the consumer, and therefore have been of primary concern for regulators. Conflicts of interest most often relate to the way in which financial advisors are compensated for their services. Commission payments for selling certain products, for example, can incentivise advisors to recommend to their clients products paying higher commissions when a lower commission product may be just as suitable. Regulators have relied upon three main tools to mitigate the conflicts of interest faced by financial advisors: standards regarding the duty of care that advisors owe to their clients, requirements for disclosure of conflicts, and limits with respect to the remuneration that advisors can receive for their services. The resulting exposure of advisors to legal liability and other penalties from non-compliance aids in the enforcement of these measures and helps to align advisors' incentives with those of their clients.

Regulators are also placing more emphasis on qualification standards required to provide financial advice in order to ensure the competency of the advisor and to ensure that advisors have the knowledge and skills needed to provide appropriate recommendations to their clients.

Most jurisdictions also have dispute resolution schemes to resolve consumer complaints in an efficient and cost-effective manner. As these schemes form an important aspect of the process in which consumers can seek financial advice, regulators have also been looking to ensure their proper functioning.

While such measures can improve the quality of financial advice, ensuring that advice remains accessible and affordable remains a challenge. Regulators are increasingly looking towards technology as a potential way to improve the accessibility and affordability of financial advice as well as to provide an alternative to overcome advisor bias, and are making sure that regulation is in place to provide the same level of consumer protection as for traditional channels.

This chapter discusses measures that policy makers can use to improve the quality of financial advice for retirement.[1] It first looks at how financial advice is typically regulated and discusses the implications of the differences in the application of the regulation for different types of financial advice. It then provides some examples of the regulatory developments relating to financial advice over the last years in several OECD jurisdictions. The objectives and potential effectiveness of each of the measures to improve the quality of financial advice are subsequently discussed, relying on literature and real-world evidence where available. The chapter then considers the impact that these measures may have on the affordability and availability of financial advice, which may create an advice gap, along with policy measures which can be taken to reduce this gap. The report concludes with a discussion of policy implications to consider when implementing regulation to improve consumer outcomes from receiving financial advice for retirement.

3.1. Scope and application of the regulation of financial advice

Regulation generally differs across the potential sources of financial advice for retirement planning. Distinctions in the regulation of financial advisors can be important, as different types of financial advice serve different purposes and have different aims. However, such distinctions also raise numerous challenges to ensuring optimal consumer outcomes. In the best case, these distinctions can allow financial advice to meet the varying needs of consumers. In the worst case, an advice or protection gap can be created where certain types of advice are not readily provided or consumers are less protected. Policy makers need to be aware of the potential for advice and protection gaps to emerge as a result of the fragmented regulation of financial advice and take measures to reduce these gaps to the extent possible.

Defining the scope of regulation

The first issue that policy makers must address is what definition of financial advice is considered to be within the scope of regulation. The type of financial advice covered is generally classified based on the extent to which advice is a personalised recommendation and/or by the range of options considered in the advisor's recommendation.

The different types of financial advice can range from being objectively factual to being fully personalised to account for the individual's specific profile and circumstances. Factual advice or guidance is when factual information is provided with no recommendation, for example the provision of general information or education. General advice is the provision of a recommendation without consideration of personal circumstances. Personalised advice can be either simplified (scaled) or comprehensive. The former provides a recommendation for an issue of limited scope for a specific individual, while the latter provides a recommendation taking into account all aspects of an individual's profile and personal circumstances.

Financial advice can also be classified depending on the range of options considered by the advisor. Execution-only services do not provide advice and simply take orders from the client. Restricted advice is provided based on a limited range of products or providers, while independent advice considers a wide range of product types from numerous providers.

There are differences across jurisdictions with respect to the type of advice that regulation of financial advisors considers to be in scope of its requirements. Generally, factual advice, guidance or education where no recommendation is provided to the consumer is excluded, as are brokers who provide an execution-only service. Some jurisdictions, as is the case in the United Kingdom, consider all advice where a recommendation is made to be in scope. Other jurisdictions, such as Australia and the European Union, consider only advice which is personalised to be within the scope of the regulation. A distinction is also often made between restricted and independent advisors, as is the case in the European Union and the United Kingdom, with different requirements imposed on each type of advisor. This distinction could be paralleled with the distinction between sales and advice, as proprietary advisors, who are restricted, arguably have the role of a salesman rather than an advisor. Following the recent introduction of the Conflicts of Interest Rule, the United States presents a case where requirements differ also depending on the purpose of investment, even for the same type of advisor. Broker-dealers providing recommendations for retirement plans are subject to more stringent duty of care standards than broker-dealers providing advice for other types of investments.

Regulation also generally differs depending on the type of product being recommended. The most common distinction is between retail investment products and insurance products, in part because the regulating bodies with jurisdiction over these sectors often differ. This distinction is especially relevant for retirement planning, where both investment products and insurance products, in particular annuity products, can play an important role in financing retirement. Some jurisdictions also make a distinction depending on the complexity or features of the product offered. This is the case for example in New Zealand, where not all types of advisors are allowed to recommend certain complex products,[2] and in the United States where variable annuities provided by life insurers are regulated as securities and are subject to specific suitability requirements.

Finally, regulation can differ depending on the type of client the advisor is providing recommendations to. The main distinction is between retail clients, usually individual investors, and wholesale clients who are presumed to have a higher level of financial knowledge. This distinction can result in different levels of protections offered to the different types of clients.

The importance of comprehensive and clear definitions of the different types of advice

First, the comprehensiveness of the definitions of what type of advice and advisors are covered by regulation is based is important to avoid protection gaps. For example, in Canada there is no real restriction on the use of the title of financial planner, and in general there is a lack of regulation concerning some aspects of financial planning. For example, in some provinces there are 'financial planners' who do not themselves sell financial products and are not overseen by the regulator or the other self-regulating bodies (Expert Committee to Consider Financial Advisory and Financial Planning Policy Alternatives,

2016). This was also found to be a potential problem in the United States, where the existing regulation does not stipulate what activities financial planners are allowed to be engaged in (Financial Planning Coalition, 2014). Clients of financial planners may therefore be much less protected than they would otherwise expect.

Any ambiguity with respect to the definition of advice and the applicable regulation in a given situation can also result in a reluctance to provide advice. Employers, for example, would be the logical source of information for consumers with occupational pension arrangements. Yet in many cases, employers have been reluctant to provide any guidance or education with respect to investment within pension plans due to concerns over regulatory liability. The Financial Advice Market Review found this to be a concern for employers in the United Kingdom, and recommended to clarify the boundary of the regulation so as to clarify what assistance employers are able to provide (HM Treasury and Financial Conduct Authority, 2016). This was also found to be true in Canada and the United States with respect to the offering of annuity products within employer sponsored plans. The United States reacted by clarifying the obligations of the employer to assess the annuity provider's financial viability and has defined a statute of limitations after which legal action cannot be taken against the employer, and Canada has proposed guidelines for providing standardised product information. The United States also enables employers to shield themselves from liability for the consequences of individuals exercising control and making their own investment decisions provided that certain conditions are met.

The line between simplified/scaled and comprehensive advice has also proven to be a barrier for consumers to have access to advice for simple needs more limited in scope, such as the advice of which funds to invest in within a retirement plan. In the United Kingdom, for example, despite having regulation applicable expressly for simplified advice for issues of limited scope, the Financial Advice Market Review (FAMR) found advisors were still reluctant to provide it in part due to liability concerns. The FAMR therefore recommended that the regulator provide further guidance for advisors to provide 'streamlined' advice (HM Treasury and Financial Conduct Authority, 2016). In New Zealand, the lack of an explicit boundary between scaled and comprehensive advice made advisors providing personalised advice reluctant to simplify their due diligence with respect to the client. As a result they would only offer fully comprehensive advice, resulting in a more costly service than consumers with simple needs were willing or able to pay (New Zealand Ministry of Business, Innovation and Employment, 2016b).

Potential implications of differences in the application of regulation

Different applications of regulation to different types of advice also present a risk that an uneven playing field could result. Moreover advisors could cherry-pick the type of advice they provide to avoid more stringent regulatory requirements. This was found to be a concern in New Zealand, where an advisor could avoid higher costs of compliance by limiting their advice to general advice only and not providing personalised advice (New Zealand Ministry of Business, Innovation and Employment, 2016b). This was also found to be the case in the United States, where advisers could avoid fiduciary duty by side-stepping one of the five conditions defined by the 1975 rule under ERISA (US Department of Labor, 2015). While the recent Conflicts of Interest rule expands the application of fiduciary duty in the United States to all retirement accounts, an opportunity for broker-dealers to avoid these requirements by not serving the retirement market may still exist until the SEC follows through with its promised regulation for a more uniform fiduciary standard for all broker-dealers.

Regulation differing across types of products or channels also presents a risk of cherry-picking. For example, when disclosures were introduced for a specific product in India, advisors began recommending an alternative high-commission product which did not require disclosure (Anagol, et al., 2013). To the extent that investment and insurance products are regulated differently, clients could become over or under-annuitised depending on the profitability of recommending insurance or not. Australia recognised the uneven playing field between retail investment advice and insurance in its recently proposed Life Insurance Reform Legislation, which intends to level the playing field between retail investment and insurance products.

Another concern is the extent to which such differences across channels could potentially result in a shift in the structure of the market. Different regulation for proprietary (or restricted) advisors compared to independent advisors could result in a competitive advantage for the former, incentivising firms to vertically integrate their businesses (Lortie, 2016; Valentine, 2013).

Finally, differences in regulation of financial advice can lead to consumer confusion about what standards are applicable for the advice they receive. In the United States, consumers demonstrated a lack of awareness regarding the differences in the types of advisors and services they offer (Financial Planning Coalition, 2014). Furthermore consumers are unaware of the standards applicable to a given type of advisor. One study in the United States showed that only 3% of consumers were aware of which advisors were subject to fiduciary duty and only 5% were aware of which advisors were required to disclose any conflicts of interest faced (Burke and Hung, 2015). A review conducted by the Financial Conduct Authority in the United Kingdom revealed a lack of understanding by consumers of the difference between restricted and independent advice (Financial Conduct Authority, 2014).

The fragmentation of regulation across different types of advisors and products can result in certain types of advice not being available to consumers or a lack of consumer protection in certain situations. While differences in regulations may be necessary to a certain extent, these advice and protection gaps should be minimised. Policy makers should keep these issues in mind when implementing tools to regulate financial advice.

3.2. Regulatory developments in financial advice

Regulators across OECD jurisdictions have been making efforts to improve consumer outcomes from receiving financial advice and address the challenges raised in the previous section. Several regulators are also opening the discussion to the evolving role of technology to increase the accessibility and affordability of financial advice and to ensure that the regulation in place is sufficient to ensure consumer protection. This section provides some examples of recent measures that have been taken in several OECD jurisdictions to provide an overview of the types of policies which are being implemented.

The Future of Financial Advice (FOFA) regulation was passed in Australia in June 2012, with implementation mandatory from July 2013. The legislation focused on mitigating conflicts of interest through limits on remuneration from commissions and improving disclosure standards for retail financial advice. The Life Insurance Reform Legislation, published in December 2015, proposed to extend the regulation of remuneration to advice for life insurance products. The regulator also issued a regulatory guide to ensure consumer protection with respect to robo-advice in August 2016.

The Client Relationship Model – Phase 2 (CRM2) entered into force in Canada in July 2013 and was gradually implemented through July 2016. The regulation aimed to improve reporting and disclosure standards for clients particularly with respect to costs and fees, including advisor compensation. Rules established by the industry's self-regulating bodies have been harmonized to align with the new regulation. In addition, the Canadian Securities Administrators (CSA) published a consultation paper in April 2016, following the initial consultation in 2013, proposing regulation regarding the introduction of a statutory best interest duty towards retail clients.

The Danish Act on Insurance Mediation passed in 2006 targeted the remuneration of independent insurance brokers in Denmark, who serve as the main intermediaries for occupational pension schemes.

In the European Union, the revised Markets in Financial Instruments Directive (MiFID II) was approved mid-2014 and is planned to be implemented in member states from January 2018. It seeks to improve upon the original MiFID regulation implemented in 2007, particularly with respect to consumer protection issues and shortcomings revealed during the financial crisis. The Insurance Distribution Directive (IDD) was published in February 2016, with implementation planned for February 2018. It applies to all insurance undertakings and intermediaries who can sell directly to their customers. Both regulations put forward standards with respect to duty of care, qualification of intermediaries, remuneration and disclosure requirements. The European Supervisory Authorities have also issued a joint discussion paper on the automation of financial advice looking at the potential benefits and risks of such innovations. The objective of this paper was to determine any additional regulatory action needed to address automated financial advice (Joint Committee of the European Supervisory Authorities, 2015).

The Finnish Insurance Mediation Act, which targeted the remuneration of independent insurance brokers in Finland, came into force in 2005 and became fully effective in 2008.

In Germany, the Act to Strengthen Investor Protection and Improve the Functionality of the Capital Market became effective in November 2012 and addressed required disclosures and advisor qualifications. The Fee-Based Investment Advice Act, effective in August 2014, created a legal class of independent advisors who do not receive potentially conflicted remuneration (Burke and Hung, 2015b).

An Amendment Decree Financial Markets in the Netherlands, banning commissions for all financial advisors, entered into force in 2013.

In 2016, the New Zealand government proposed several modifications of the 2008 regulation of financial advisors in order to address the identified shortcomings. Planned changes include the simplification of advisor classifications, extending requirements to provide advice in the consumer's best interest and improving disclosure requirements. In addition, the changes seek to broaden the definition of advice in order to accommodate technological innovations, and require that entities providing such robo-advice be licensed and held to the same requirements as other types of advisors. (New Zealand Ministry of Business, Innovation and Employment, 2016).

The Retail Distribution Review (RDR) came into effect in the United Kingdom in January 2013, forbidding financial advisors from receiving commission payments and increasing qualification standards. The regulation on remuneration and transparency was extended to platforms in April 2014. The Financial Advice Market Review, completed in March 2016, made several recommendations to continue to improve the affordability and accessibility of financial advice. To embrace the use of technology in providing advice, the regulator launched "Project Innovate" to encourage firms to develop lower cost advice models aimed at the mass-market, particularly with respect to simplified advice to help address the advice gap. Following this review the Financial Conduct Authority is establishing an Advice Unit to assist in the development of such models (HM Treasury and Financial Conduct Authority, 2016).

The Dodd-Frank Act of 2010 charged the United States Securities and Exchange Commission (SEC) with assessing the effectiveness of the current regulation in ensuring appropriate financial advice for consumers. The SEC was asked to consider making the regulation regarding fiduciary duty consistent for all types of financial advisors, though the SEC has yet to do so and any adopted framework would not change the existing requirements under ERISA for advice on tax preferred retirement investments. Beginning in 2009, the Department of Labor undertook a project to address the problems of conflicts of interest in financial advice for retirement, and in April 2016 it published a final Conflicts of Interest Rule which extends fiduciary duties to all types of advisors providing financial advice for all types of retirement plans. With respect to technological innovations, FINRA, the industry self-regulatory body, recently published a report to clarify the application of its rules with respect to digital investment advice and share effective practices (FINRA, 2016). A new rule proposed by the SEC would require developers of algorithmic trading to be registered as a securities trader, and be subject to the same qualification requirements as securities traders.

These policy measures have generally sought to improve and update existing regulation to account for the current financial realities. The discussion that follows will assess in more detail the advantages and challenges of each of types of tools implemented, drawing on examples from the measures taken in the various jurisdictions in addition to evidence found in the literature as a basis for this discussion.

3.3. Policy measures to improve consumer outcomes from financial advice

Policy makers have implemented several measures to make sure that financial advice leads to optimal outcomes for consumers. First, there are measures to mitigate any conflicts of interest that the financial advisors may face. These are duty of care standards, disclosure requirements and explicit limits on remuneration structures. These three measures are complementary and are generally combined when implemented in order to improve their effectiveness. Secondly, policy makers can ensure the competency of the advisor to provide quality advice by establishing qualification standards for financial advisors. Finally, dispute resolution facilitates consumers' access to redress in the event that poor financial advice is received, and can lead to the imposition of liability on advisors for failure to provide appropriate financial advice, which aids in the enforcement of the requirements.

Policy measures to mitigate conflicts of interest in financial advice

Mitigating the conflicts of interest in financial advice is of primary importance for improving consumer outcomes. The influence of the financial advisor on consumers' decisions can be significant, and consumers tend to trust the financial advice provided to them. Moreover, consumers often lack awareness of any potential bias in the advice they receive. A survey of eight EU member states found that 58% of investors felt that their investment decision was influenced by an advisor's recommendation, and the majority of investors reported high levels of trust in their advisor (Chater et al., 2010). Over half of the consumers felt that their advisor had no bias, and over a quarter of individuals did not even consider any potential conflicts of interest that their advisor could face (Chater et al., 2010). Measures to ensure that advice is appropriate and to mitigate conflicts of interest must therefore be the foundation of any policy to improve consumer outcomes from financial advice. The main policy measures implemented to mitigate conflicts of interest are duty of care standards, disclosure requirements and limits on the remuneration that advisors receive.

Duty of care standards

Duty of care standards impose legal requirements on financial advisors to act ethically when providing a recommendation to a client. Basic requirements, including for general financial advice, usually include an obligation for the advisor not to mislead or deceive the client and to act with care, skill and diligence in providing a recommendation. On top of these requirements, an advisor providing personal advice is usually required to perform some sort of due diligence to ensure that the advice is appropriate for a particular client. This involves taking into account factors such as age, personal situation, financial situation, financial knowledge, investment experience, risk appetite and investment objectives. The specific factors required to be considered can nevertheless vary from one jurisdiction to the next. Generally speaking, however, the extent to which these factors need to be taken into account is defined through either a suitability requirement or a best interest requirement.[3]

Suitability requires a recommendation to be reasonable given the personal situation of a client, but not necessarily that it is the best product for their needs. Suitability does not require that advisors put the client's best interest above their own. As such, a product paying a higher commission could be considered as suitable as the otherwise equivalent lower commission product. Suitability also allows for a reduced option set to be considered, as the advisor is not required to consider all possible types of products, but to simply believe that the one recommended is appropriate.

Suitability requirements are more compatible with some type of advice than others. Sales-only or restricted advice is more often subject only to a suitability requirement, as are insurance agents. One reason for this is that the range of options they consider in their recommendation is limited.

However, providers of products can also be held responsible for insuring suitability rather than placing full responsibility on the advisor, mitigating somewhat this conflict of interest. In the United States, the insurance provider is responsible for making sure that the appropriate procedure is in place to determine suitability. The Insurance Distribution Directive (IDD) in Europe introduces an additional suitability check by requiring that providers ensure that the products developed are appropriate for market that the product targets given the typical risks this market faces.

Less common is a requirement that intermediaries ensure suitability even for non-advised transactions. The Mutual Fund Dealers Association (MFDA) in Canada requires that members should determine suitability even for unsolicited transactions, and where the transaction seems unsuitable they must inform the client.

Best interest, on the other hand, requires that advisors provide the best recommendation for the client given the client's needs, and that advisors put the client's interests ahead of their own. As such, best interest requirements inherently imply that advice be free from bias, making conflicts of interest an important issue to address.

The approach to address conflicts of interest can range from prohibiting conflicts of interest altogether to requiring the appropriate management of the conflicts in order to prevent potential harm to the client. Written conflicts of interest policies may also be required to formalise the internal procedures for managing any conflicts of interest. Regulation in the United States prohibits conflicts of interest unless appropriate consumer protections are in place to mitigate the potential impact of the conflict of interest. The Investment Industry Regulatory Organization of Canada (IIROC) takes the reverse approach, and first requires that members have a written conflicts of interest policy requiring that advisors should address conflicts of interest in a fair and transparent manner in the best interests of their client, and then if this is not possible the conflict of interest should be avoided. The IIROC provides guidance on how conflicts of interest can be addressed, but the rule remains principle-based and flexible.

A best execution standard, required by MiFID II in Europe, takes another approach to addressing conflicts of interest. This standard is enforced in addition to a suitability requirement, and requires that all sufficient steps must be taken to obtain the best product for the client, considering all costs, including commission.

Regulation in many jurisdictions is currently moving towards a more uniform and broad application of a best interests standard and the establishment of formal procedures for mitigating any conflicts. Canada and New Zealand are considering implementing more uniform best interest standards for all types of advisors. The United States recently issued a rule extending best interest standards to all types of advisors providing advice for retirement, and are considering extending this to all broker-dealers. The IIROC in Canada and MiFID II in Europe both require a written conflicts of interest policy to be in place, and MiFID II requires that this policy be reviewed annually.

Enforcement of duty of care standards[4]

The success of duty of care standards to improve consumer outcomes will in part depend on the extent to which advisors fully comply with due diligence requirements and the effectiveness of the conflicts of interest policies to identify and mitigate all potential conflicts the advisors face. As the continuous monitoring and enforcement of standards on an individual or transactional basis is normally not feasible, targeted reviews using methods such as mystery shopping can be one tool for supervisors to use to ensure compliance. Such exercises can also help to identify where the regulatory requirements may not be sufficiently clear, and be used as an opportunity to provide feedback to advisors regarding the quality of their advice.

Several jurisdictions have performed investigations to assess how well financial advisors assess the suitability of their recommendations to clients. One such investigation employed mystery shoppers to assess the quality of advisors' recommendations given the requirements in place under the Markets in Financial Instruments Directive (MiFID) for European Union member states (Synovate, 2011). The study found that less than 10% of advisors gathered sufficient information to make a suitable recommendation, particularly with respect to the client's financial knowledge, experience investing and financial situation. Furthermore most advisors were not sufficiently comprehensive in assessing the risk profile of the client and did not clearly explain the risks of the recommended product. However, the due diligence of advisors tended to be more thorough in member states which were more financially developed. Nevertheless, the majority of recommendations were deemed to be unsuitable, primarily due to high levels of risk (Synovate, 2011). A more recent investigation carried out in the United Kingdom found that while in general advisors demonstrated good practices, this was not consistent across firms and there were several instances of poor due diligence (Financial Conduct Authority, 2016b). A study in the Netherlands found that 40% of banks and investment firms did not collect sufficient information on their clients to be able to make a suitable recommendation (AFM, 2016).

Reviews of the effectiveness of policies to manage conflicts of interest have found similarly disappointing results. A review of IIROC members in Canada found that in many cases the conflicts of interest policies in place were not adequate to effectively identify and address conflicts of interest (IIROC, 2016). The Financial Conduct Authority found that advisors in the United Kingdom were often not effectively managing the conflicts of interest they faced, as demonstrated by their platform selection for clients (Financial Conduct Authority, 2016b).

Even where regulatory requirements are clear, however, another explanation for the lack of effectiveness of policies to manage conflicts of interest is the potential lack of awareness of advisors that they are acting in their own best interests. Bias is very difficult for individuals to correct, even when making a conscious effort to do so, and individuals are often not aware of the extent of their bias (Moore, et al., 2010). Furthermore, individuals often do not believe that they are biased even when their actions point to the contrary (Bazerman, et al., 1997). Self-interest is an automatic and unconscious process which is difficult to overcome with the controlled thought processes which are used to apply ethical and professional standards, and automatic processes tend to override those which are controlled.

Indeed evidence indicates that social norms and culture play an influential role in the effectiveness of policies to manage conflicts of interest. The Financial Conduct Authority found that firm culture plays an important role in the effectiveness of the due diligence process, and firms with a culture to challenge the status quo demonstrated better due diligence processes (Financial Conduct Authority, 2016b). A review by the Central Bank of Ireland on investment firms found that those with a stronger culture of compliance were more aware of the conflicts of interest and better managed these conflicts (Central Bank of Ireland, 2016). Another study on registered financial advisors in the United States found that firms who hired financial advisors with a record of misconduct were also more likely to have higher rates of past misconduct, and that misconduct at the top levels of the firm increases the likelihood of the misconduct of advisors (Egan et al., 2016).

The influence of culture and social norms implies that there should be a role for professional bodies to set standards that their members are expected to follow in order to establish positive social norms for the advisor profession. Because of a lack of awareness of bias, even the threat of legal consequences may need to be complemented with other mechanisms to be fully effective in mitigating conflicts of interest. Social norms influencing advisor and firm culture are likely to be more influential, as internalising ethical and professional standards would help these values to become a part of the automatic thought process to more effectively mitigate bias (Moore and Loewenstein, 2004).[5]

Challenges to the implementation of duty of care standards

Critics of extending the best interest standard cite concerns that more stringent duty of care standards would significantly increase the costs of compliance and reduce the availability of advice for low to moderate wealth consumers. Advisors would incur costs in terms of the additional time needed to perform the appropriate due diligence on clients to ensure that the advice is in their best interests. Second, administrative burden could increase, particularly with respect to conflicts of interest policies and other administrative requirements. Advisors could also face increased risk of legal liability. The resulting increases in cost could make advice less affordable for lower wealth consumers. In addition, advisors may not be able to recommend products which pay commissions due to the conflicts of interest they present.

Compliance costs could indeed increase as a result of more stringent duty of care standards. One study in the United States showed that a larger proportion of broker-dealers in states imposing a best interest standard (fiduciary duty) felt that costs of regulatory compliance were significant (Finke and Langdon, 2012). As an indicator of the potential cost of increased due diligence, a study in Australia showed that comprehensive personal advice cost six times more than scaled advice which is limited in scope (ASFA, 2014).

Increased compliance costs could potentially limit the access to advice for low to moderate wealth groups. A survey in the United States by the National Association of Insurance and Financial Advisors reported that nearly two-thirds of members indicated that they would reduce their services to less affluent clients if compliance costs increased by more than 15%, and nearly one third would limit the types of products they recommended (National Association of Insurance and Financial Advisors, in Partnership with LIMRA, 2012). However, another study showed no difference in the proportion of clients served with incomes under USD 75 000 per year for broker-dealers in states imposing best interest requirements compared to other states (Finke and Langdon, 2012).

There is little evidence indicating the impact of increased duty of care standards on the ability to recommend products paying commissions. To the extent that a requirement to avoid all conflicts of interest is not implemented, which would effectively ban products paying commissions, advisors should still be allowed to recommend them provided that the conflicts of interest are managed. A study in the United States showed that broker-dealers in states imposing a best interest standard were just as able to recommend products paying commissions as advisors in other states (Finke and Langdon, 2012).

Nevertheless, the potential for increased compliance costs highlight the need for regulation to provide clear guidance as to the level of due diligence required in order to limit the impact on the affordability and availability of advice. This will allow financial advisors to know when they have satisfied the requirements and minimise the cost of the necessary due diligence. The distinction between comprehensive personal advice and scaled advice also needs to be very clear in order to keep advice affordable for requests more limited in scope, such as investments within a retirement plan. This will provide financial advisors assurance that they will not be held liable for financial circumstances of their clients which are outside of the scope of the advice they provide.

Duty of care standards should form the foundation of any policy aiming to mitigate conflicts of interest in financial advice. Standards need to be in place to ensure that appropriate due diligence is performed and self-interest is mitigated in order to ensure the suitability of recommendations for clients. Nevertheless the level of due diligence required needs to be clearly defined in order to ensure that the additional costs of compliance do not increase the cost of advice to unreasonable levels, particularly for requests which are relatively straightforward and limited in scope. Policy makers also need to be aware of the role of culture and social norms in the effectiveness of policies to mitigate conflicts of interest, and encourage the development of professional standards. In addition, cultures of compliance can be encouraged through targeted monitoring and enforcement. Such enforcement could also provide feedback to improve clarity in the regulatory requirements, facilitating overall compliance.

Disclosure requirements

Disclosure requirements complement duty of care standards and are often required as a means to manage conflicts of interest. Disclosure aims to make the existence of any conflicts of interest more transparent for the consumer as well as to ensure that consumers understand the limitations with respect to the advice they receive.

Disclosure has historically been the primary method used to address conflicts of interest and most jurisdictions have implemented some sort of disclosure requirement.[6] Most often disclosure involves revealing any conflicts of interest faced or the nature of the remuneration that advisors receive. While the amount of remuneration is also commonly required to be disclosed, some jurisdictions only require this information to be disclosed at the request of the client. MiFID II recognises the limitations of disclosure and treats it more as a last resort solution, not allowing firms to overly rely on disclosure to manage their conflicts of interest.

With recent reforms, advisors are increasingly being required to also disclose the type of advice that they provide; whether it is independent or not and the nature and/or scope of the service provided. Suitability reports may also be required explaining why the recommendation is suitable for the client. In the United Kingdom, suitability reports are required to be provided to consumers explaining why the recommendation from the advisor is suitable given the client's request and needs as well as information received from the client. The report must also explain any potential disadvantages to the client from following the recommendation. MiFID II, in addition, will require disclosure of whether the advisor will continue to assess the ongoing suitability of the recommendation.

Enforcement of disclosure requirements

Here again clarity regarding regulatory expectations is important to facilitate the implementation and enforcement of disclosure requirements. Several reviews have shown that advisors often do not accurately disclose information even with disclosure requirements in place. In Europe, one investigation showed that less than 5% of advisors disclosed any conflict of interest to their clients, that there was a general lack of communication regarding remuneration and that fees did not seem to be fully and accurately disclosed (Synovate, 2011). The Financial Conduct Authority (FCA) found that following the implementation of the Retail Distribution Review in the United Kingdom, the majority of firms were not adequately disclosing the cost of advice. However, a follow-up review did see significant improvements in disclosure practices after the FCA had provided additional guidance on good practices (Financial Conduct Authority, 2014b).

Challenges to the implementation of disclosure requirements

Increased disclosure requirements can potentially increase the cost of providing advice, though this can be mitigated through efficient processes and procedures. For example, the Financial Advice Market Review in the United Kingdom found that firms were spending significant time on preparing suitability reports. As a result the Financial Conduct Authority will continue to work with the industry to better streamline this process and simplify the reports in order to minimise the additional burden of preparing the reports and the regulatory uncertainty regarding the information which is required to be included (HM Treasury and Financial Conduct Authority, 2016).

To reduce compliance costs and help consumer comprehension, there is also a trend towards simplifying the information disclosed, making disclosures easier for the consumer to understand and more standardised across firms and products. In the United States, for example, the Department of Labor has issued detailed regulations and standards on fee disclosure and transparency of expenses by private pension funds. Germany requires that a brief and comprehensible disclosure regarding product features, risks and cost be provided to clients before the transaction is executed. In Canada, the CRM-2 legislation requires that all advisor compensation cost be broken down and reported in a transparent and standardised manner. Model reports have been developed to aid firms to do so, and provide a line-by-line breakdown of commissions by type along with clear explanations of each type. Planned changes in New Zealand seek to simplify disclosure requirements, making them easier for consumers to understand and helping them to understand the limitations of the advice they receive (New Zealand Ministry of Business, Innovation and Employment, 2016).

Increasing the simplicity and standardisation of disclosures is also a result of the acknowledgement that consumers have difficulty to understand the fees that they pay. A recent study of workplace pensions in the United Kingdom revealed a poor understanding of fees charged by the provider (Price Bailey and Ipsos MORI, 2016). A study in Australia showed that less than 15% of people paying for advice through commissions are actually receiving advice (Australian School of Business, 2010). Australia has since implemented a requirement that consumers must opt-in every two years to continue paying ongoing fees for advice, as well as a requirement to disclose the services that the consumer is entitled to. A survey in the United States revealed that 60% of clients did not understand how their financial advisor was charging them (Cerulli Associates, 2013). Furthermore, 31% believed that the advice they received was free (Ody, 2011).

Nevertheless, while simplified and standardised disclosure may help to improve consumer understanding and outcomes, it is likely not sufficient in itself. There is little evidence demonstrating the effectiveness of disclosure of potential conflicts of interest to improve consumer decision-making and outcomes.

First, consumers often demonstrate a lack of attention to such disclosures of conflicts of interest, even when presented in a simplified manner. One study in the United States revealed that consumers did not avoid loads on products, even when these loads were disclosed in a simplified way, and that this disclosure resulted in no change in investment outcomes (Beshears et al., 2009). Prior to the Retail Distribution Review reforms, the United Kingdom required that advisors provide clients with a menu detailing the cost of compensation and the average market price. This menu was also shown to be ineffective in improving consumer outcomes (Butterworth et al., 2007).

On the other hand, when consumers do pay attention, there is the risk that the disclosure of conflicts of interest may lead them to overweight this information in their investment decision. A study in Europe demonstrated that disclosure of conflicts in a face-to-face situation led to an automatic reaction of distrust in the advice, rather than a proper assessment of the advice itself (Chater et al., 2010). A study in the United States for mortgage disclosures showed that consumers placed too much weight on the information provided on the broker's commissions, leading them to choose a more expensive mortgage (Lacko and Pappalardo, 2004).

Consumers also demonstrate a lack of understanding regarding the implications of a disclosed conflict. Online subjects in a study in eight European Union member states did not react to the disclosure of the nature of the remuneration of the advisor unless the implications of the conflict of interest were explicitly spelled out, and even then a strong reaction was only elicited if this warning was provided in a bold red font (Chater et al., 2010).

Another study showed that individuals receiving disclosures regarding only the nature and amount of advisor compensation (and no explanation of the implications for the advice received) did not sufficiently discount the advisor's advice (Cain et al., 2005).

A potential unintended outcome of making the implications of the conflict of interest clear, however, may be a perception of increased pressure for the consumer to follow advice. Another study revealed that following a disclosure of a conflict of interest and an explanation of its implications, consumers felt increased pressure to follow the advice. Explanations provided for this phenomenon were that the consumers did not want to signal that they did not trust the advisor, and they felt a desire to help the advisor achieve a positive outcome and be compensated (Sah et al., 2013).

While disclosure does not necessarily improve consumer decision-making, it may provide an incentive for advisors to mitigate or avoid the conflicts of interest they face and therefore improve the quality of the advice provided. One study showed that advisors more often prefer to avoid any conflicts of interest when they are required to disclose them (Sah and Loewenstein, 2014). Another study showed that increased transparency of commissions that agents received for mutual funds helped to mitigate the conflict of interest of the agent and improved returns (Edelen et al., 2012).

However, disclosure may also have a negative impact on the quality of advice provided. One study showed that advisors provided more biased advice when disclosing a conflict of interest that they were unable to avoid, as they felt they had a "moral license" to be more biased because they had been honest to the client and fulfilled their obligations of transparency (Sah and Loewenstein, 2014). Nevertheless this was a case when the implications of the conflict were also explained rather than the conflict being simply disclosed. This highlights the importance and complementarity of duty of care standards in mitigating advisor bias, but also implies that providing more information or improving client understanding may not necessarily be more beneficial for the client in terms of outcomes. Where additional details are disclosed, they may be better disclosed in secondary statements which the consumer can review at their leisure, removed from any pressure to comply with the advice.

Despite disclosure requirements relating to conflicts of interest being ubiquitous, their effectiveness in improving consumer decision-making to follow advice seems limited. Nevertheless there still seems to be value in increased transparency, which can provide incentives for advisors themselves to mitigate the conflicts of interest that they face. However policy makers need to be sure that regulatory requirements are clearly communicated to facilitate the implementation of such requirements and limit the costs. Given the limitations of disclosure, however, additional measures are needed to mitigate the conflicts of interest in financial advice.

Remuneration limits

Limits on remuneration structures have been imposed where duty of care standards and disclosure requirements have been deemed insufficient to resolve the negative impact to consumers of conflicts of interest.[7] These limits can range from caps to complete bans on certain types of remuneration, or can impose other structural requirements or conditions on the compensation received by the advisor.

Caps on the allowable level of compensation can take the form of either hard limits or soft limits. The problems that these caps intend to address, however, vary from one jurisdiction to another. Chile imposed a hard limit on commissions of 2% for annuity sales as a response to escalating commissions which seemed unresponsive to competitive pressure. Proposed legislation in Australia, on the other hand, would impose hard limits on both upfront and ongoing commissions that insurance intermediaries can receive in response to an investigation finding a correlation between high commissions and poor quality of advice (ASIC, 2015). Soft limits have been imposed in the Netherlands and in the United Kingdom, where fees charged for advice must be representative of the actual cost of advice, and intend to prevent vertically integrated firms from having a competitive advantage through the subsidisation of advice from its product charges. In the United States, the cost of advice and commission payments must be kept to a "reasonable" level.

Other jurisdictions have imposed outright bans on certain types of commission payments. Australia, the Netherlands and the United Kingdom have implemented some of the broadest bans by banning all conflicted remuneration for retail investment advice, which generally includes not only commission payments but also compensation based on volume targets as well as kickbacks. Denmark and Finland have limited commission bans to independent insurance brokers. More limited bans on specific types of remuneration have also been introduced, for example Australia has banned fees based on a percentage of assets under management for leveraged investments only, and Canada is considering a ban on trailing commissions paid beyond the period of initial investment.

Still other jurisdictions have imposed limits or conditions on the structure of the allowable compensation. Australia has introduced a claw back provision for insurance sales, where the advisor must pay back a portion of the commission in the event that the product is terminated within a certain period. In an effort to avoid excessive switching between pension providers, Mexico has introduced a conditional provision reducing the agent's compensation if the client switches pension providers within 30 months. Both the Netherlands and the United Kingdom have imposed limits with respect to the allowable time period that a client can pay the advisor fee for fee-based advice.

Challenges for the implementation of remuneration limits

The main goal of any regulation imposing limits on the remuneration of financial advisors is to better align the interest of the agent with those of the client, reducing the bias of the advisor and improving the quality of advice. Minimising the remuneration that the advisor receives from commissions in particular would reduce their incentive to recommend products paying higher commissions over those that do not.

Indeed, much evidence shows that the quality of advice is influenced by remuneration structures. One survey on independent financial advisors in Germany showed that advisors having a lower portion of their salary coming from commissions provided better quality advice (Bluethgen et al., 2008). Another study in Australia concluded that fee-for-service advice provides higher value to clients than commission-based advice (Rice Warner Actuaries, 2011). A study on advisors in the United States showed that advisors receiving compensation in the form of commissions or as a percentage of assets under management had higher rates of misconduct (Egan et al., 2016). Further evidence is shown following changes in regulation imposing certain remuneration structures. The implementation of the conditional reduction in the remuneration of agents in Mexico resulted in a reduction of switching pension funds by over 20%. Following the implementation of the Retail Distribution Review in the United Kingdom banning commission payments, there were significantly more flows to products which had paid lower commissions prior to the regulatory change (Financial Conduct Authority, 2014).

Trailing commissions in particular have been shown to go unnoticed by consumers, potentially resulting in higher total costs. Generally speaking, trailing commissions deduct a regular percentage of assets under management from the clients account, and are therefore less noticeable to the consumer than upfront fees which are usually larger and deducted immediately. One study in India showed that the cost of a closed end fund, where trailing commissions were allowed, was three percentage points higher compared to an open ended fund where trailing commissions were prohibited (Anagol and Kim, 2012). In Australia, only 15% of consumers paying for ongoing advice through a regular fee deducted from their account were actually receiving advice (Australian School of Business, 2010). The opt-in clause required by the FOFA regulation to continue paying this fee sought to address this problem. Another study on mutual funds in Canada showed that trailing commissions are associated with an increase in inflows and a decrease in performance of the fund. Nevertheless, trailing commissions can reduce the incentive for the advisor to encourage churning; the same study in Canada showed that outflows were also lower for funds with trailing commissions (Cumming et al., 2015).

Fee-based remuneration presents an alternative to compensation based on commissions, and removes the incentive to recommend a product paying a higher commission. However, these remuneration structures also present their own challenges. Advisors charging fees based on a percentage of assets under management may have the incentive to cater only to higher wealth clients, perhaps one driver of the shift towards this market observed in the United Kingdom following the ban on commissions. Flat-fee advisors may also be less incentivised find the most appropriate product for their client given the additional effort required. One study in Europe showed that flat-fee advisors were less likely to recommend successful investment outcomes to their client than advisors receiving commissions, as they were more indifferent to the client's outcome (Chater et al., 2010). Finally advisors charging hourly fees may have the incentive to inflate the amount of time spent on a client, and additionally a flat or hourly fee may deter clients from seeking advice at all.

Nevertheless, most evidence shows that limits on the remuneration of financial advisors are likely to improve consumer outcomes for those who do seek advice. However, these types of limits may also result in unintended consequences of a reduction in the number of advisors, an unwillingness of advisors to continue to serve lower wealth clients, or consumer reluctance to pay upfront for advice.

The potential reduction of the number of advisors due to reduced profitability is a potential concern for the availability of financial advice. The overall number of advisors in the United Kingdom fell by nearly 10% from 2011 to 2015, though the number of advisors did increase during the second half of this period (APFA, 2016). Part of the reduction is also likely due to increased qualification standards imposed by the regulation. Changing business models also contributed to a reduction in the number of advisors, however; the number of advisors from banks decreased by nearly two-thirds from 2011 to 2014, coinciding with the exit of several banks from the advice channel (APFA, 2016). On the other hand, only 7% of firms reported a decrease in the number of advisors in Australia following the reforms (ASIC, 2014).

Limits on remuneration have not been shown to have a significant impact on profitability. There is some evidence that the commission ban in the United Kingdom reduced product costs beyond the level of the commission payment due to increased transparency and competition (Financial Conduct Authority, 2014). Nevertheless, revenues for both investment and insurance business have increased since the reforms (APFA, 2016). As another example, in Finland where commissions were banned for independent insurance brokers, their market share of statutory pension insurance decreased from 16.2% in 2003 to 9.2% in 2014. However, while total broker compensation did decrease somewhat following the implementation of the ban in 2008, it has since recovered to previous levels (Makynen, 2015).

However, changing business models may lead advisors to be more unwilling to serve clients with lower levels of wealth. There is some evidence of this in the United Kingdom, where 69% of advisors said that they had turned away a client in the last year, usually due to the fact that it would have been uneconomical to provide the client advice. Many advisors also indicated that the client's sources of wealth other than retirement were also taken into consideration when deciding to accept the client. In addition, firms requiring a minimum level of wealth of 100 000 GBP to provide advice doubled within two years to 32% of firms in 2015 (HM Treasury and Financial Conduct Authority, 2016). However, 26% of clients of advisory firms surveyed at the end of 2015 had pension wealth of less than 30 000 GBP, indicating that there are still some advisors willing to serve lower wealth clients (Financial Conduct Authority, 2016c).

Fee-based advice, particularly in the form of fee-for-service or hourly rates, may lead to consumer reluctance to pay for advice. This seems to largely due to the lack of awareness by consumers as to how much they pay for advice through commissions, and the perception of an upfront fee as a sure loss regardless of the ultimate decision that they take. Several surveys assessing consumer's willingness to pay for advice confirm this. One survey showed that 47% of Australians prefer to pay for advice through commissions, compared to 26% who preferred upfront or hourly fees (Ody, 2011). Another showed that 75% of Australians were not willing to pay more than AUD 250 for advice, and that demand was higher for simplified advice; the actual cost of full personal advice was 1 AUD 190 for industry funds, and AUD 220 for simplified advice (ASFA, 2014). In the United Kingdom, only 8% of consumers were willing to pay over GBP 500 for advice, and only 14% willing to pay between GBP 200 and 500; the actual cost of advice is around GBP 150 per hour, and advice for pension investments requires on average nine hours of the advisor's time (HM Treasury and Financial Conduct Authority, 2016). As further evidence of consumer reluctance to pay for advice, non-advised sales in the United Kingdom have increased, representing over half of the transactions for personal investment firms in 2014-15, compared to around 25% in 2010-11 (APFA, 2016). In an effort to mitigate this reluctance to pay upfront for advice, the Netherlands and the United Kingdom allow for the client to take a 'credit' and pay the advisor fee over a limited period of time. The Netherlands has also taken additional measures, requiring that the consumer take a competency test before being allowed to invest directly without advice (Oxera, 2015).

Limits on remuneration aim to reduce the conflicts of interest that advisors face in receiving commission payments from the products they recommend, however such limits also present challenges to maintain the availability of advice and consumer demand for advice. While consumer outcomes for those who seek advice generally seem to improve with such regulation, the accessibility of advice could reduce if financial advisors change their business models to target higher wealth clients and consumers may be reluctant to pay for advice. As such, the appropriate limits will depend on the specific problems observed in a given market and measures will need to be taken to reduce the impact on the advice gap.

Qualification standards

Qualification standards need to be imposed on financial advisors to ensure the competency of the advisor to provide that advice. Generally, there are requirements for financial advisors to be registered with the supervisory body, which can include some minimum standards in order to obtain a license to operate. Standards meant to verify the competence of the advisor may include minimum levels of educational attainment, completion of exams or requirements to follow courses for continued professional development.

The registration of financial advisors is relatively common, and can be a valuable tool for the supervisor to monitor their behaviour. A study on registered financial advisors in the United States showed that 1 in 13 advisors have a record for misconduct, but a third of these have more than one instance of misconduct (Egan et al., 2016). Therefore past misconduct may increase the likelihood of future misconduct, and the supervisory body needs to be aware of these instances to improve future monitoring.

Beyond monitoring conduct, registration of advisors can serve to highlight their particular qualifications or competencies for consumers and can facilitate the search for a financial advisor appropriate for specific needs. For example, the Australian regulator has a register for financial advisors where consumers can search for advisors and see details of their qualifications and expertise. As another example, the Personal Finance Society in the United Kingdom has a special register for financial advisors who are better qualified to provide financial advice later in life (Financial Conduct Authority, 2016).

Educational standards for financial advisors seem to have been relatively low historically. Furthermore, standards are not generally consistent for different types of advisors, making it difficult for consumers to judge the competency of their financial advisor.

Many jurisdictions have been moving to not only increase educational standards for financial advisors but also to make them more uniform. Having a minimum uniform standard is important given the lack of consumer awareness of the different standards that advisors are held to. Australia, Canada and New Zealand are in the process of making efforts to increase qualification standards for advisors as well as increase uniformity. The Retail Distribution Review in the United Kingdom already increased the standards for advisors, and MiFID II is clearly defining the knowledge that advisors should have and demonstrate through experience and an appropriate qualification. Continued professional development (CPD) is also increasingly being required, and has already been implemented in the United Kingdom. MiFID II in Europe and the Professional Standards of Financial Advisors in Australia will also implement CPD requirements for advisors. Greece implemented new standards for insurance intermediaries in 2014, requiring that advisors complete a specified number of approved courses each year for the renewal of their professional license (EIOPA, 2015).

Evidence from the United Kingdom has shown that increased educational standards have impacted the professionalism of advisors. More financial advisors are going beyond the minimum standards set and there is increased focus on providing ongoing services to clients. Membership of professional bodies has also increased (Financial Conduct Authority, 2014).

However, some other jurisdictions have encountered challenges in enforcing professional standards of knowledge and education. An investigation in France found that insurance intermediaries were not receiving sufficient training to meet regulatory requirements. Insurance providers in Spain have faced the challenge of maintaining sufficient levels of qualifications given the high turnover of the telemarketing sector, which they rely upon to reach out to consumers (EIOPA, 2015).

Qualification standards are necessary in order to ensure that financial advisors are competent to give appropriate financial advice to clients, and many jurisdictions have been aiming to increase these standards as well as make them more uniform for different types of advisors. The registration of advisors can play an important role in matching advisors to consumers and aiding supervisors in monitoring advisor conduct. However, once again, clear definitions of what constitutes advice and who is allowed to provide it are needed in order to overcome the challenges in maintaining these standards for the profession.

Dispute resolution

Mechanisms need to be in place to allow consumers to resolve any complaints related to the advice received.[8] Dispute resolution schemes are often put in place to offer a more timely and efficient resolution of consumer complaints than going through the court system.

Regulation often requires that financial intermediaries belong to a dispute resolution scheme that consumers can access in the event that they feel they have been harmed by financial advice received. Some jurisdictions have a centralised function that serves to resolve such disputes. In the United States, for example, consumers having a complaint against a broker-dealer can normally seek redress through an arbitration process managed by FINRA, who has the power to grant a monetary settlement as well as suspend or cancel the registration of the party providing the investment advice for non-compliance. In the United Kingdom, the Financial Ombudsman Service deals with consumer complaints. If the firm is unable to compensate the client for a valid claim against them, the client may be able to claim from the Financial Services Compensation Scheme. The European Commission has centralised a cross-border dispute resolution network called FIN-NET for the countries in the European Economic Area. The members of the network are responsible for handling disputes out of court between consumers and the providers of financial services, including investment firms and insurance companies, and they also facilitate cross-border complaints.

Other jurisdictions have several schemes operating with various financial intermediaries. Australia, for example, has three such schemes, one of which focuses specifically on complaints related to superannuation, the Superannuation Complaints Tribunal. New Zealand has numerous dispute resolution schemes, and advisors are required to be associated with one. In Canada, IIROC regulated advisors must have membership in an arbitration programme to resolve any potential disputes with clients.

The existence of numerous dispute resolution schemes can present challenges to ensuring the consistency of the process to handle consumer complaints and the rules applied. This seems to be a potential problem in Canada, where the process of pursuing a complaint varies across the different sectors, with each having a different approach and procedure (Expert Committee to Consider Financial Advisory and Financial Planning Policy Alternatives, 2016). A review of the regulation in New Zealand also raised this concern. The review found that schemes do not necessarily apply rules consistently, which could provide opportunities for arbitrage and potentially reduced economies of scale (New Zealand Ministry of Business, Innovation and Employment, 2016b).

Transparency regarding the process to resolve complaints is also important from the perspective of the financial advisor. The Financial Advice Market Review in the United

Kingdom found that some advisors were reluctant to provide advice due to future liability concerns coming from to the lack of a time limit within which consumers are allowed to file a complaint and uncertainty around the rules that would be applied. As a result, the review recommended that the process that the Financial Ombudsman Service follows should be made more transparent (HM Treasury and Financial Conduct Authority, 2016).

Dispute resolution schemes play an important role in facilitating consumer access to redress in the event that the financial advice received is not appropriate. Nevertheless, in order for these schemes to operate effectively, the process followed to resolve disputes needs to be transparent and consistent across the various schemes in operation. Consumers also need to be made aware of the process which they should follow in order to have access to redress from any harm inflicted from inappropriate financial advice.

3.4. Minimising advice gaps

While the policy measures discussed above can be effective in increasing the quality of advice, they may also inadvertently affect the availability and affordability of advice, increasing the advice gap. The drivers of this advice gap include a shortage of advisors supplying advice in certain markets, higher costs of compliance and/or the reluctance of consumers to pay for advice. Policy makers need to ensure that any potential reduction in the availability or affordability of advice does not outweigh the benefits of improved consumer outcomes from financial advice. There are several measures that policy makers can take to reduce the impact of regulation on the advice gap and encourage innovative solutions to address these issues, particularly for lower wealth consumers.

The potential shortage in the supply of advice in certain markets can be driven by uncertainty around regulatory liability, an un-level playing field and/or potential differences in the profitability of providing advice. Each of these can affect the willingness of advisors to serve certain markets thereby affecting the number of advisors that consumers have access to.

Uncertainty around regulatory liability can stem from a lack of clarity in the definitions of advice and the scope of application of the regulation. For example, uncertainty regarding the boundary between guidance and advice can lead to reluctance to provide any information to consumers at all. This has proven to be an issue in several jurisdictions when it comes to employers providing their employees information about their investment options for pension plans. Another advice gap observed in some jurisdictions has been the lack of provision of simplified advice for specific investment matters more limited in scope. The lack of clarity for the due diligence requirements for comprehensive versus simplified advice has led to a reluctance by advisors to provide simplified advice due to a concern over legal liability. Improving the clarity of definitions and legal requirements can reduce advisor's uncertainty around whether they are fully complying with regulations and reduce their concerns of future legal liability.

A lack of uniformity in the application of regulation can lead to an un-level playing field and present opportunities for cherry-picking by advisors to serve only some markets over others. For example, differences regarding duty of care requirements could lead advisors to only serve the markets where regulation is lighter and compliance costs lower. The lack of uniformity of duty of care standards has been raised as a concern, for example, in New Zealand and the United States. Where disclosure requirements differ, advisors may also be incentivised to only offer products which do not require disclosure of conflicts.

Increased uniformity of requirements for different types of advisors and products would reduce incentives to serve only less regulated markets.

Where profitability differs among consumers, advisors may be incentivised to serve only those which are potentially more profitable. This could result, for example, where advisors are compensated primarily from fees based on assets under management which result in higher fees from higher wealth clients. This has been a concern in the United Kingdom, for example, following the ban on commission payments. As such, the benefits of any limits on compensation must be weighed against the potential reduction in the access to advice for lower wealth clients, and innovative business models to serve these clients should be encouraged to be developed.

A second driver of the advice gap could be increased costs of compliance with regulation for advisors, which may also increase the cost of advice, reducing the affordability of advice for lower wealth clients. These increased costs can be due to increased due diligence requirements to fulfil the duty of care standard in place, increased administrative costs due to disclosure requirements, or increased risk of legal liability if regulatory requirements are not sufficiently met. For example, several jurisdictions such as New Zealand and the United Kingdom identified that advisors may have been performing higher due diligence than necessary for simplified advice, making the cost of providing such advice unreasonable given its limited scope. Again, the clarity of regulatory requirements is essential to ensure that advisors know when they have fulfilled requirements and do not spend excessive resources to exceed them, and the proportionality of regulation with respect to due diligence for simplified and comprehensive advice is needed to keep costs down for simplified advice. Regulators can also work with advisors to help streamline processes and ensure that requirements are met in an efficient and cost-effective manner.

Perhaps the most challenging driver of the advice gap for policy makers to counter is the reluctance of consumers to pay for advice, particularly fee-based advice in the form of fee-for-service or hourly rates. Many consumers are not aware of how much they pay for advice, particularly when advisors are compensated through more opaque remuneration structures such as commissions. Disclosure requirements for advisor remuneration and limits on more opaque compensation structures can make the price of advice much more transparent to consumers. However, making the cost more transparent may lead to reluctance by consumers to use financial advisors. The amount that consumers are willing to pay upfront for advice is often less than the cost of providing the advice. Flexibility around how the fee is paid could help to reduce the sticker shock of seeing the full price of advice. For example, the Netherlands and the United Kingdom allow the consumer to take a limited "credit" from the advisor and pay the fee over a specified period of time. Nevertheless, the undervaluation of advice by consumers is not an easy problem to overcome.

Given the reluctance of consumers to pay for advice, innovative solutions will need to be found to reduce the cost of advice, or at least the perception of high cost, particularly for lower wealth segments. Technology-based advice has the potential to increase the accessibility of advice as well as reduce the cost of providing it for basic retirement savings needs. In addition, technology-based advice avoids the problem of conflicts of interest by relying on objective and transparent models using generally accepted investment theories. However, policy makers need to ensure that the regulation in place encompasses these channels so that the same level of consumer protection is in place as for advice provided in person.

3.5. Regulation of technology-based advice

Financial advice that relies on technology has the potential to help bridge the advice gap which can result from measures taken to mitigate conflicts of interest and ensure the competency of advisors. The growth of technology can facilitate in particular the provision of simplified and streamlined financial advice at a lower cost. Furthermore, the use of objective and automated models provides an alternative to overcoming advisor bias. Regulators have been seeking ways to promote innovative solutions for the provision of advice while assessing how such advice platforms would fit within the existing regulation of financial advice and ensuring that appropriate consumer protections are in place.

Several jurisdictions have been encouraging technological solutions to help close the advice gap. The Financial Conduct Authority in the United Kingdom launched 'Project Innovate' to encourage firms to develop lower cost advice models aimed at the mass-market, particularly with respect to simplified advice. The Financial Advice Market Review further recommended that the regulator establish an Advice Unit to assist in the development of such models (HM Treasury and Financial Conduct Authority, 2016). Similarly, the Netherlands Authority for the Financial Markets and the Dutch Central Bank have launched an "Innovation Hub" to support financial innovation and answer questions regarding regulatory requirements. An Innovation Hub has also been established in Australia to support FinTech start-ups. In addition, Australia, Singapore and the United Kingdom are also introducing 'regulatory sandboxes' for businesses to experiment with innovative products and services in a controlled environment.

Such innovations do not always neatly fit into the existing regulation of financial advice, however. A review of the current regulation in New Zealand identified that the regulation as currently written may present a barrier to the potential role of technology in providing financial advice, as it requires that advice be provided by a "natural person". Planned changes seek to broaden the definition of advice in order to accommodate technological innovations, and require that entities providing such robo-advice be licensed and held to the same requirements as other types of advisors (New Zealand Ministry of Business, Innovation and Employment, 2016). Current regulation in Canada explicitly limits the acceptable role of technology in providing advice, as under the current regulation, fully automated services are not allowed, and any robo-advice service must also provide some access to personalised advice from an advisor (Lortie, 2016).

Regulators in several jurisdictions have been assessing how technology-based advice should be regulated going forward. In Australia, the regulator has issued a consultation document and a draft regulatory guide with respect to robo-advice. The proposed guide maintains that the qualification requirements for providers of robo-advice be the same as those for normal advisors, and lays out the requirements for testing the algorithms used and the governance controls and processes in place. In the United States, the Department of Labor has established conditions for which model-based asset allocations would not violate the fiduciary duty for pension plans under the ERISA regulation, which includes the independence of the financial expert developing the models (US Department of Labor, 2001). More recently, the financial advice industry's self-regulatory body published a report to clarify the application of its rules with respect to digital investment advice and share effective practices. It highlights the importance of the oversight of the algorithms used in digital tools to ensure that an appropriate governance framework is in place and that the resulting advice is appropriate for the client (FINRA, 2016). In addition, a new rule proposal by the Securities Exchange Commission would require developers of algorithmic trading to be registered as a securities trader, and be subject to the same qualification requirements as securities traders. In Europe, MiFID II will require that firms engaging in algorithmic trading have effective risk controls in place and perform stress testing on the algorithms. The European Supervisory Authorities have issued a joint discussion paper on the automation of financial advice looking at the potential benefits and risks of such innovations in order to determine any additional regulatory action needed to address automated financial advice (Joint Committee of the European Supervisory Authorities, 2015).

Key themes raised in these regulatory assessments are the need for consistency with the regulation of face-to-face financial advice and the need for proper risk and governance controls to be in place. First, the type of advice being provided by the platform needs to be clear within the definitions provided by the regulation in order to determine which standards apply, for example to what extent the advice is general or personalised. If the advice is determined to be personalised advice, clear processes would need to be in place with respect to how suitability for the client is determined. The providers of these platforms should also be held to the same qualification standards in order to be sure that they understand the implications of the advice provided by their platforms and are competent to ensure that it is appropriate. Finally, the algorithms used for automation need to be extensively tested, and controls need to be in place to ensure that the procedures in place continue to function properly. With adequate consumer protection measures in place, technology has great potential to increase the affordability of and access to financial advice and help to close the advice gap.

3.6. Conclusions

The various measures which policy makers can take to improve consumer outcomes from financial advice for retirement are complementary as each addresses a different aspect which influences the quality of financial advice. Duty of care standards, disclosure requirements and remuneration limits aim to ensure that conflicts are appropriately managed, understood or eliminated completely. Qualification standards aim to ensure that the advisor has the appropriate knowledge to provide advice. Finally, mechanisms for dispute resolution are needed to facilitate consumers' access to redress in the event of a complaint. Policy makers must therefore consider how to implement these measures together.

Nevertheless, each of these policy measures presents challenges for policy makers to ensure their effectiveness in improving the quality of financial advice for retirement. Furthermore, these measures can potentially lead to an advice gap, reducing the availability and/or affordability of advice, particularly for consumers with low to moderate retirement wealth.

Enforcement is the key to making duty of care standards effective in improving the quality of advice. Periodic monitoring and enforcement of due diligence processes and procedures to identify and manage conflicts of interest can provide feedback to advisors where their processes are not in line with regulatory requirements and help to identify areas of improvement. This could be accomplished, for example, through mystery shopping exercises. Such reviews can also be used as an opportunity to clarify regulatory requirements and share best practices. The exposure to legal liability if poor advice is provided also helps to align advisors' incentives with their clients and helps with enforcement. In addition, enforcement can help to promote a culture of compliance within firms. An increased role of industry bodies in setting standards for the profession could also help to establish positive social norms, helping advisors to internalise these values and overcome their unconscious biases.

Disclosure requirements are important to promote transparency. However, their value may lie more in their potential to influence advisor behaviour rather than the optimal use of disclosed information by consumers to improve their decisions to follow advice. Increased transparency can help incentivise agents to avoid and/or manage the conflicts of interest they face, helping to make duty of care standards more effective. However, more information is not necessarily better in terms of improving consumer outcomes. While the full cost that the consumer will pay should certainly be disclosed, a detailed breakdown of the amount of the advisor's compensation may not be necessary in the primary disclosure document. Secondary disclosure statements can provide detailed information which the consumer can review at their leisure, removed from any pressure to comply with the advice.

Limits on the remuneration advisors receive can help to better align the interests of the advisor and the client. The appropriate limits depend on the problems observed in the particular market and their complementarity with other policies to mitigate conflicts of interest as they change the incentive structure of the advisors. For example, moving towards a fee-based model may overcome the conflict of interest from commission payment, but it may also decrease the incentive for advisors to serve clients with lower wealth.

Qualification standards help to ensure that advisors are competent to provide advice to clients. Minimum qualification standards should be uniform across all advisor types in order to ensure adequate consumer protection. Beyond minimum standards of competency, however, advisors could specialise in certain areas to meet specific consumer needs, such as investing for retirement. A centralised register of financial advisors could facilitate consumers' search for an advisor, and could allow both a verification of their credentials as well as a filter to search for advisors providing advice for specific needs.

Consumers also need a consistent and transparent procedure to facilitate the resolution of their complaints. The process and rules of such schemes need to be consistent and transparent in order to ensure that all schemes are applying the same standards and that no arbitrage opportunities exist.

Policy makers will also need to consider how to limit the impact of these measures on the advice gap. First, to ensure the availability of advice for all markets, improving the uniformity in the application of regulation can help to reduce opportunities for cherry-picking by advisors to serve only less regulated channels over others. Clarity in the scope of regulation and the definitions and rules applied is also important to reduce advisors' uncertainty with respect to legal liability for providing advice, reducing advisor reluctance to provide advice in more ambiguous situations.

To minimise the costs of compliance with regulation and promote the affordability of advice, clarity in regulatory requirements is essential to ensure that advisors know when they have fulfilled requirements and do not spend excessive resources to exceed them. Regulators can work together with advisors to help streamline processes and ensure that requirements are met in an efficient manner. In addition, the proportionality of regulation with respect to due diligence for simplified and comprehensive advice is important to allow advisors to provide lower cost advice for more straightforward requests.

Consumer undervaluation of advice and their reluctance to pay for it is potentially the most challenging aspect of the advice gap for policy makers to address. Flexibility around how upfront fees are paid could help to reduce the sticker shock of seeing the full price of advice. However more innovated solutions will need to be found to reduce the cost of advice, particularly for individuals with lower levels of wealth and less complex financial planning needs.

Policy makers should encourage and support innovative business models which can provide advice services for lower wealth clients. Technology-based advice in particular has the potential to increase the accessibility and affordability of advice for straightforward financial planning for retirement. Furthermore its objectivity presents an alternative to overcome the behavioural biases of advisors. However, policy makers need to ensure that the regulation in place encompasses these channels so that the same level of consumer protection is in place as for traditional channels.

While the policy measures discussed in this chapter can improve the quality of financial advice and consumer outcomes, there are numerous challenges to ensure their effectiveness and to minimise any impact on the advice gap. While not all of these challenges are easily resolved, the implications discussed here can help policy makers to implement policies that will be effective and promote the availability and affordability of financial advice for retirement.

Notes

1. The chapter does not focus on the evidence of the influence that conflicts of interest can have on financial advice, as this has been covered extensively in other research (e.g. Burke et al., 2015).
2. The Ministry of Business, Innovation and Employment of New Zealand has made recommendations to simplify the classification of advisors.
3. Jurisdictions may differ in the language used to refer to these two concepts and their exact definitions. As used here, best interest requirements are more stringent than suitability requirements and these terms will continue to be used as defined in this section throughout the chapter.
4. For a more general overview of enforcement frameworks see the Effective Approaches to Support the Implementation of the Remaining G20/OECD High-Level Principles on Financial Consumer Protection.
5. Professional standards are also an effective approach to implement the second OECD/G20 High Level Principle on Financial Consumer Protection on the Role of Oversight Bodies.
6. The fourth OECD/G20 High Level Principle on Financial Consumer Protection on Disclosure and Transparency recommends disclosing conflicts of interest.
7. The sixth OECD/G20 High Level Principle on Financial Consumer Protection on Responsible Business Conduct of Financial Services Providers and Authorised Agents states that "the remuneration structure for staff of both financial services providers and authorised agents should be designed to encourage responsible business conduct, fair treatment of consumers and to avoid conflicts of interest."
8. The ninth OECD/G20 High Level Principle on Financial Consumer Protection on Complaints, Handling and Redress states that "Jurisdictions should ensure that consumers have access to adequate complaints handling and redress mechanisms that are accessible, affordable, independent, fair, accountable, timely and efficient".

References

AFM (2016) *Kwaliteit Beleggingsdienstverlening 2015: Resultaten van het onderzoek en goede praktijkvoorbeelden.*

Anagol, S., S. Cole and S. Sarkar (2013), *Understanding the Advice of Commissions-Motivated Agents: Evidence from the Indian Life Insurance Market.*

Anagol, S. and H.H. Kim (2012), "The Impact of Shrouded Fees: Evidence from a Natural Experiment in the Indian Mutual Funds Market", *American Economic Review*, Vol. 102/1, pp. 576-593.

APFA (2016), *The Financial Adviser Market: In numbers.*

ASIC (2015), *Consulation Paper* 245: Retail insurance advice reforms.

ASFA (2014), *ASFA survey on the provision of financial advice by superannuation funds*, Sydney.

ASIC (2014), *Review of the financial advice industry's implementation of the FOFA reforms.*

Australian School of Business (2010), *Financial Planning: What is the Right Price for Advice?.*

Bazerman, M.H., K.P. Morgan and G.F. Loewenstein (1997), "Opinion: The Impossibility of Auditor independence", *Sloan Management Review*, Vol. 38/4.

Beshears, J. et al. (2009), *How Does Simplified Disclosure Affect individuals' Mutual Fund Choices?.*

Bluethgen, R., Meyer, S. and A. Hackethal (2008), *High Quality Financial Advice Wanted!*

Burke, J. and A. Hung (2015), *Trust and Financial Advice*, Rand Corporation.

Burke, J. and A. Hung (2015b), *Financial Advice Markets: A Cross Country Comparison*, RAND Corporation.

Burke et al. (2015), *Impacts of Conflicts of Interest in the Financial Services Industry*, RAND Corporation.

Butterworth, D., K. Malcolm and M. Tiden (2007), *An Empirical Investigation into the Effects of the Menu.*

Cain, D.M., G. Loewenstein and D.A. Moore (2005), "The Dirt on Coming Clean: Perverse Effects of Disclosing Conflicts of Interest", *Journal of Legal Studies*, Vol. 34.

Calcagno, R. and C. Monticone (2015), "Financial Literacy and the Demand for Financial Advice", *Journal of Banking and Finance*, Vol. 50, pp. 363-380.

Central Bank of Ireland (2016), *Themed Inspection highlights Conflict of Interest risks in investment firms.*

Cerulli Associates (2013), *U.S. Retail Investor Advice Relationships 2013.*

Chater, N., S. Huck and R. Inderst (2010), *Consumer Decision-Making in Retail Investment Services: A Behavioural Economics Perspective – Final Report.*

Cumming, D., S. Johan and Y. Zhang (2015), *A Dissection of Mutual Fund Fees, Flows, and Performance.*

Debbich, M. (2015), *Why Financial Advice Cannot Substitute for Financial Literacy?*

Edelen, R.M., R.B. Evans and G.B. Kadlec (2012), "Disclosure and agency conflict: Evidence from mutual fund commission bundling", *Journal of Financial Economics*, Vol. 103, pp. 308-326.

Egan, M., G. Matvos and A. Seru (2016), *The Market for Financial Adviser Misconduct.*

EIOPA (2015), *EIOPA Fourth Consumer Tredns Report.*

Expert Committee to Consider Financial Advisory and Financial Planning Policy Alternatives (2016), *Financial Advisory and Financial Planning Policy Alternatives: Preliminary policy recommendations.*

Financial Conduct Authority (2016), *Ageing population and financial services*, London.

Financial Conduct Authority (2016b), *Assessing suitability: Research and due diligence of products and services*, London.

Financial Conduct Authority (2016c), *FCA survey of firms providing financial advice*, London.

Financial Conduct Authority (2014), *Post-implementation review of the Retail Distribution Review – Phase 1*, London.

Financial Conduct Authority (2014b), *Retail investment advice: Adviser charging and services*, London.

Financial Planning Coalition (2014), *Consumers are Confused and Harmed: The case for regulation of financial planners.*

Finke, M. and T. Langdon (2012), *The Impact of Broker-Dealer Fiduciary Standard on Financial Advice.*

FINRA (2016), *Report on Digital Investment Advice.*

HM Treasury and Financial Conduct Authority (2016), *Financial Advice Market Review: Final Report*, London.

IIROC (2016), *Managing Conflicts in the Best Interest of the Client.*

Joint Committee of the European Supervisory Authorities (2015), *Joint Committee Discussion Paper on automation in financial advice.*

Lacko, J.M. and J.K. Pappalardo (2004), *The effect of mortgage broker compensation disclosures on consumers and competition: A controlled experiment.*

Lortie, P. (2016), *A Major Setback for Retirement Savings: Changing how financial advisers are compensated could hurt less-than-wealthy investors most.*

Makynen, T. (2015), *Negative Effects of the Prohibition of Commission in Finland*, Velden.

Moore, D.A. and G. Loewenstein (2004), "Self-interest, Automaticity, and the Psychology of Conflict of Interest", *Social Justice Research*, Vol. 17/2.

Moore, D.A., L. Tanlu and M.H. Bazerman (2010), "Conflict of Interest and the Intrustion of Bias" *Judgement and Decision Making*, Vol. 5/1, pp. 37-53.

National Association of Insurance and Financial Advisors (in Partnership with LIMRA) (2010), *Facts at a Glance: Results from a LIMRA survey of NAIFA members*, Falls Church, Virginia: NAIFA.

New Zealand Ministry of Business, Innovation and Employment (2016), *Final Report: Review of the Financial Advisers Act 2008 and the Financial Service Providers (Registration and Dispute Resolution) Act 2008.*

New Zealand Ministry of Business, Innovation and Employment (2016b), *Options Paper: Review of the Financial Advisers Act 2008 and the Financial Service Providers (Registration and Dispute Resolution) Act 2008.*

Ody, E. (2011), "Investors Prefer Commissions to Account Fees, Study Says", Bloomburg Business, 7 June.

Oxera (2015), *Regulating remuneration systems: effective distribution of financial products*, Oxera.

Price Bailey and Ipsos MORI (2016), *Workplace Pensions – The Members' Perspective: An examination of public interest and awareness of pension scheme arrangements and retirement options.*

Rice Warner Actuaries (2011), *Value of IFFP Advice.*

Sah, S. and G. Loewenstein (2014), "Nothing to Declare: Mandatory and Voluntary Disclosure Leads Advisors to Avoid Conflicts of Interest", *Psychological Science*, Vol. 25/2, pp. 575-584.

Sah, S., G. Loewenstein and D.M. Cain (2013), "The Burden of Disclosure: Increased Compliance with Distrusted Advice", *Journal of Personality and Social Psychology*, Vol. 104/2, pp. 289-304.

Synovate (2011), *Consumer Market Study on Advice within the Area of Retail Investment Services – Final Report*, Synovate Ltd..

US Department of Labor (2015), *Fiduciary Investment Advice: Regulatory Impact Analysis.*

US Department of Labor (2001), *Advisory Opinion*, 14 December 2001, *www.dol.gov/ebsa/regs/AOs/ao2001-09a.html*

Valentine, T. (2013), "The Problems with Investment Advice", *JASSA*, Issue 4, pp. 42-46.

Chapter 4

Policy considerations for life annuity products

This chapter discusses the issues that policy makers should consider to support life annuity products as a key instrument to finance retirement and protect individuals from the risk of outliving their assets. First, there is a need for consistency in the scope, definition and terminology used to refer to annuity products. There is also a need for coherence in the design of the framework of the pension system in order to further the role of annuity products to protect individuals from longevity risk. Continued innovation in product design highlights the need for regulatory requirements to adapt, but also for consumers and their financial advisors to be able to understand the complicated product features which may result. Finally, the appropriate incentives for annuity providers to mitigate the risks they face where necessary should be in place in order to ensure the sustainability of these products.

The shifting retirement landscape has led to increased risk borne by individuals in financing their retirement, bringing to the fore the importance of the role that annuity products can play. Annuity products provide a guaranteed income stream for life, protecting individuals from the longevity risk of outliving their assets and the investment risks from market downturns. As such, policy makers need to consider life annuity products in the design of the pay-out phase for pensions to mitigate some of the risks that individuals are facing in financing their retirement. Indeed, for countries where a significant proportion of retirement assets are invested in DC plans, the OECD recommends that individuals use part of their assets accumulated for retirement to purchase a life annuity in order to protect themselves from longevity risk.[1]

The menu of annuity products available is growing, often resulting in more complex features meant to appeal to the demands of consumers for increased flexibility or better value. While traditional life annuities protect individuals from longevity risk, they are often perceived as expensive and their illiquidity limits any flexibility to address contingencies such as the need to cover health care expenses. Moreover, individuals tend to be reluctant to give up a large part of their retirement savings in exchange for a fixed income stream. In response, annuity providers are developing products which offer more flexibility to access the underlying assets or lower cost through risk-sharing mechanisms that in turn reduce the level of the guarantee offered.

The increasing complexity of annuity product design presents a challenge for policy makers to establish appropriate policies to ensure the sustainability of these products as well as to make sure that the features of these products are understood by consumers. While higher guarantees and/or more flexibility make products more attractive for consumers, these features also come at an increased cost. Policy makers therefore need to understand these products and the types of guarantees and options that they offer in order to ensure that an appropriate balance is struck and that a regulatory framework is in place to encourage and support the use of annuity products.

This chapter discusses the main issues that policy makers should consider to support the role of annuity products as a key instrument in financing retirement. First, there is a need to clarify the definition of what constitutes an annuity product and to establish consistency in the language used to discuss them. There is also a need for coherence in the design of the framework for the pension system in order to further the role of annuity products to protect individuals from outliving their savings in retirement. Continued innovation in product design highlights the need for regulatory requirements to be flexible and able to adapt to future changes, but also the need for consumers and their financial advisors to be able to understand the more complicated product features which are resulting. Finally, new risks presented by these products also require that the annuity providers manage these risks, and policies need to provide the appropriate incentives to mitigate these risks where necessary in order to ensure the sustainability of these products.[2]

4.1. The need to define a common language: what is a life annuity product?

The definition of a life annuity product at first glance seems simple. It is a product which offers a stream of income payments to be paid to the individual for life. Nevertheless the literature and discussion of annuities, annuity income, and annuity markets is fraught with misunderstanding and a lack of comparability. For example, defined benefit (DB) pension arrangements provide a stream of income in retirement for life, yet would not generally be thought of as an annuity product. There are also annuity products (e.g. annuities certain) that provide a stream of income but do not protect individuals from the risk of outliving their assets. Other products like deferred annuities may never be converted into a stream of income payments for life, and instead may be taken as a lump-sum.

There is therefore a need to clarify what is meant by the term "life annuity product". The current lack of consistency with respect to the language and definitions used to discuss these products presents a large barrier for cross country comparison of annuity markets and products and any discussion around their role in retirement. This section presents some criteria with which to clarify the scope and define the concept of what an annuity product is, and introduces the terminology which will be used describe products and their features in this chapter.[3]

Clarifying the scope

The distinction needs to be made between annuity income and annuity products in order to define the scope of what is considered to be an annuity product. Policy makers often refer to a target level of "annuitisation" for individuals in retirement, in other words the appropriate proportion of available income in retirement which should be guaranteed. However, this proportion can also potentially include income received from public pensions and income received from defined benefit pensions in addition to income received from annuity products. Therefore, in order to assess the role annuity products play in providing retirement income, these different components of the overall level of annuitisation must be separated out.

Four criteria could be used to distinguish the scope of what is considered to be an annuity product among the various sources of income in retirement.

- An annuity product should be fully financed by the contributions or premiums put towards its purchase. This would exclude annuity income coming from PAYG financed systems, where current contributions cover current annuity pension payments.
- Annuity payments should be calculated on an actuarially fair basis, implying a direct link between contributions paid and the level of income received. Defined benefit schemes for which benefits are defined in terms of final salary or the number of years employed would therefore not be considered as an annuity product.
- The provider of the annuity product should be the entity which promises to make payments to the individual or member. This makes the distinction between instruments used for de-risking pension plans as opposed to functioning more directly as a solution to provide income to an individual in retirement. As a result, bulk annuities and reinsurance are out of scope of this discussion.
- The employer should not be the guarantor of the promised payments. This would exclude income which is provided by the employer as part of the employment contract from being considered an annuity product, such as "cash balance" hybrid pension plans or book reserve plans.

Defining an annuity product

The definition of an annuity product must also be clear in order to distinguish these products from pension savings products which may not provide for income in retirement and from other drawdown products which provide no longevity guarantees. This is necessary in order to assess the role of the income guarantees that annuity products offer compared to other types of pension and retirement products.

The first criteria to clarify the definition of an annuity product should be that it provides a longevity insurance component, as protection from longevity risk is one of the main benefits provided by annuity products. As such, drawdown products with no lifetime guarantees are not considered to be annuity products. Annuity certain products, where payments are only guaranteed for a specified number of years, are also not included as they can be more likened to fixed income investments.

In addition to including longevity insurance, the definition of an annuity product needs to address deferred savings products which include the option or mandate to be converted into annuity income at a future date, since whether these contracts are actually annuity products can be ambiguous. In some cases the product may never result in an annuity income being paid, and in others the contract covers only the accumulation phase. To clarify the definition, where receiving a future income stream from a deferred annuity is optional, the annuity conversion rate should be defined at the onset of the contract. Where this is not the case, the product could be better viewed as a savings vehicle with an immediate annuity purchased at the end of the accumulation period. Alternatively, where receiving a future income stream from a deferred annuity is mandatory, the provision of the future income should be established in the same contract that was established for the accumulation of the assets. As such, the annuity product could then be viewed as a whole, rather than a savings product with limited pay-out options at retirement.

Features of annuity products

Given this scope and definition of an annuity product, annuities can nevertheless vary widely in their structure and the guarantees and options they offer to consumers. The plain vanilla, traditional life annuity product provides guaranteed regular payments to an individual for life in exchange for a non-refundable upfront premium. This product thereby guarantees a stable income to the individual and protects them from the risk of outliving their assets in retirement. This basic annuity structure, however, can vary along several dimensions: the timing of the payments, the timing of the premiums, and whether the product is sold at an individual or group level.

Annuity products can either be immediate, with payments beginning right after the premium is paid, or deferred, with payments beginning at some future point in time. Immediate annuities tend to be bought with assets accumulated at retirement to provide payments through retirement. Deferred annuities are generally bought at younger ages to provide payments once the individual is retired, though they may also be bought at retirement to provide old age longevity insurance and ensure that the individual will have an income if they live longer than expected.

The premiums for annuity products can be paid all at once, in a single premium, or divided into regular premium payments. Single premiums are typical for immediate annuity products, while regular premium payments are more common for deferred products, allowing individuals to contribute over time and build up the level of future income, similar to other retirement savings products.

Finally, annuity products may be purchased at an individual retail level or for a group of individuals. Individual annuities are more commonly purchased by individuals within personal defined contribution pension schemes, for example, or other voluntary personal pension arrangements. Group annuities, on the other hand, are more commonly arranged by employers for a group of their employees.

Beyond the basic structures outlined above, annuity products can offer various guarantees for the individual annuitants. These guarantees can insure the individual against several risks, namely longevity, death, investment and/or the loss of purchasing power.

The insurance against longevity risk is the risk most commonly associated with annuity products, as annuity products which provide payments for the lifetime of the individual insure against the longevity risk of outliving their assets in retirement.

Annuity products may also offer a guaranteed payment to the surviving beneficiaries of an annuitant in the case of death. This can take the form of a lump-sum payout contingent on the death of the annuitant, the provision for a lifetime payment to the surviving spouse, or the provision of a guaranteed period during which payments continue for the specified number of years regardless of the survival of the annuitant.

Investment guarantees are also common guarantees provided by annuity products, either implicitly through the guarantee of a specified level of income or explicitly through a guaranteed minimum return on the assets underlying the annuity product. These types of guarantees provide insurance against the investment risk of a decrease in asset value which could significantly reduce the level of assets available for financing retirement.

Annuities can also provide protection against the loss of purchasing power from inflation by indexing the guaranteed payments to the inflation rate, guaranteeing a level of income in real terms rather than nominal terms.

In addition to guarantees, annuity products can also offer varying levels of flexibility to the consumer, providing options with respect to the access to underlying assets and the timing and/or level of payments. For the traditional annuity product, the consumer completely relinquishes the premium assets to the annuity provider, and has no ability to get out of the contract or change the terms on which the income will be received. Variations on this traditional product, however, can offer additional flexibilities to the consumer such as control over investment decisions, the ability to withdraw from or surrender the product, or the ability to vary the level or timing of income received during the pay-out phase.

A common terminology

In order to fully understand the features and risks of different types of annuity products and be able to discuss the role of policy in supporting these products, there is a need to establish a common terminology for different types of products. The lack of a common terminology is a particular problem, for example, when it comes to variable annuity products. The term "variable annuity" is commonly applied to a wide variety of products, therefore two policy makers from different jurisdictions or organizations can find themselves discussing the challenges and risks for "variable annuities", yet actually be referring to two different products with completely different risk characteristics and profiles. Therefore, policy makers need to have a common language in order to be able to have coherent discussions with respect to the risks presented by the products and the role of policy to ensure their sustainability.

Table 4.1 proposes to group the different types of annuity products into three different categories based on payment features and risk profile, and uses a terminology that could form a common basis for guiding the discussion around annuity products. While in theory various combinations of annuity types could be possible (e.g. inflation indexed enhanced annuity), these combinations are not commonly found in the market.

Table 4.1. **Classification of annuity products**

Product type	Annuity type	Product description
Fixed payment	Level/Escalating/De-escalating	Annuities which guarantee pre-defined payments beginning immediately or deferred to some point in the future. Payments can be level or be scheduled to increase (escalate) or decrease (de-escalate) over time by a defined amount.
	Advanced Life Deferred Annuity	Deferred annuities which are bought around retirement age with payments that are deferred to begin at a more advanced age, usually over age 75.
	Joint	Annuities with payments contingent on the survival of two lives.
	Enhanced	Annuities which pay out a higher income level to individuals deemed to have a shorter life expectancy due to health or behavioural factors.
Indexed payment	Inflation-indexed	Annuities whose payments are indexed to the level of inflation experienced in each period.
	Participating	Annuities which offer a minimum guaranteed level of income to the annuitant while offering additional bonus payments depending on an actual return or profit measure.
	Variable Payout	Annuities for which the initial payment is calculated using a reference rate of return defined in the contract and subsequent payments are adjusted by the ratio of the actual return on assets over the reference return.
Retirement savings with guaranteed income option	Variable Annuity	Deferred annuity products with a guaranteed income option which offer flexibility with respect to how the assets are invested or accessed by the consumer.
	Fixed Indexed Annuity	Deferred annuity products with a guaranteed income option which offer returns which are indexed to the market as well as flexibility with respect to how the assets accessed by the consumer.

The first category of annuity products includes annuities promising fixed payments to the annuitant which are clearly defined from the onset of the contract and for which the underlying return does not change over time. These types of annuities typically offer full longevity protection to the individual as well as an implicit guaranteed return on the premium paid. However, the annuitant generally has no flexibility with respect to the payments made or how the underlying assets are invested and no additional benefit is received if investment returns are higher than expected. The main risks for the annuity provider for these types of products are longevity risk and investment risk. With respect to investment risk, the largest risk is reinvestment risk to the extent that the duration of the liabilities exceeds that of the assets, and assets would need to be reinvested at rate lower than that which is guaranteed.

The second category of annuity products includes those with indexed payments which vary depending on an external measure. These products allow annuity payments to increase or decrease depending on factors such as inflation or profits. This also means that the underlying return can vary over time, though a minimum rate is usually guaranteed. Annuitants can be exposed to volatility and unpredictability in their annuity payments, but can also benefit from changes in market conditions while having a certain minimum level of security. For products in this category, the mechanism with which payments are indexed and the level of risk-sharing offered play major roles in the overall risk exposure and the way in which the risk is managed by the annuity provider.

The final category of annuities is somewhat of a hybrid category, and includes products whose primary function is arguably retirement savings but which also offer the option of electing to receive a guaranteed level of income during retirement. These types of products can therefore also offer longevity protection. The return on these products depends on market performance, though minimum guarantees are typically offered. Furthermore, they offer the highest level of flexibility to the annuitant, providing access to the underlying assets and participation in positive market returns, as well as potential flexibility in the level of annuity income that is received. Nevertheless, this flexibility results in an increased risk to the annuity provider in terms of unpredictability of consumer behaviour, which complicates the management of the underlying investment risks. Furthermore the dynamic nature of the guarantees involved necessitates a rather complex risk management strategy to mitigate the investment risk exposure for the annuity provider. These factors can increase the cost of such guarantees for the consumer.

Harmonising the language used to discuss annuity products could lead to the additional benefit of having a common standard for collecting and reporting data on annuity markets to be able to compare the size and trends of annuity markets across jurisdictions. There is currently no common standard for classifying annuity products, which also makes it difficult to understand the relative importance of the different types of annuity products across jurisdictions. However, the variables collected also need to be more comprehensive. For example it would be useful to have data on the rate at which deferred products with an annuity option are actually converted into an income stream in order to have a clearer view on consumer preferences and how these products are used in practice.

Once a common definition and language has been agreed upon, policy makers will better be able to define clear objectives with respect to the desired role of annuity products within the retirement landscape and implement policies to support this role.

4.2. Designing a coherent framework for retirement

Policy makers need to consider numerous elements in designing the framework to support the desired role of annuities within the retirement landscape. This first involves considering how annuity products fit in the pension system given the rules in place. Limits on product design and pricing may also potentially be considered in light of the needs of individuals and the risks they face for their retirement. Finally, encouraging the demand for annuity products can be a challenge, and policy makers must consider the most efficient way to do so given the potentially heterogeneous needs of the population.

Policy makers first need to identify where annuities should play a role in the retirement system by considering the existing pension gap and the risks that individuals will have to bear, particularly given the shift towards more individual responsibility. The risks faced will determine the types of guarantees and flexibilities which annuities could provide to add value and increased security for the individual. Protection from longevity risk may be most important for the payout phase, though some flexibility and liquidity may also be needed to cover unexpected expenses. Minimum return guarantees may be important particularly during the accumulation phase to protect the individual from the timing risk of retiring following a market downturn.

The rules relating to the accumulation and drawdown of pension savings need to accommodate the products which can fulfil the needs identified. For example, plan sponsors can be reluctant to make annuity products available within their plans due to duty of care requirements which could lead to legal action against the sponsor if the plan member feels the annuity product was not appropriate. This concern of plan sponsors was found to be an issue in Canada and the United States. Such requirements therefore need to be clearly defined particularly with respect to annuity products to avoid ambiguities as to whether the plan sponsor has fulfilled its responsibilities towards its members.

Another consideration is any minimum or maximum distribution or withdrawal limit imposed. These limits need to allow for the appropriate use of annuity products to manage investment and/or longevity risk. For example, until recently, advanced life deferred annuities purchased within qualified defined contribution plans[4] in the United States did not count towards the minimum withdrawal requirement and therefore could not be used optimally to manage longevity risk. Since 2014, these types of annuities have been allowed to count towards the minimum distribution requirement if the payments begin by age 85 and the annuity premium does not exceed the minimum of 25% of the account balance or USD 125 000. This allowance is expected to increase the demand for these types of deferred annuity contracts.

Limits on product features or design could potentially be considered where it is in the consumers' best interest and where the consumer may otherwise be less likely to protect themselves from the risk in question. One example could be requiring that married individuals be offered joint annuities, as is the case in Chile, in order to ensure that the surviving spouse will continue to receive income even after the death of their partner. Individuals may be less likely to choose a joint annuity on their own either due to a lack of awareness of the option or because it reduces the guaranteed income level. Another restriction could be to limit the guaranteed payment period, a feature generally preferred by consumers but which also limits the benefit of longevity risk pooling that annuities can offer. A ten year limit on the guarantee period was previously imposed in the United Kingdom.

Limits on the guarantees offered could also be potentially considered with the objective to limit the risk to the annuity provider. For example, restrictions could be imposed on the age at which guaranteed annuity conversion rates can be offered, as the risk of these guarantees significantly increases with the length of the deferral period for which they are offered. Israel has imposed such limits on annuity providers. Other jurisdictions, such as Germany, impose a maximum discount rate allowed to be used to price the annuity in order to ensure that the guaranteed rate is sustainable.

Nevertheless, any limits imposed should not unduly increase the risk to the annuity provider or the cost to the consumer. For example, requiring that annuities be indexed to inflation could certainly benefit the consumer as these types of annuities are generally not preferred over fixed level annuities due to the present-bias of consumers and a lack of foresight as to the effects of inflation on purchasing power. However, these annuities also tend to be relatively more expensive than fixed level or escalating annuities. Furthermore, if inflation-linked bonds are not widely available for the annuity provider to invest in to match this liability, an accumulated concentration of exposure to inflation risk could present a solvency risk. Another example of a limit on product features could be requiring that consumers are able to change their annuity provider. Given the long-term duration of the annuity contract, it could potentially be beneficial to allow the consumer to change their mind if they are able to get a better value elsewhere. However, such flexibility also increases the risk to the annuity provider and therefore the cost to the consumer. Transaction costs for the consumer could also be expected to increase. Alternative policy measures should therefore be considered if the objective is to encourage annuity providers to offer competitive rates.

Any limits with respect to market segmentation, where certain risk factors are used for pricing annuity products, should be implemented with caution, particularly where the purchase of an annuity is voluntary. Such restrictions can potentially result in certain subgroups of the population being excluded from the annuity market due to anti-selection, where only consumers having higher life expectancies will purchase annuities. The most prevalent restriction on market segmentation is the restriction on gender-based pricing, as is the case in Europe, where gender is not allowed to be used as a risk factor to price annuities. This increases the price of annuities for males, who could then decide that annuities are too expensive given their lower life expectancy compared to females and drop out of the market. Eventually if males continue to not purchase annuities, this could result in the price for all annuities converging to the price based on female mortality, eroding any intended benefits. This seems to have occurred in Germany, where pricing by gender has not been allowed since 2006. Annuity prices following this ban were closer to the prices charged to females prior to the new regulation (von Gaudecker and Weber, 2006). Furthermore, if regulation does not allow the annuity provider to adjust its mortality assumptions to reflect the actual mortality experience, the annuity provider could face solvency problems as the premiums paid would not be sufficient to cover the liability owed.

Experience in the United Kingdom has shown that market segmentation can be beneficial to consumers in some cases. Enhanced annuities, widely available in the United Kingdom, offer higher incomes to individuals having health or lifestyle conditions which reduce their life expectancy. This product provides a solution to a population sub-group who would otherwise have been disadvantaged from the purchase of a regular annuity. Nevertheless these products remain uncommon outside of the United Kingdom, so perhaps more could be done to encourage their development (OECD, 2016).

Any mandate for the purchase of an annuity should be considered with caution, as the need for the protection that annuities can offer is likely to differ significantly across socioeconomic groups. A one-size-fits-all approach may therefore not be appropriate. This would likely penalise the lower income groups who would likely not have saved enough to purchase a meaningful level of income. In 2012, for example, when the purchase of an annuity was still mandatory for defined contribution plans in the United Kingdom, approximately 16% of annuities sold to pensioners were for funds of less than GBP 5 000, which would translate into a monthly income of less than GBP 20 (Financial Conduct Authority, 2014).[5] It could also result in over-annuitisation of assets for other groups who need to maintain some flexibility and liquidity from their assets. These issues could partially be addressed by allowing more flexibility to withdraw accumulated assets when they do not meet or when they exceed certain thresholds. For example, while the purchase of an annuity is not mandatory in Chile, it is not allowed if individuals do not have enough assets accumulated to get an annuity payment above a minimum level of income. In this case, they have to take a programmed withdrawal and the government provides the longevity insurance when the account is exhausted.

Nevertheless, making the purchase of an annuity mandatory can be effective at increasing the demand for annuity products, and can also help to spur innovation from annuity providers looking to gain market share. This was seen to be the case in the United Kingdom, which now has one of the largest annuity markets, and competition for market share has resulted in the prevalence of enhanced annuities. However, given the sharp reduction in the purchase of annuities following the recent pension reforms which removed this requirement, it also presents a case study on the challenge of encouraging consumer demand for annuity products particularly when these products are perceived as a poor value. Indeed, annuity demand fell by 61% in the second quarter of 2015 compared to the second quarter of the previous year (ABI, 2015).

As an alternative to a hard mandate, policies are increasingly being used in the retirement landscape to "nudge" consumers towards the desired behaviour, namely with automatic enrolment to save for retirement and default investment strategies. This mechanism in particular relies on the inertia of individuals to go with the "default" option. These types of policies have been effective and useful for getting people to save during the accumulation phase. However, they need to be designed very carefully if applied for the purchase of an annuity in the decumulation phase. Experience in the United Kingdom presents evidence that providing a "default" annuity option, in this case the annuity provided by the individual's existing pension provider, resulted in consumer apathy and a disengagement from the process, and often resulted in consumers not getting the best product available to them. Furthermore, this tendency resulted in a lack of competitive pressure on annuity providers leading to lower value product for consumers (Financial Conduct Authority, 2014; 2015). Low-cost centralised default annuity providers could potentially be introduced to maintain competitive pressure among annuity providers. In Sweden, for example, the state Premium Pension Authority is responsible for providing the annuity. In Singapore, the Central Provident Fund provides a low-cost annuity option to compete with private annuity providers.

Rather than offering consumers the option to opt-out of a default, another approach is to make consumers actively compare products and make a choice. This approach seems to be effective at increasing engagement in the decision as well as competitive incentives for annuity providers. For example, once individuals have indicated that they plan to retire in Chile, the pension fund transmits their information to an electronic platform (the SCOMP) which then provides consumers comparable information regarding their options to take a programmed withdrawal from a pension fund or take a life annuity from an insurance company (Stanko and Paklina, 2014). The individual is therefore forced to choose an option, making them much less prone to the effects of inertia and staying with their current pension provider, and encouraging them to actively consider the option to purchase an annuity. Indeed, in 2015 approximately 50% of pensioners had life annuities provided by an insurance company (Superintendencia de Pensiones, 2015).

More traditional fiscal incentives can also be used to encourage individuals to purchase annuity products. For example, deferred tax treatment in the United States has contributed to the widespread use of variable annuity products as retirement savings vehicles. Both the Czech Republic and Estonia encourage the purchase of annuities over other payout options of pension plans by offering more favourable tax treatment for annuity payments (OECD, 2015). In Korea, annuitisation of retirement savings was found to be 15 percentage points higher for savings vehicles where lump-sums are taxed compared to vehicles were lump sums are tax-free (Lee, 2016). However, while preferential tax treatment has been effective in encouraging annuitisation in some cases, it is not always effective in overcoming individuals' preferences for lump-sums or for increased flexibility. In the United States, for example, guaranteed withdrawal benefits have remained the most popular option for payouts from variable annuities in the United States despite the taxation of the entire gain upfront (Geneva Association, 2013; IRI, 2011).

4.3. Keeping up with innovation: Ensuring sustainable and suitable annuity products

Product innovations by annuity providers may be part of the solution to encourage demand for annuity products. Much of these innovations have involved increasing the flexibility offered by the product or increasing its perceived value through risk-sharing. However policy makers must have a framework in place to keep up with these innovations and ensure that the products remain sustainable for the annuity provider and suitable for the consumer.

Product innovations involving more flexibility and risk-sharing have led to increasingly complex annuity products. Increased flexibility in particular introduces additional risk for the annuity provider which needs to be provisioned for, and reserving and capital requirements which can adapt to new product features are needed in order to ensure that the products are sustainable. Increased risk sharing, on the other hand, highlights the importance of ensuring that consumers themselves are able to understand the products they purchase and the costs and risks that they entail in order to select the most suitable product for their needs. Given product complexity, consumers may also need to rely on financial advice therefore this advice should also lead to a suitable recommendation for the consumer.

The evolution in the design and features of annuity products and the new risks which they present has made clear the need for capital requirements to be more flexible and comprehensive in the risks which are accounted for in these requirements. The increasingly dynamic nature of annuity products and their guarantees requires reserve and solvency capital requirements that are also more dynamic in order to reflect the underlying risks and ensure sufficient assets to back the annuity providers' liabilities. Static approaches based on formulas are no longer adequate for the new generations of annuity products.

Approaches based on principles for the calculation of reserve and solvency capital requirements are needed to allow for the flexibility in calculations to capture changing provisioning needs in light of innovations in annuity product design. This type of approach has been widely adopted in particular in light of the dynamic nature and risks presented by variable annuities, and allows for the use of stochastic scenarios and the recognition of the behavioural risks coming from increased flexibility offered by these annuity products. Reserve and solvency calculations could also be complemented with additional stress and scenario testing to ensure that the nature of all risk exposures and the interaction of these risks is recognised and understood.

The increased complexity and dynamic nature of annuity products also requires the communication of product features and risks to consumers through effective product disclosures in order to ensure that consumers understand the product that they are purchasing. This disclosure needs to clearly communicate the main features of the annuity product, any risks that this product entails for the consumer and all applicable fees relating to the product's purchase and use.

Disclosure requirements should therefore also move to an approach based on principles, focusing not only on the type of information which is included but also how it is included. Regulation often stipulates the minimum information that is required to be included in annuity product disclosures, but given the constant innovation with respect to product features and guarantees, minimum requirements could quickly become insufficient. The key features highlighted and metrics used should be presented in a manner which is in line with the goals of the product and the risks it is meant to insure against. To ensure that the consumer is aware of any risks from the annuity product, disclosures should convey not only the expected payments but also the potential negative outcomes to which the consumer could be exposed to in the event of low profits or poor market performance, particularly for annuity products with risk-sharing arrangements. All costs and fees for the annuity products should be fully and accurately disclosed at the onset of the contract as well as at the time at which they are incurred. The effectiveness of product disclosures may vary with the type of product, the context and the median with which the information is presented. Disclosures should therefore be tested for effectiveness in the context in which they will be used in order to ensure that the targeted consumers do indeed understand the essential information provided.

Given the increasing complexity of annuity products, the role of financial advice in helping consumers to understand the different types of products and select the product which is most suitable is increasing in importance. Ensuring that the financial advisor reliably and effectively communicates product features and risks to the consumer and can match these with the consumers' needs is therefore necessary.[6] Policy makers can address this issue from several angles. First is to ensure that the advisors themselves understand the products available, secondly is to ensure that their advice is suitable for the consumer and finally is to provide the consumers with tools to better judge whether they are getting appropriate advice.

Policy makers first need to ensure that financial advisers are also keeping up with the innovation in the annuity product market and not only are aware of the products available but also have the knowledge to understand the underlying mechanisms of the product. Several jurisdictions address this through ongoing education and examination requirements for advisors to ensure that they are sufficiently trained on the products they sell and are able to make appropriate recommendations.

Various approaches can be taken to help ensure that product advice is in the best interest of the consumer and that they end up with a suitable product. The most common approaches focus first on duty of care standards for financial advice and secondly on the way in which advisors are compensated for their services. First, duty of care sets a standard for the advice itself, but the way in which it is defined and enforced can vary. At one end of the spectrum, it can be defined as a strict legal standard such as fiduciary duty, which offers legal recourse to the affected consumer in the event that the product was not in their best interest. Less stringent standards, however, require only a determination of whether the product is reasonably suitable for the consumer. Regulation of compensation structures, on the other hand, aims directly to mitigate any potential conflicts of interest for the advisor which could inadvertently or otherwise result in less suitable advice for the consumer. Measures taken to address this issue can vary from banning commissions completely, banning certain commission structures or imposing a cap on the commission. However, while such measures may help to improve the quality of financial advice by better aligning the interests of the advisor and the consumer, there is a risk that such limits could lead to a reduced take-up of financial advice. The costs and benefits should therefore be carefully weighted when considering limits on compensation, and the appropriate measure to take will depend on the particular problems observed in the market.

Finally, policy makers can try to provide consumers with the tools with which to assess the advice received. This is most often done through the required disclosure of commissions paid to the advisor. Nevertheless consumers do not necessarily use and act on this information to assess any potential incentives to recommend one course of action over another, nor do they call into question the advice they receive, so this measure alone is not likely to be effective at improving consumers' decisions. Another tool is the cooling-off period implemented in some jurisdictions, which allows the consumer time to digest the advice and product information and change their mind regarding their purchase. Nevertheless the effectiveness of this measure also relies on the quality and clarity of the product disclosure and information provided.

4.4. Encouraging appropriate risk management

Ensuring the sustainability and suitability of products in the evolving annuities landscape also involves ensuring that the risks resulting from these products are able to be managed appropriately by the annuity providers. Risk exposures are determined by product design and the features and flexibility the products offer as well as how the market or longevity experience evolves going forward. Annuity providers need to ensure that they will be able to make the payments promised to annuitants, even in the event where experience deviates from expectations, for example lower than expected investment returns. The framework that policy makers put in place must encourage annuity providers to have a clear view of their risk exposures and mitigate the risk where needed. This framework should encourage the appropriate risk management of annuity products through the accounting framework, investment limits and the capital requirements which are in place.

Policy makers need to be aware of the potential impact that accounting standards can have on the risk exposures from the different types of annuity products in order to identify any potential misalignment of risk management incentives or areas which may need additional monitoring. For example, the accounting framework will directly affect the risk exposures from participating annuity products in particular, as the calculation of the surplus to be shared with the annuitants will depend on the accounting measure used. Historical valuation methods will result in more balance sheet stability, as unrealised gains and losses are not recognised and therefore would not be shared with the annuitant. On the other hand, fair value methods which better reflect the financial position of the entity will result in higher levels of volatility both for the annuity provider's balance sheet as well as for the payments to the annuitant. To manage this potential volatility and reduce its risk exposure from an economic point of view, the annuity provider may establish a buffer reserve to smooth payments to the annuitant by retaining some of the profits during good periods to be paid out during less profitable periods. However, supervisors need to closely monitor and understand the calculations underlying such smoothing mechanisms in order to ensure fairness and transparency of the profit participation. Furthermore, any minimum participation rate imposed by regulation must take into account the interaction between the participation rate, the accounting measure and any smoothing mechanism imposed to ensure that the annuity provider is able to manage the resulting volatility exposure and solvency risk.

The accounting framework can also have an impact on the risk management strategy implemented for annuity products where dynamic hedging strategies for market risks are used, such as with variable annuities. Such strategies rely on the measurement of the annuity liability value at a given point in time, which is determined by the accounting measure used. Dynamic hedging strategies based on Generally Accepted Accounting Principles (GAAP) or statutory measures of the liability can result in an under-hedging of certain risks compared to hedging on an economic basis. Supervisors may therefore want to also monitor economic measures of the balance sheet so as to not provide a disincentive for annuity providers to more fully hedge their risk exposures on an economic basis.

Policy makers should also ensure that annuity providers are able to effectively use and implement appropriate strategies to mitigate their risk exposure. For example, investment in financial derivatives should be allowed where these instruments can be used to hedge risk exposures. However, supervisors should also ensure the effectiveness of such strategies. Some jurisdictions address this by requiring that annuity providers submit a plan for their use of derivatives as well as their resulting investments. This allows supervisors to ensure that these instruments are being used as part of an effective hedging strategy and not for speculative purposes, as well as to monitor annuity providers' overall exposure to derivatives.

In addition to ensuring the effectiveness of any risk mitigation strategy, policy makers should also be aware of any potential increase in risk as a result of the strategy. For example, the use of over-the-counter (OTC) derivative instruments to hedge market risks can also increase the counterparty risk exposure of the annuity provider. Such exposures are generally addressed through concentration limits to counterparty exposure. However recent regulation implemented such as the Dodd-Frank Act in the United States and the European Market Infrastructure Regulation (EMIR) in Europe have sought to reduce this risk through centralised clearing and collateral requirements. While such measures can be effective in reducing counterparty exposure, they may also increase liquidity risk or duration mismatching as a result of the collateral requirements. Therefore policy makers must find a balance so as to ensure that the overall reduction of risk results from risk mitigating measures so as to not reduce the incentives for annuity providers to mitigate their risk exposures.

Capital requirements, including both reserve and solvency capital requirements, should recognise the risk reduction from any risk mitigation strategies in order to serve as an incentive for annuity providers to hedge their risk exposures. This includes, for example, the recognition of reinsurance coverage as well as investment strategies which minimise the asset-liability duration gap or otherwise reduce the investment risk exposure of the annuity provider. Partial risk reduction may also be recognised, such as for dynamic hedging strategies where the hedge is approximate by nature. For example, both Canada and the United States only partially recognise the risk reduction from dynamic hedging strategies in reserve and solvency capital requirements for variable annuity products, as the effectiveness of these strategies is not expected to be perfect.

4.5. Policy considerations

Annuity products and the guarantees that they offer may provide part of the solution to address the increasing investment and longevity risks that individuals are facing. Product innovations enhancing the attractiveness of these products for consumers through increased flexibility or lower cost through risk-sharing mechanisms which reduce the level of guarantees broaden the menu of options available and the ability for these products to meet the varied needs of consumers.

Nevertheless, in order for these products to provide an effective solution, policy makers must consider the challenges that these products present with respect to their underlying risks and their increasing complexity in order to ensure the sustainability of these products for annuity providers and their suitability for consumers.

The first barrier for policy makers to overcome is the lack of consistency with respect to what is meant by an annuity product and the terminology used to describe the different types of products. The definitions and classifications presented in this chapter could serve as a starting point to arrive at a common language for discussing the role of annuity products and the related policy considerations. The proposed classification could also serve as a basis for comparable data collection on the size and composition of annuity markets.

Policy makers also need to design a coherent pension framework which facilitates the expected role of annuity products to provide income in retirement. The rules around the accumulation and drawdown of pension assets need to accommodate the annuity products which can meet individuals' needs at the various stages of their retirement planning. Limits on annuity product design or features, including limits on factors used for pricing, should not be imposed without considering the impact on the cost and risk exposure of the annuity product.

Moreover, the use of annuity products needs to be encouraged. Given the heterogeneous needs of society, particularly between high and low socioeconomic groups, a one-size-fits-all prescription is not likely to be appropriate. Default options can increase take-up, but need to be carefully designed so as to maintain competitive pressure among annuity providers. The effective provision of information on the options available and engaging individuals in the decision of whether to purchase an annuity is another option. Fiscal incentives can also be a useful tool to encourage demand for annuity products.

Approaches based on principles are better suited than approaches based on static formulas to ensure that capital requirements are able to adapt to changing product features. The continued innovation in annuity product design requires the regulatory framework to be more flexible and adaptive to changing risk exposures and risk drivers in order for capital requirements to remain sufficient to back the annuity liabilities and guarantee the sustainability of these products.

Policy makers also need to make sure that consumers are purchasing products which are suitable for their needs, particularly given the increased complexity of products that has accompanied innovation. Product disclosures should not only provide a minimum level of information regarding the product features, risks and costs, but also ensure that this information is easy for the consumer to understand. Policy makers can help to make sure that financial advice for these products is suitable through qualification and education requirements for advisors, duty of care standards or potentially limits on compensation structures. Commission disclosure requirements and cooling-off periods can also provide the consumer with tools to better assess the quality of the advice they receive.

Finally, the regulatory framework should ensure that the tools to manage risk and the incentives to do so are in place in order to encourage appropriate risk management by annuity providers. Supervisors should ensure that the relevant accounting measures are monitored to ensure a realistic view of risk exposures and to provide an incentive to manage risks effectively. Hedging should be facilitated, but the strategies should be monitored to ensure their effectiveness in reducing overall risk exposures. Any requirements to control the risks from the strategies themselves should also ensure that overall risk reduction still results, so as to avoid reducing incentives to hedge. Finally, capital requirements should reflect the reduction of risk from any effective risk mitigation measures in order to align with the incentives of annuity providers to manage their risk exposures.

Implementing effective policy to support the annuity products to finance retirement requires that the mechanisms and risks these products present be understood by all stakeholders. Annuity providers must recognise and understand the dynamics of risk to ensure that their products are sustainable, consumers must understand how the products function in order to select the most suitable, and policy makers need to be able to monitor the risks to ensure the continued relevancy of the regulatory framework in place. As such, the framework put in place should be designed to keep up with innovation and adapt to the changing retirement landscape.

Notes

1. The OECD Roadmap for the Good Design of DC Pension Plans, *www.oecd.org/finance/private-pensions/50582753.pdf*.
2. For a more thorough discussion of the issues relating to annuity products and their guarantees, see OECD (2016).
3. The discussion throughout focuses on life annuity products. Providing protection from outliving one's resources (i.e. longevity risk) is one of the most important goals of pension arrangements (see the The OECD Roadmap for the Good Design of DC Pension Plans)
4. 401(a), a 403(b) plan, a governmental 457(b) plan or a traditional IRA
5. Based on the estimation that 60% of annuitants get an annuity from their existing provider, and 27% of these have pension pots under 5 000 GBP. The FCA indicates that for premiums less than 5 000 the rates are around 4.25%, and the rates are around 5.1% for premiums between 5 000 and 10 000.
6. Chapter 3 discusses these issues in more detail and provides examples of the types of measures which have been taken in various jurisdictions.

References

Financial Conduct Authority (2015), *Retirement income market study: Final report – confirmed findings and remedies.*

Financial Conduct Authority (2014), *Thematic Review of Annuities.*

Geneva Association (2013), *Variable Annuities – An analysis of Financial Stability*, The Geneva Association, Geneva.

The Investment Research Institute (2011), *The Tax Advantage of Annuities: How Tax Deferral and Guaranteed Lifetime Strategies Can Benefit All Consumers.*

Lee, K. (2016), "Analysis of payout choice from individual deferred annuities in Korea", *Journal of Pension Economics & Finance*, Vol 15/2, pp. 224-248.

OECD (2016), "Fragmentation of retirement markets due to differences in life expectancy", in OECD, *OECD Business and Finance Outlook 2016*, OECD Publishing, Paris, *http://dx.doi.org/10.1787/9789264257573-11-en.*

OECD (2016), *Life annuity products and their guarantees*, *www.oecd.org/daf/fin/private-pensions/AnnuityProducts2013.pdf.*

OECD (2015), *Stocktaking of the Tax Treatment of Funded Private Pension Plans in OECD and EU*, *www.oecd.org/tax/tax-treatment-funded-private-pension-plans-oecd-eu-countries.htm.*

Stanko, D. and N. Paklina (2014), "Supervising the Distribution of Annuities and other Forms of Pension Pay-Out", *IOPS Working Papers on Effective Pensions Supervision*, No.21, *www.iopsweb.org/WP_21_Supervising-Distribution-Annuities-Pension%20Pay-out%20.pdf.*

Superintendencia de Pensiones (2015), *Boletín Estadístico Electrónico* N° 219, Santiago.

von Gaudecker, H.-M. and C. Weber (2004), "Surprises in a Growing Market Niche: An Evaluation of the German Private Life Annuities Market", *The Geneva Papers on Risk and Insurance*, Vol. 29/3, pp. 394-416.

Chapter 5

The role of financial education in supporting decision-making for retirement

Ageing populations and fiscal pressures have led many governments to reform their pension systems in ways that are making individuals increasingly responsible for managing their retirement wealth, as well as investment and longevity risks. This chapter starts by providing an overview of the main challenges people face when they take decisions for retirement. The chapter then looks at the role of financial education in addressing people's lack of financial literacy for retirement, analysing how financial education needs for retirement vary across different features of pensions systems and discussing the main existing initiatives. It concludes with practical tools to support policy makers.

Ageing populations and fiscal pressures have led many governments to reform their pension systems, in particular by reforming pay-as-you-go schemes in ways that are likely to extend working lives and reduce benefits for future generations. At the same time, defined-contribution (DC) private pension schemes started taking the place of defined-benefit private pension (DB) schemes for new entrants, bringing more uncertainty over benefits and further increasing the burden on individuals. As a result, individuals are becoming increasingly responsible for managing these risks and their resources in order to support themselves beyond their working lives. In this context, it is essential that individuals have the necessary skills to make their own retirement plans and manage their resources in retirement.

This chapter provides an overview of individual decision-making challenges for retirement, with a focus on those related to a lack of financial literacy, and discusses financial education initiatives to support individuals in planning and managing their resources in retirement. The chapter provides background analysis for the update of the 2008 OECD Good Practices for Financial Education Relating to Private Pensions (OECD, 2008a) as part of the consolidation of all OECD policy instruments on financial education, and more generally to support policy makers in the implementation and improvement of financial education initiatives for retirement. In doing so, it draws on extensive work by the OECD and the International Organisation of Pension Supervisors (IOPS) on the characteristics of pension systems and on the benefits of increasing levels of financial literacy for improving retirement planning.[1]

Section 5.1 describes the main challenges people face in planning for retirement and managing their retirement resources, in both the accumulation and payout phases. The main challenges are related to a lack of financial literacy (including lack of awareness, knowledge, motivation, confidence and skills) as well as to several behavioural biases (such as present-based time preferences, status quo bias, limited attention) that undermine people's ability to plan, save and take retirement decisions.

Section 5.2 focuses on those challenges related to the lack of financial literacy that can best be addressed by financial education, while recognising that financial education may not be able to overcome behavioural biases. Depending on the structure of each pension system, decision-making is likely to be more difficult and to require greater financial literacy for: i) private pensions than for public pensions; ii) personal pension plans than for occupational plans; and iii) defined-contribution (or notional defined-contribution) schemes than for defined-benefit schemes. The section also briefly discusses the financial education needs of specific population subgroups.

Section 5.3 looks at how financial education can play a role in addressing the lack of financial literacy for retirement, as part of a broader policy mix to encourage retirement planning and facilitate decision-making around pensions. This section gives an overview of the financial education initiatives and tools for retirement developed in different countries, discussing how they can address the financial education needs for retirement described in

Section 5.3. Tools to increase awareness and provide information about pensions are widespread; they include online information, pension statements, comparison tools and pension calculators. Instruction, training and generic advice have the potential to address a wider spectrum of challenges, even though they are relatively less widespread. Research evidence highlights examples where individual pension statements about public and/or private pensions, as well as retirement planning seminars, have successfully increased people's financial and pension knowledge and induced changes in behaviour.

Section 5.4 concludes by proposing two practical tools to support policy makers in identifying financial education needs for retirement and in improving their financial education efforts in pensions and retirement decision-making.

The chapter covers OECD member countries as well as relevant non-OECD countries, including those that replied to a stocktaking questionnaire on policy advances in regards to financial education for retirement sent to members of the OECD International Network on Financial Education (OECD/INFE) and of the OECD Working Party on Private Pensions.[2] The chapter adopts the notions of financial literacy and financial education developed in previous OECD and INFE work.[3]

5.1. Decision-making challenges for retirement

This section looks at the challenges people face in making decisions about their retirement.[4] Recent pension reforms have made individuals increasingly responsible for the management of their own retirement wealth. During the 1990s and 2000s several countries made public pension benefits more actuarially fair and more closely linked to working histories.[5] At the same time, the pension reform process substantially increased workers' uncertainty with regard to their replacement rates and shifted investment and longevity risks onto them, typically by adopting defined-contribution (DC) formulae instead of defined-benefit (DB) ones for new entrants.[6] Overall, reforms made future pensions not only less generous but also more uncertain and difficult to understand for individuals, thus making planning ahead more cumbersome.

A stocktaking survey circulated in 2014 among members of the OECD/INFE and the OECD Working Party on Private Pensions revealed that policy makers around the world agree that their citizens face a number of difficulties in taking decisions about their retirement funding, such as:

- *Planning and estimating retirement income needs.* People have a hard time figuring out how much money they would need to maintain their standard of living in retirement and underestimate their retirement income needs. Policy makers highlighted that many people are unaware that they are likely to face a low income in retirement, do not know how to assess their future financial needs, do not know how to make plans for retirement, know they should save more but do not take steps to do so, and are unaware of the level of saving required for an adequate living standard. Planning difficulties may also include not understanding pension information sent by pension providers.
- *Assessing risks related to pensions and long-term investment.* Policy makers across a majority of countries and economies reckoned that people do not know how to assess risk and reward, including in the pensions context.
- *Understanding and assessing retirement products.* People do not know which types of products (including pensions and annuities) they should use to meet their retirement goals, nor do they know how to assess the performance of these retirement products.

The research literature suggests a series of factors that may explain why people have difficulties in planning for retirement, estimating retirement income needs and choosing retirement products. Focusing on demand-side factors, this literature points to a combination of lack of general financial knowledge, lack of domain-specific knowledge and various psychological biases that undermine people's ability to plan ahead, save for retirement and take other related decisions. These biases include present-biased time preferences, status quo bias, a tendency to be affected by how choices are framed, limited attention and difficulty in dealing with complex choices, overconfidence about one's own ability, over-optimism about the financial environment, a difficulty in formulating accurate beliefs about risk, social pressure and peer effects on individual choices, and more generally the impact of emotional states on decision-making (Knoll, 2010; Yoong, 2011).

Challenges in decision-making for retirement are related to a combination of limited financial literacy, such as poor pension knowledge and limited skills, as well as to behavioural and psychological biases that affect decision-making irrespective of people's financial knowledge.

Low financial knowledge and pension-specific knowledge

A quite large body of evidence suggests that knowledge of concepts necessary to perform saving calculations, such as compound interest rates, the time value of money, the difference between real and nominal values, and the principle of risk diversification, should not be taken for granted in the population at large (Atkinson and Messy, 2012; Lusardi and Mitchell, 2011). Furthermore, surveys in various countries have shown that many savers do not know which type of private pension they have and possess limited knowledge of important characteristics of their own pension arrangements (Banks and Oldfield, 2007; Barrett, Mosca and Whelan, 2013; ILC-UK, 2015; Money and Pensions Panel, 2013).

Several studies – mainly about the United States – indicate that knowledge about Social Security is also scanty (EBRI and MG&A, 2006; Financial Engines, 2014; Greenwald et al., 2010; Gustman and Steinmeier, 2004) and that workers are also poorly informed about their private pension plans (Mitchell, 1988; Gustman and Steinmeier, 1989; Gustman and Steinmeier, 2004; Gustman, Steinmeier and Tabatabai, 2008; Dushi and Iams, 2010). This is especially true with regards to DC pensions, which give more responsibility to workers than DB ones (Gustman, Steinmeier and Tabatabai, 2008; Dushi and Iams, 2010).

Pension-specific knowledge is also related to having a correct understanding of life expectancy. Reviewing evidence mostly coming from the United Kingdom and the United States, O'Connell (2010) highlights that many people have a tendency to underestimate their expected lifespan with respect to population life tables, and that women are generally more likely than men to underestimate their likely longevity.

Present-biased time preferences

Research has shown that for many individuals time preferences are not constant and tend to vary depending on whether choices between imminent goods versus future goods are closer or farther in the future (Laibson, 1997). More precisely, many people prefer a larger, later reward to a smaller, sooner reward when the choice lies in the future, but may then change their mind when the two options are nearer to the present, opting for the smaller, immediate reward instead of the larger future reward. In the context of retirement saving, this bias implies that relatively small transaction costs, burdensome paperwork and in general situations where large delayed benefits are accompanied by small short-term costs, can be a real barrier to action, including participation in retirement savings plans (O'Donoghue and Rabin, 1999, 2001; Choi et al., 2004).

Shopping around is another example of a situation where large delayed benefits accompanied by small short-term costs may create a barrier to action. Despite that nine out of ten consumers in the UK were aware they could shop around for annuities, only two-thirds of individuals reported doing so, with potential losses on their expected retirement benefits (FCA, 2014). Procrastination appears also to affect employees' ability to take advantage of matching contributions in DC plans. In general, matching contributions by employers and the state have contributed to raising coverage and contribution rates in private pensions in various countries (OECD, 2012a), but many individuals who would be eligible do not take advantage of them (Choi, Laibson and Madrian, 2011).

Reference dependence, status quo bias and framing

According to Kahneman and Tversky (1979)'s prospect theory, individuals do not evaluate their wealth in an absolute sense, but rather in relative terms with respect to a reference point. In particular, this is related to the observation that individuals are hurt by a loss more than they feel good for a gain of the same amount (loss-aversion). Other manifestations of loss aversion include the observation that some individuals ascribe a higher value to objects that they already possess more than they would be willing to pay for the same object (endowment effect), and that in general people tend to stay in their current situation when presented with the choice of doing something or doing nothing (status-quo bias). This bias may explain why people have a tendency to stick to the default option in terms of pension plan participation, contribution rate and investment allocation (Madrian and Shea, 2001; Agnew, Balduzzi and Sunden, 2003).

Another consequence of such "reference-dependence" is that the presentation of choices (framing) is very important, as individual preferences over two options may be reversed when the same issue is framed in a different way. Framing has been used to explain low demand for annuities: when consumers think in terms of consumption, annuities are seen as valuable insurance, whereas when consumers think in terms of investment risk and return, the annuity is perceived as a risky asset, because the payoff depends on an uncertain date of death (Brown et al., 2008).

Limited attention, menu effects and choice overload

Another aspect that creates serious challenges to people's ability to plan ahead for their retirement relates to limited attention, in the sense that individuals may not have the cognitive capacity to process all information in the environment. Limited attention means that individuals may rely on information that is more readily available and salient in their decision-making, and may adopt simplifying heuristics and rules of thumb for managing complex sets of information. When presented with a large menu of investment options, individuals may engage in naive and inefficient diversification strategies (Benartzi and Thaler, 2007; Huberman and Jiang, 2006), may avoid choice completely (Iyengar, Huberman and Jiang, 2004), or may turn to simpler options (Iyengar and Kamenica, 2010).

5.2. Financial education needs for retirement

Financial education has shown that it can improve people's financial knowledge and behaviour. It is not the only instrument to ensure individuals are adequately planning their finances for retirement, and it is unlikely to overcome their behavioural biases, but governments are increasingly recognising its role and including it in the policy mix to support retirement saving and decision-making. Within this context, financial education can support individuals in making sure they have:

- sufficient financial **knowledge**, including a good understanding of the characteristics of public and private pensions in the country (and of taxation rules regarding retirement saving), of the risks related to pension systems and retirement, and of the key financial concepts relevant for retirement planning;
- **attitudes** oriented towards the long term, as well as the motivation and confidence to plan ahead and take other retirement-related decisions;
- the **skills** to engage in various behaviours, both in the accumulation and payout phase, in order to have adequate income in retirement. Such decisions include estimating retirement income needs, taking decisions about participation, contribution and payout of pension schemes, and shopping around for pension products.

Many of these financial education needs are relevant irrespective of the financial (or real) instruments used for retirement saving, whether within or outside of a pension system. But given that in many countries, and especially OECD ones, pension systems constitute the most important channel for managing retirement savings, it is important to take into account how these financial education needs vary depending on the features of national pension systems.[7]

Financial education needs for retirement according to pension system characteristics

Previous OECD work provided a preliminary overview of individual financial education needs in relation to different types of retirement saving (OECD, 2008b: Table 5), highlighting how financial education needs varied according to the type of pension schemes available in the country (DB vs. DC, and protected vs. unprotected). This section expands and revises that first analysis by describing the financial education needs for retirement faced by consumers according to a more comprehensive set of pension system characteristics.

Figure 5.1 offers a general framework to think about financial education needs for retirement planning according to the design of a pension. It provides a summary of financial education needs for retirement, analysing how these vary according to the features of a pension system. The rows in the table identify what people should know and understand, what kind of attitudes they should have, and what skills and behaviours they should demonstrate to be able to take effective decisions for retirement in the context of their national pension system. The columns identify the main features of pension systems, and especially the distinction between public vs. private, mandatory vs. voluntary, occupational vs. personal, and DB vs. DC schemes.[8]

The figure highlights a number of key patterns that can be split across public pensions, private pensions, or aspects common to both and that are described in the rest of this sub-section. Depending on the structure and features of a pension system, decision-making about retirement is likely to be more difficult and to require greater financial literacy for: i) private pensions than for public pensions; ii) personal pension plans than for occupational plans; and iii) defined-contribution (or notional defined-contribution) schemes than for defined-benefit schemes.

Figure 5.1. **Financial education needs for retirement**

FINANCIAL EDUCATION NEEDS FOR RETIREMENT		FINANCIAL EDUCATION NEEDS for retirement according to pension system characteristics								
		Public PAYG			Private					
					Mandatory			Voluntary		
		Non-contributory / Flat	DB earnings-related	NDC	Occupational		Personal	Occupational		Personal
					DB	DC	DC	DB	DC	DC
KNOWLEDGE AND UNDERSTANDING										
Basic understanding of pension RULES, including public and private pensions rules, retirement saving taxation, rights and responsibilities related to pensions		Yes	Yes	Yes	Yes	Yes	Yes	Yes	Yes	Yes
Basic appreciation of RISKS related to pension systems and retirement:	Demographic/longevity risk	No	Yes	Yes	Some	Yes	Yes	Some	Yes	Yes
	Political risk	Yes	Yes	Yes	Yes	Yes	Yes	Yes	Yes	Yes
	Inflation risk	No	Some	Some	Some	Some	Some	Some	Some	Some
	Investment risk	No	No	Some	No	Yes	Yes	No	Yes	Yes
Understanding of FINANCIAL KNOWLEDGE CONCEPTS relevant for retirement planning:	Inflation	No	Yes	Yes	Yes	Yes	Yes	Yes	Yes	Yes
	Time value of money	No	Yes	Yes	Yes	Yes	Yes	Yes	Yes	Yes
	Interest compounding	No	Some	Yes	Yes	Yes	Yes	Yes	Yes	Yes
	Relation risk-return	No	No	Some	Some	Yes	Yes	Some	Yes	Yes
	Effect of costs and fees on capital	No	No	No	Some	Yes	Yes	Some	Yes	Yes
Basic numerical abilities		No	Yes	Yes	Yes	Yes	Yes	Yes	Yes	Yes
ATTITUDES AND PREFERENCES										
Motivation and confidence to plan ahead, shop around and take retirement-related decisions		No	Some	Yes	Yes	Yes	Yes	Yes	Yes	Yes
Long-term orientation		No	Some	Yes	Yes	Yes	Yes	Yes	Yes	Yes
SKILLS AND BEHAVIOUR										
ESTIMATE RETIREMENT INCOME NEEDS both in accumulation and payout phase		Yes	Yes	Yes	Yes	Yes	Yes	Yes	Yes	Yes
TAKE DECISIONS regarding the ACCUMULATION phase:	Participation in a scheme	No	No	No	No	No	No	Yes	Yes	Yes
	Provider	No	No	No	Maybe	Maybe	Maybe	Maybe	Yes	Yes
	Contribution rate/level	No	Maybe	Maybe	Maybe	Maybe	Maybe	Yes	Yes	Yes
	Investment allocation	No	No	No	No	Maybe	Maybe	Maybe	Yes	Yes
TAKE DECISIONS regarding the PAYOUT phase:	When starting to receive benefits	Maybe	Yes	Yes	Yes	Yes	Yes	Yes	Yes	Yes
	What payout option	No	No	No	Maybe	Yes	Yes	Maybe	Yes	Yes
	Which provider	No	No	No	Maybe	Maybe	Maybe	Maybe	Yes	Yes
SHOP AROUND across providers/products both for contribution/accumulation and payout phase		No	No	No	Maybe	Maybe	Yes	Maybe	Maybe	Yes

Legend:

Yes	Cells in a darker colour indicate a stronger financial education need.
Maybe/some	Cells in a middle colour indicate that there may be a financial education need depending on countries' regulation and /or scheme
No	Cells in a lighter colour indicate a minor financial education need.

Financial education needs common to most public and private schemes

In most schemes, public and private, individuals need to have a basic understanding of how their pension system is structured and how it affects them, how their long-term savings are taxed, and to which risks their public and private pensions are exposed to. In particular, individuals need to have a basic understanding of, and an appreciation of how they are affected by:

- *The main rules governing the public and private schemes* under which they are (or can be) covered, the level of mandatory contributions that they are paying, eligibility rules for benefits, how benefits are computed, how contributions and benefits in different schemes are taxed, as well as issues regarding portability of pension plans, and their costs and fees. This may also include being aware of the consequences of job changes on public and private pensions and retirement benefits. All these elements are crucial to form expectations about future retirement benefits and ultimately to be able to plan how much to save in voluntary pensions or other forms of saving.
- *A set of risks related to pension systems* in the aggregate, such as demographic/longevity risk, political risk, investment risk and inflation risk, and how they can impact their individual retirement situation. Demographic/longevity risk refers to the uncertainty surrounding mortality and life expectancy and the possibility of outliving one's resources: only individuals in DC schemes are usually exposed to longevity risk, but individuals in all schemes should at least be aware of population ageing trends in order to understand why and how pension systems are being reformed. Political risk refers to the uncertainty about pension rules: individuals in all schemes should appreciate the fact that current pension rules may be subject to further reform should circumstances change. Investment risk refers for example to the risk that returns would be lower than expected. Inflation risk refers to the risk that benefits may lose value over time; it may apply to all schemes but may be weaker or stronger across country/scheme depending on the extent to which retirement benefits are indexed to inflation.
- *Basic numeracy and financial knowledge* about how (pension) wealth evolves over time, such as interest compounding, inflation, time value of money, the relation between investment risk and return, and how costs and fees in private pensions affect the accumulated capital and benefits in retirement. Knowledge of inflation is especially important to understand mechanisms of pension indexation. Knowledge on how best to allocate assets accumulated in retirement to protect from longevity risk, in particular in DC plans, is essential as well.[9]

In addition, individuals covered under all public and private schemes need to have attitudes oriented towards the long term, as well as the motivation and self-control to plan ahead. Another element common to individuals covered under most schemes is the need to figure out their retirement income needs both in the accumulation and in the payout phase.

Financial education needs related to public pensions

Only a few aspects are left to individual choice in public pensions, while most aspects are fixed by law. People need to have the awareness, knowledge, attitudes and skills to take decisions about retirement age and voluntary contributions for their public pensions.

The major decision that is left to individuals is their own retirement age. Many countries have a statutory or 'normal' retirement age, but allow the possibility of early and/or deferred retirement, with related provisions for reduced/increased benefits upon early/

deferred retirement. The decision about retirement age is crucial because many countries link the amount of retirement benefits to the age of retirement (in an approximately actuarially neutral way).[10] Decisions about retirement age require individuals to have a basic understanding of how benefits are computed. In earnings-related DB systems it is relatively easy for individuals to figure out how much they will receive in retirement and to plan ahead because benefits are usually computed according to a formula based on past earnings and years of service. In contrast, in NDC schemes benefits are computed based on the entire contribution history, on an internal interest rate (that can be for example based on GDP growth) and on an annuity conversion factor depending on life expectancy (usually using unisex mortality tables), making it more difficult for workers to estimate the amount of their benefits in relation to pre-retirement earnings.

Another potential element of choice in public systems – in countries that allow these possibilities, such as Belgium, France, Italy and Germany – is whether to pay additional voluntary contributions in the system, and whether to pay *ex-post* contributions (such as, for instance, for periods spent in higher education, etc.).

Financial education needs related to private pensions

Individuals may need to take many more decisions concerning private pensions, in contrast with public pensions. They therefore need to have the awareness, knowledge, attitudes and skills to take a potentially large set of decisions in relation to their private pensions. The larger the role of private pensions in the total retirement income of individuals, the stronger the case for financial education. What people need to know and be able to do varies according to the features of private pension schemes, and in particular whether they are mandatory or voluntary, occupational or personal, DB or DC.

Mandatory versus voluntary private pensions.[11] An increasing number of countries are mandating the participation of workers (or groups of workers, such as private sector employees) in some form of individual or collective private pension plan. Voluntary participation in DC schemes is possible in most countries.

In mandatory private pensions, individuals do not have to decide whether to participate, but they may need to be able to choose (depending on countries) the pension provider, the contribution level, the investment allocation, when to start receiving benefits and in which form to receive them. On the contrary, voluntary plans usually offer the greatest amount of flexibility and therefore require the greatest financial skills to take sound decisions in both the accumulation and drawn down phases. Such plans usually allow the greatest deal of choice with respect to participation, plan/provider, level of contribution, investment allocation, time of payout, and payout type. Moreover, the number of available personal plans, as well as of possible investment allocations, can be quite large, adding to the complexity of making a choice. Interestingly, in a few countries like the Czech Republic and Denmark, the decision to join and the amount of contributions paid into private pensions also affects the contribution rate and/or the amount received from public pensions.

Among voluntary plans, it is also important to distinguish between opt-in vs. opt-out (that is, plans where the individual has to make an active decision to enrol vs. plans where the individual is automatically enrolled by default but may decide to leave the plan). Exploiting individuals' tendency to remain in the status quo, participation in the latter is typically higher than in the former. In both cases, however, individuals needs to be sufficiently financially literate: in the case of opt-in plans they need to decide whether to join the plan (possibly comparing it against other plans or investment options); in the case of opt-out plans individuals should be able to figure out whether the auto-enrolment is good for them and whether any accompanying default option (such as default investment allocation or default contribution rate) is appropriate to their situation.

Occupational versus personal private pensions. Generally speaking, personal plans offer a greater amount of choice than occupational plans, therefore requiring greater financial skills. For instance, in occupational plans the choice of provider or plan is typically more limited based on the company or industry where the worker is employed. Moreover, fees and costs are likely to be higher in personal plans than in occupational plans, meaning that workers need to contribute more or to accept riskier investment strategies to have the same level of accumulated capital at retirement.

DB versus DC private pensions.[12] There is a risk in DB schemes that the sponsoring employer could become insolvent, but, generally speaking, DC plans offer a greater amount of choice, imply a greater amount of risk for individuals, and require more financial skills than DB plans. People should have sufficient financial knowledge and skills especially in relation to the following elements:

- *Benefits calculation*: it is relatively straightforward for individuals to get an idea of how much they will receive in retirement in DB plans, because benefits are usually computed according to a formula based on past earnings. Also, individuals do not have to bear investment and longevity risks. By contrast, individuals with a DC plan should be aware that benefits depend on the performance of the underlying investments and that it is more difficult to forecast the amount of retirement benefits. As individuals may have the possibility/responsibility to choose their investment allocation, they should also have an appreciation of investment risk in financial markets.
- *Payout options*: DB plans are often paid out in the form of annuities with limited choice for the individuals.[13] In DC plans, by contrast, individuals should be capable of choosing between different payout options, such as lump sums, annuities, programmed withdrawals, or any combination. In addition, individuals should have the awareness, motivation, confidence and skills to select the best provider to buy their payout product, which may be different from the intermediary who managed the accumulation stage of their pension, and, if they choose an annuity, to choose between single or joint annuities, indexed or fixed, with or without guarantees, etc.[14] Decision about the payout product requires an understanding of the characteristics of the different products available, and an understanding of longevity risk. Moreover, individuals should also appreciate how interest rates at the time of retirement may impact their annuity.
- *Costs and fees*: in DB plans, plan members have a promise on the level of pension they will receive and plan sponsors are in most cases responsible for meeting the costs, meaning that management costs affect retirement benefits in a rather indirect way. Members of DC plans, on the contrary, should be aware that they are directly charged a fee for administration and asset management services. These costs can have a substantial negative impact on future retirement income. Individuals should keep costs into account when estimating their retirement income needs but complicated fee structures may make comparisons across different plans difficult (Ionescu and Robles, 2014).

Specific financial education needs of given population subgroups

Depending on national specificities, some groups are likely to face specific challenges in planning for retirement, meaning that they may need specific (or enhanced) financial literacy skills, including especially:

- *Young people, and especially young workers*: They should recognise the importance of starting to plan and save for retirement from a young age, as a way to benefit as much as possible from interest compounding; they need to understand their options and how to manage their pension savings to provide a suitable level of income in retirement; and since they are likely to have several employers over their lifetimes, they also need to be aware of the issues they may face when trying to move existing pension savings or start new plans, and the cost of holding money in multiple funds.
- *Women*: They typically earn less over their lifetimes than men, have longer life expectancy, and are consistently found to have lower financial knowledge and lower confidence in their financial abilities than men (OECD, 2013b), meaning that they may be particularly in need of financial education for retirement planning. Since they are more likely than men to have career breaks due to maternity leave and childrearing, they need to understand the potential impact on their future retirement benefits of pausing contributions.
- *Pre-retirees*: They need to be aware of the choices that they will be faced with at retirement, such as when to draw on their pension, how to use any lump sum received and how to choose an annuity. They should be aware that the amount of benefits they will receive may also depend on the time when they start receiving benefits, in terms of interest rates and investment returns.
- *Self-employed*: In many jurisdictions, the self-employed are required to pay lower payroll contributions to finance their public pension, leading to a greater need to accumulate voluntary retirement saving through private pensions or other means. Moreover, decisions about private pensions are usually more difficult for the self-employed than for employees, because the self-employed do not have access to occupational plans, they may not be covered by mandatory private pensions (e.g., in Australia and Mexico), and they are often not covered by auto-enrolment and other default options. All this means that the self-employed need to be particularly skilled in planning and managing their retirement savings and retirement income.

5.3. Policy responses and the role of financial education

As discussed above, individuals face many issues when planning for retirement. Depending on the national pension system, they may have to decide when and how much to contribute to private pension plans, where to invest, when to begin withdrawing a pension, how these pension benefits should be managed, as well as whether and how to save outside of the pension system. Retirement decisions also interact with the whole financial situation, including labour market status, health, wealth, housing situation, and desired living standard. In taking these decisions, individuals are affected by their own financial knowledge, attitudes and skills, as well as by psychological biases.

Financial education has a role to play in supporting retirement planning, saving and overall decision-making. In a context where mistakes can be particularly painful and with so many variables to consider, it is not surprising that much of the population feels ill-prepared or overwhelmed and is therefore unwilling to make a start on this process. Policy makers and other pensions' stakeholders therefore can contribute to encouraging and supporting appropriate retirement behaviour in planning, saving and decumulating one's savings (OECD, 2008a, 2012b).

Policy responses to support decision-making for retirement

Governments use combinations of various instruments to address people's retirement decision-making challenges.[15] Lewis and Messy (2012) provide examples of how governments influence whether and how to save, including saving for retirement. Yoong (2011) also reviews a number of behaviourally-motivated approaches taken by governments or suggested by research to promote retirement saving. Overall, policy responses to encourage retirement saving and support decision-making include:

- **Compulsion.** Ways of increasing retirement savings may include mandating workers to contribute to supplementary private pension schemes, increasing contribution rates in public and private pensions, increasing retirement ages or postponing the minimum age of benefits withdrawal (in DC or NDC systems).
- **Soft compulsion.** Several governments have started introducing default mechanisms around key private pensions' decisions, such as participation (auto-enrolment in a plan if no choice is made [OECD, 2014; Paklina, 2014]), choice of plan/provider (default plan/ fund/provider if no choice is made, such as in Australia and Chile), contribution level (minimum default contribution, such as in New Zealand, the United Kingdom and the United States [OECD, 2014]), investment allocation (default allocation, such as in Chile, Estonia and New Zeland), payout product (default payout options, such as in Hungary, India, Nigeria, Portugal and Thailand [Stańko and Paklina, 2014]).
- **Fiscal incentives.** Governments encourage private pensions saving through tax incentives, including by allowing individuals to deduct their contributions to funded pensions from their personal income tax base, and by exempting from tax (or taxing at a preferential rate) the returns on investments.
- **Matching contributions.** The state and/or employers in various countries match employees voluntary plan contributions up to a certain percentage (OECD, 2012a, 2014; Soto and Butrica, 2009; DiCenzo, 2014).
- **Simpler and low-cost products.** For instance, Australia, Brazil and the United Kingdom offer low-cost DC plans with simpler features as a way to facilitate choice.
- **Other tools to simplify decision-making.** In order to take into account individual limited attention and aversion to too much information, researchers have devised campaigns and tools based on social marketing (Lusardi, Keller and Keller, 2009) and tools to simplify the enrolment process (Beshears et al., 2013).
- **Voluntary commitment devices.** Building on people's awareness of their own tendency to procrastinate, mechanisms such as Save More Tomorrow (Thaler and Benartzi, 2004) allow people to lock themselves into commitments like withdrawal restrictions or savings rates.

Many of the policy interventions described above are designed to create a shift in behaviour to achieve improved well-being in later life. Policy makers are increasingly including financial education to the policy mix, in order to raise awareness, facilitate access to information, provide (or make it easier for people to acquire) financial skills, as well as to provide easier access to unbiased generic advice. Governments typically provide financial education as a complement to other measures to increase retirement saving and support overall decision-making about retirement. Financial education can be useful to increase awareness and understanding of other policy measures. The relevance of financial education does not diminish in the presence of default mechanisms and other tools to simplify decision-making, as the default option is almost never the best choice for everyone and people may need to be able to judge whether and how to make an active choice to modify it.

Financial education initiatives for retirement

Policy makers have recognised the role of financial education in supporting individuals to make their own choices and plans for the future. National strategies for financial education are becoming increasingly widespread, and frequently aim at supporting recent pension reforms implemented in the country (Grifoni and Messy, 2012; OECD/INFE, 2015b). Several countries, such as Australia, Brazil, Chile, Indonesia, Latvia, Netherlands, New Zealand, Serbia and Spain, are tackling financial education for retirement under their national strategy for financial education. An early milestone of the National Strategy for Financial Literacy in Canada was the publication of a strategy to enhance the financial literacy of current and future seniors. A strategic approach has the advantage of ensuring that the population has the opportunity to improve basic competencies, such as budgeting, as well as addressing related issues such as credit management, before focusing specifically on retirement saving. In some cases, governments mandate private pension funds to deliver financial education to their members (see Box 5.1).

Box 5.1. **Compulsory provision of financial education for retirement**

In New Zealand, newly licensed default fund KiwiSaver providers as of 1 July 2014 are required to offer investor education to their members. The default providers have to deliver education to their members in the form of investment information, as well as helping them make appropriate investment choices for their individual circumstances. The different default providers have proposed different approaches to investor education, including proactive communication campaigns, seminars, financial advice and online tools for members (MBIE New Zealand, 2015).

In Colombia pension fund managers are obliged by law to address education campaigns to their members. Those campaigns must be made by accredited professionals who are ready to give the best information about payout products, annuities, asset allocation information and anything the members must know to be well informed and ready to take the next step when choosing a payout product (Stańko and Paklina, 2014).

This section discusses how different financial education tools can address various financial education needs. Figure 5.2 summarises these tool and splits them into information and awareness, instruction, and advice following the OECD (2005c) definition. Moreover, financial education initiatives vary in the extent to which they:

- Address **personal vs. general issues.** For instance, communication and awareness campaign provide general information to a broad audience while personal statements sent by post provide personalised information about one's own situation.

Figure 5.2. **Financial education tools for retirement**

FINANCIAL EDUCATION NEEDS FOR RETIREMENT		FINANCIAL EDUCATION TOOLS								
		INFORMATION and AWARENESS						INSTRUCTION		ADVICE
		General			Personalised					
		Websites	Awareness campaigns and events	Comparioson tools	Pension statements	Online personal info	Calculators and simulators	Retirement planning seminars	Non-retirement financial literacy training	Counseling / advice
KNOWLEDGE AND UNDERSTANDING										
Basic understanding of pension RULES, including public and private pensions rules, retirement saving taxation, rights and responsibilities related to pensions		X	X	X	X	X	X	X		X
Basic appreciation of RISKS related to pension systems and retirement:	Demographic/longevity risk	X	X				X	X		X
	Political risk	X	X					X		X
	Inflation risk	X	X				X	X	X	X
	Investment risk	X	X				X	X	X	X
Understanding of FINANCIAL KNOWLEDGE CONCEPTS relevant for retirement planning:	Inflation						X	X	X	
	Time value of money						X	X	X	
	Interest compounding						X	X	X	
	Relation risk-return						X	X	X	
	Effect of costs and fees on capital						X	X		
Basic numerical abilities								X	X	
ATTITUDES AND PREFERENCES										
Motivation and confidence to plan ahead, shop around and take retirement-related decisions				X	X			X	X	X
Long-term orientation		X	X		X	X	X	X	X	X
SKILLS AND BEHAVIOUR										
ESTIMATE RETIREMENT INCOME NEEDS both in accumulation and payout phase				X	X	X	X	X		X
TAKE DECISIONS regarding the ACCUMULATION phase:	Participation in a scheme	X	X	X	X	X	X	X		X
	Provider	X	X	X	X	X	X	X		X
	Contribution rate/level	X	X	X	X	X	X	X		X
	Investment allocation	X	X	X	X	X	X	X		X
TAKE DECISIONS regarding the PAYOUT phase:	When starting to receive benefits	X	X	X	X	X	X	X		X
	What payout option	X	X	X	X	X	X	X		X
	Which provider	X	X	X	X	X	X	X		X
SHOP AROUND across providers/products both for contribution/accumulation and payout phase				X				X	X	

Legend:
X (shaded) — This financial education tool can be useful to address this need.

- Are **passive or active.** For instance websites and other sources usually provide information on which individuals can base their own decisions, while training workshops also foster more practical skills that can be readily applied by individuals.
- Have **short-term or long-term goals.** For instance awareness campaigns around a pension reform aim at having a rather immediate impact, while financial education workshops are geared towards equipping participants with skills that can be used also in the future.

Table 5.1 summarises financial education initiatives undertaken in various countries and economies and Table 5.2 provides weblinks to selected financial education resources for retirement planning.

General information and awareness

There are ways of providing general information about retirement options and increasing awareness of retirement issues. They include: i) general information, mostly through websites, ii) awareness campaigns covering retirement issues and or related to specific events/reforms, and iii) comparison tools.

Websites are by far the most common way of providing information concerning retirement. All countries for which information was available have one or more websites providing general descriptive information on how the pension system is structured and operates. Some websites also offer printable booklets with similar information. While in most cases information is disseminated across multiple websites, some countries have developed specific websites providing information about all types of public and private pensions in one place, including PensionsInfo.dk in Denmark, Pensionikeskus.ee in Estonia, Info-retraite.fr in France, Manapensija.lv in Latvia, Mijnpensioenoverzicht.nl in the Netherlands and Minpension.se in Sweden. All pension funds in the Netherlands have to provide information to existing and new participants about the most relevant aspects of the pension scheme through an online standardised template (pension123.nl). As this makes comparisons across funds easier, it is especially useful for employees changing job.

Regular public awareness and communication campaigns are another way of raising awareness around the need to save for retirement (see Atkinson et al., 2012, for a more extensive overview about National Pension Communication Campaigns). Pension3Day is organised every year by Money Wise in the Netherlands, involving over 250 partner organisations to raise awareness of pension issues among employers and entrepreneurs. The Pensions Superintendence of Chile developed a series of videos to give information and promote private pension schemes.

One-off events and campaigns can be used to build consensus around a specific reform, increase trust in pension authorities, and encourage specific behaviours, such as voluntarily joining a new system, increasing contributions or postponing retirement (Atkinson et al., 2012). In the Czech Republic, both the government and the private sector launched several initiatives on raising awareness of the importance of savings for retirement following a pension reform in early 2013. Romania undertook various campaigns to increase knowledge of the private pension system and to inform and educate participants about their rights, obligations, and the role of the supervisory authority ("Time passes in your favour" in 2007-08; "Learn to choose! Private pension, a young decision" in 2010-12). The United Kingdom launched the Pension Wise campaign, including a website to provide information and guidance about a new pension reform entered into effect in April 2015 (pensionwise.gov.uk).

Table 5.1. **Summary of financial education initiatives for retirement by country**

	INFORMATION and AWARENESS								INSTRUCTION	ADVICE
	General			Personalised						
	Websites	Awareness campaigns and events	Comparison tools	Public pension statements	Private pension statements	Online personal info – Public pension	Online personal info – Private pensions	Calculators and simulators	Retirement planning seminars	Counselling/advice
OECD										
Austria	x			x	x	x	x	x		x
Australia	x				x	x	x	x	x	
Belgium	x			x	x	x				
Canada	x				x	x		x		
Chile	x	x	x		x		x	x	x	x
Czech Republic	x	x							x	
Denmark	x		x	x	x	x	x			
Estonia	x		x		x	x	x	x		
Finland	x			x		x		x		
France	x			x		x		x		x
Germany	x			x	x	x	x			x
Hungary	x		x	x		x		x		
Ireland	x		x		x			x		
Israel	x				x					
Italy	x	x		x	x	x				
Japan	x			x	x	x	x			
Latvia	x		x			x	x	x	x	
Mexico	x	x	x	x	x		x	x	x	
Netherlands	x	x		x	x	x	x	x	x	x
New Zealand	x	x	x	x	x	x	x	x	x	
Portugal	x					x				
Slovak Republic	x					x	x			
Spain	x		x	x	x	x		x		
Sweden	x			x	x	x	x			
Switzerland	x			x	x					
Turkey	x				x		x			
United Kingdom	x	x		x	x	x	x	x		x
United States	x	x	x	x	x	x	x	x	x	x
Others										
Hong Kong, China	x		x		x			x		
Indonesia	x	x			x	x	x		x	
Romania	x	x	x		x	x				
Serbia	x								x	
Thailand	x							x	x	
33	33	10	12	18	23	24	16	18	11	7

Note: This table is updated as of July 2016.

StatLink http://dx.doi.org/10.1787/888933426794

Comparison tools compare private pension plans performance, costs, investment allocation, and other plan features in a standardised way (without necessarily using user-specific parameters). Such comparison tools can be considered at the intersection of financial education and financial consumer protection tools, as they lower the cost of obtaining information about pension plans, reduce the complexity of making a choice, and

Table 5.2. **Selected financial education resources for retirement planning**

Events/awareness campaigns	
Chile	*www.youtube.com/watch?v=54dkaORVa0Q* and *www.youtube.com/watch?v=BzdCiVDcfyE*
Indonesia	(videos in Spanish)
Netherlands	*https://youtu.be/vsUTNU1SpD8* (video – in Indonesian)
United Kingdom	*www.wijzeringeldzaken.nl/pensioen3daagse/* (in Dutch)
	www.pensionwise.gov.uk
Tools to compare pension plans/annuities	
Chile	*www.scomp.cl/* (in Spanish)
Netherlands	*http://pensioen123.nl/* (in Dutch)
New Zealand	*http://fundfinder.sorted.org.nz/*
United Kingdom	*www.moneyadviceservice.org.uk/en/tools/annuities*
Personal pension situation on demand	
Australia	*https://my.gov.au*
Denmark	*www.pensionsInfo.dk* (in Danish)
Estonia	*www.pensionikeskus.ee*
France	*info-retraite.fr* (in French)
Latvia	*www.manapensija.lv*
Netherlands	*www.mijnpensioenoverzicht.nl* (in Dutch)
Sweden	*www.minpension.se* (in Swedish)
Calculators/simulators	
Austria	*www.pensionskontorechner.at/* and *http://pensionsrechner.arbeiterkammer.at/* (in German)
Australia	*www.moneysmart.gov.au/tools-and-resources/calculators-and-apps*
Canada	*https://srv111.services.gc.ca/generalinformation/index* (Canadian Retirement Income Calculator – Government of Canada)
Chile	*www.spensiones.cl/apps/simuladorPensiones/* (in Spanish)
France	*www.marel.fr/* (in French)
Hong Kong, China	*www.mpfa.org.hk/eng/mpf_education/mpf_calculators/index.jsp* (MPFA)
	www.thechinfamily.hk/tools/retirement/en/main/index.jsp (IEC)
Mexico	*www.consar.gob.mx/calculadora/inicio.aspx* (in Spanish)
Netherlands	*www.wijzeringeldzaken.nl/Wat-moet-ik-doen-voor-mijn-pensioen/* (in Dutch)
	www.nibud.nl/consumenten/schijf-van-vijf/ (in Dutch)
New Zealand	*www.sorted.org.nz/calculators/retirement*
Portugal	*www4.seg-social.pt/pensoes* (in Portuguese)
United Kingdom	*www.moneyadviceservice.org.uk/en/tools/pension-calculator*
United States	*www.socialsecurity.gov/OACT/anypia/index.html*

Note: This table is updated as of July 2016.

help consumers shopping around, and at the same time can make disclosure requirements more effective and improve market competition. For instance, the Commission for Financial Capability in New Zealand created the Kiwisaver Fund Finder (fundfinder.sorted.org.nz) where users can select funds according to riskiness, fees, past returns, and services offered. The Money Advice Service website in the United Kingdom compares annuity prices, supporting consumers' in their right to shop around for an annuity via the so-called Open Market Option. Individuals are asked a set of standard questions regarding the type of annuity they would like and receive comparative quotations from the providers. Though providers take part on a voluntary basis, all the main insurance companies active in the annuities market are represented (Stańko and Paklina, 2014). The Pension Superintendence in Chile developed a sophisticated (and mandatory) online system to compare (and obtain quotations on) annuities and other withdrawal options from different companies (Stańko and Paklina, 2014; Iglesias-Palau, 2009).

Websites, booklets, awareness campaigns, and comparison tables can be a good way to provide information about legislation and regulation on how the pension system works, the main rules and characteristics of public and private schemes, and any related issue, like fiscal incentives for retirement saving. They can also be a useful way to explain the main risks related to different types of pensions, including demographic, political, and investment risks, and the reasons for pension reforms. At times of pension reforms and other changes, when also private sector campaigns and media coverage may be going on, campaigns by public authorities can be crucial to offer complete, unbiased and reliable information, thereby reducing uncertainty and lowering information costs. Public campaigns can also make the need to save for the long term more salient and help people focus on the need to take action. Overall, having clear and sufficient information about pension rules and about retirement products is a key starting point for planning ahead.

It is important that care is taken in how information is provided in order to make sure it is effective. For instance, information should be easily available, it should be clear, with minimum jargon and with explanatory glossaries readily available, and it should not be overwhelming. It is also preferable to offer all relevant information about different schemes in one place, such as a single website covering all pension schemes, public and private, mandatory and voluntary. Information initiatives from the public and private sector should also be coordinated. As highlighted in Atkinson, et al. (2012), it may be relevant to delay providers' sales campaigns while a pension communication campaigns is in progress, to ensure that marketing campaigns of private operators do not overshadow government information. It may also be relevant to experiment with different delivery channels to learn which ones are more effective. For instance, Heinberg et al. (2014) provide experimental evidence that videos may be more effective than print material to deliver information about retirement planning.

As regards comparison tools, IOPS (2011) highlights the importance of reporting standardised cost measures, including as many costs as possible, and of showing investment performance over a suitably long time horizon (with warnings about the use of past performance). It also emphasises that a risk measure (such as a volatility measure) may be of assistance, particularly when used to select investment options and if supported by explanatory material.

Standardised and comparable information on private pension plan costs and fees is especially important. Complex fee structures make it harder for members to compare across pension funds and to get a clear image of the way these fees can reduce their future retirement benefits (Ionescu and Robles, 2014). Some Latin American countries have improved transparency and comparability by allowing only one type of fee. In Mexico commercial pension fund managers (AFOREs) can only charge fees on assets under management, while in Chile Administradoras de Fondos de Pensiones (AFPs) can only charge a proportional fee as a percentage of salary for every contribution made to the system. Italy and Hong Kong, China imposed a legal requirement for pension funds to publish a synthetic cost indicator. While these measures belong to regulation rather than to financial education, they reinforce the importance of standardised and comparable information.

Personalised information and awareness

There are several ways of providing personalised information about retirement options and increasing awareness of retirement issues. They include i) information sent out proactively by the state or pension providers about the individual's pension situation, ii) information about the individual pension situation available at all times or sent out on request, and iii) pension calculators and simulators.

Personalised letters (pension statements) give information about workers' pension situation and can differ across countries in terms of coverage, timing and extent of information. For instance, the Social Security Statement sent by the US Social Security Administration and the Orange Envelope provided by the Swedish Pension Agency only cover public pensions, while pension statements in Denmark cover benefits from both public and private sources. In terms of timing and frequency, some countries start sending pension statements to relatively young people, while other countries send them only to pre-retirees. The French public pension authority for private employees has progressively increased over time the number of cohorts that receive information letters (Conseil d'Orientation des Retraites, 2016). In Germany public pension statements become more detailed from the age of 55. Some statements only provide accounting information up to the time of writing (such as the number of years the worker has been contributing, the balance accumulated, etc.) while others also contain forward-looking information and projections about future retirement benefits under different scenarios (Larsson, Sundén and Settergren, 2008).

Personal information available online at all times usually provides an alternative to pension statements. While unsolicited information in the form of statements can prompt people to become more informed and to act, online information available on demand allows people to explore their situation further at their own convenience. In Australia, Denmark, Estonia, Latvia, the Netherlands, and Sweden workers can access personal information about multiple pension schemes through a single website, but more often people have to put together information and projections coming from different websites in different formats, and potentially computed according to different assumptions.

Calculators and simulators can also provide useful personalised information, typically about expected retirement age, expected retirement benefits, or life expectancy (in the case of the United States Social Security Administration). Retirement calculators provide complementary information to that delivered through pension statements. Calculators are usually based on information (age, income, pension fund balance, etc.) provided by the user rather than on administrative data, which can make their estimates less precise, but allow users to experiment with how their retirement benefits would change if they changed the key system parameters (typically, retirement age, amount of contributions, etc.) or if external parameters (rates of return, interest rates, inflation, etc.) changed. This allows users to focus on the key choice variable rather than on the calculation process. For instance, pension calculators available on the Money Advice Service website in the United Kingdom and the pension calculator on Manapensija.lv in Latvia give estimates of retirement benefits including from public pensions, workplace schemes, and private pension contributions. In the Netherlands, the Money Wise platform offers an online tool giving a customised pension situation and tips for action. The pension simulator available on the website of the Superintendence of Pensions in Chile can be used both with user-provided information and with administrative data and it provides an interesting example of how to communicate information about pension risk (and about the uncertainty that is inherent in projections) in a way that is as easy as possible for people to understand, and that prompts them to action if necessary (Antolín and Fuentes, 2012).

Evidence on the impact of social security pension information is mixed. Information appears to increase knowledge but greater knowledge does not always translate into behaviour changes. Chan and Stevens (2008) find that well-informed individuals are more responsive to pension incentives, while ill-informed individuals tend to respond to their own misperception of the incentives, rather than being unresponsive to any incentives at all. Mastrobuoni (2011) analyses survey responses of workers age 55-64 before and after the step-wise introduction of the US Social Security Statement in 1995. The author finds that the Social Security Statement improved workers' knowledge about their benefits, but he also finds that this improved knowledge has negligible impact on retirement behaviour: workers do not change their expected retirement age, their claiming behaviour or their responsiveness to incentives after receiving the statement. Biggs (2010) analyses the same survey data over a longer time span (1994-2008) and argues that the Statement did not produce an immediate increase in knowledge of retirement benefit levels but that continued receipt of the Statement over a number of years may have reduced individual errors in predicting benefits. Smith and Couch (2014) analyse the impact of the Social Security Statement on younger workers (up to 46 years old), using data from Gallup surveys. They find that Statement receipt is associated with large and statistically significant increases in knowledge of Social Security programs and benefits. Liebman and Luttmer (2015) carry out a field experiment providing information about Social Security provisions to a sample of older US workers, and find that the intervention increased labour force participation one year later, mostly among female respondents. Miranda Pinto (2012) studies the Pension Projection Statements sent by Chilean pension fund managers (AFPs), showing that individuals who received the pension projection in two consecutive years (2005 and 2006) were more likely to delay retirement than those who received the projection in only one of those years.

Designing effective pension statements for DC pensions can be even more challenging. Rinaldi and Giacomel (2008) and Antolín and Harrison (2012) note the difficulty of providing an explanation of complex DC risks and of conveying uncertainty about future benefits projections in a way that is at the same time short, simple and clear. Regulatory disclosure requirements may further undermine the objective of producing statements that are brief and free from jargon. The European Insurance and Occupational Pensions Authority (EIOPA) highlighted good practices on the provision of information about DC pension schemes, stressing the importance of providing information in 'layers' from the most pressing messages to the useful but less pressing legal information; and testing whether plan members find information attractive, comprehensible and how they would act after having read the information (EIOPA, 2013).

Research has also shown the importance of combining general and personalised information. For instance, Goda, Manchester and Sojourner (2012) find that providing individuals with income projections for retirement together with general information and material about the retirement plan to guide people in making changes to their contribution had positive effects on the contribution rate. On the contrary, the authors of the study did not find strong evidence that the plan materials and information or the income projections alone led to significant changes in the contribution rates. Similarly, Song (2012) found that, when educating adults about interest compounding, providing only projections of expected pension benefit levels given different contribution levels alone was less effective than providing both information about general principles of compounding and the projections.

Pension calculators and simulators are another important complement to personalised information as they can provide forward-looking information under different scenarios, make the long-term benefits of saving more salient, help workers in estimating their retirement income needs, and supporting all the related decisions where workers have a margin of choice. Moreover, some calculators also offer the possibility to learn about the effects of interest compounding and inflation on accumulated funds or benefits, and if built for that purpose, can also allow users to better appreciate investment risk or longevity risk. Communicating benefits only by means of written statements is increasingly recognised as inflexible and limited, while online interactive calculators appear to offer a more flexible delivery format that avoids information overload, as it allows plan member to access information in accordance with their needs, and that can improve awareness of the connections between contributions and retirement income, among other factors. In a survey to investigate to what extent the 2011 Orange envelope is read and understood, the Swedish Pensions Agency (2011) found that many people were interested in learning about their total pension situation (including occupational pensions), and many would be interested in accessing pension information online. Similarly, market research from AVIVA (2012) conducted in France, Ireland, Italy, Poland, Spain and the UK about consumers' preferences for pension statements showed that people would welcome integrated pension statements with information about different pension schemes in the same letter, as well as an interactive pension calculator.

Instruction

Seminars and workshops about retirement planning can be made available to different audiences (employees in the workplace, members of a pension fund, or even people not currently in work), can be organised by different stakeholders (including pension/financial regulators, pension providers, and employers), and may take different forms (including formal training, e-learning, community activities and so on). In some cases, general financial literacy training also covers retirement issues or enhances dimensions of financial literacy that are relevant for retirement (such as, for instance, the power of interest compounding).

The Department of Human Services in Australia set up the Financial Information Service (FIS), which provides free education to a variety of audiences including on retirement topics (such as, for instance, understanding superannuation, investing for retirement and fees and charges for aged care). In the Netherlands, the Money Wise platform provides an online toolkit to employers for them to use in the delivery of pension education to their employees. Many employees turn to their employer for information about their pension and many employers struggle with good ways of fulfilling this need: the toolkit contains standardised presentations, animations, tools, and promotional materials that employers can use, and tailor to their specific situation and needs. In Serbia, the National Bank organises lectures for people throughout the country, covering topics such as saving through life insurance and voluntary pension funds. The Security Exchange Commission (SEC) in Thailand has a new workplace project called "Kind-hearted Employers" which provides face-to-face classroom training in the workplace to enhance employees' skills in relation to money management. In the United States retirement planning seminars are often offered in the workplace by employers. In a survey of about 400 human resource professionals across the US, more than one half reported that their organisation provides financial education to their employees. According to the same survey, of the employers providing some form of financial education, eight in ten provide retirement planning seminars (SHRM, 2014). In Nigeria too employers organise pre-retirement planning programmes.

Retirement seminars (and general financial literacy training) can address a wide spectrum of financial education needs, as they can be used to provide (general) information about pension systems, can help participants acquire financial knowledge and key financial skills relevant for retirement, can explain the risks that individuals may be exposed to through pension schemes and suggest how to manage them, can support workers in estimating their retirement income needs, can teach participants not only *what* to do but also *how* to go about doing it, and ultimately help them taking decisions about their pensions. Training also has the potential to make the benefits of long-term saving more salient, possibly helping in spurring motivation and reducing inertia, and provide instruments to better manage the complex information around pensions, even though not all individuals attending a seminar would take action via increased participation and higher savings after the training (Choi et al., 2002). As it can be difficult to encourage participation in workshops and seminars, particularly when the initiative requires that people give up their leisure time or actively seek appropriate courses, the availability of workplace education may facilitate participation, especially if provided during working hours.

Evaluation evidence suggests that workplace financial education can be an effective way of changing behaviour. The review of financial education programmes for long-term saving and investment contained in Atkinson et al. (2015) highlights examples where workplace education can lead to increased enrolment and/or contribution into pension schemes, both amongst participants and their co-workers. Experimental evidence on retirement seminars delivered at the workplace is limited, but other non-experimental evidence provides encouraging results. Using a national sample (US Health and Retirement Study), Lusardi (2002), finds that retirement seminars held by employers have positive effects on employees at the lower end of the savings distribution. Similarly, using a survey of employers, Bernheim and Garrett (2003) and Bayer, Bernheim and Scholz (2009) find that retirement seminars had a significant effect on raising participation and contribution to savings plans. Clark, and co-authors (2003, 2006, and 2008) examine a typical one-hour retirement savings seminar by a single provider, TIAA-CREF, at various different institutions. Using before-and-after surveys of participants, the authors find that the seminar affected workers' stated retirement goals, albeit with only limited behaviour change afterwards.

Seminars about retirement planning appear to be offered in fewer countries than other financial education initiatives for retirement, such as the provision of information (Table 5.1). Possible reasons may include the fact that seminars are more costly to provide and organise, or the fact that they tend to be organised by employers rather than by public authorities. Another reason may be because financial literacy skills for retirement are often covered in general financial literacy training (that span several topics, from budgeting to long-term planning). In this respect, countries with a national strategy for financial education are better placed to improve dimensions of financial literacy relevant for retirement planning through a variety of means, even though they may not be specifically targeted to address retirement issues.

Advice

Within the definition of financial education (OECD, 2005c), advice involves providing consumers with counsel about generic financial issues and products so that they can make the best use of the financial information and instruction they have received, rather than offering recommendations regarding individual financial products and services (OECD, 2008b). One-to-one generic counselling and advice, if provided by an independent source, offers the possibility to provide personalised guidance and at the same time address any specific gaps in information, knowledge and potentially in skills.[16]

In Chile, the 2008 pension reform introduced pension advisors, whose main role is to guide and advise individuals through the retirement process. Pension advisors help individuals with assessing the different risks faced during retirement and with the selection of a suitable pension payout. In addition, the Chilean Pension Regulator answers questions from plan members through the web, a call center and in person. Since 2010, France has introduced a free individual face-to-face interview with a pension advisor for individuals aged 45 and over ('entretien info retraite'). The Pension Wise campaign in the United Kingdom is part of a major package of reforms. As a part of this campaign, the government is making available a free, 45-minute guidance session, to be delivered by an impartial provider, either face-to-face or over the phone, to support savers to make informed choices.

Similarly to teaching offered through workshops and seminars, generic advice can address a wide range of financial education needs, provided that advisors are unbiased or that conflicts of interest are adequately managed.[17] Counselling and advice can be used to help workers find relevant information, and can to some extent point to gaps in financial knowledge and skills (even though teaching about financial literacy may not be possible due to time constraints). The main advantage of advice is to guide workers in managing risks, estimating their retirement income needs and in taking decisions about their pensions. It is important that advice is unbiased and easily available, possibly through different channels (face-to-face, telephone, on line, etc.).

Addressing specific target groups through financial education

Retirement planning affects everyone, which explains why national strategies and tools for a relatively broad audience are seen as effective policy mechanisms for increasing retirement saving. However, within such strategies, it is often necessary to identify specific target groups who could benefit from more tailored support. Depending on national specificities, priority groups with specific needs are likely to include young people, women, pre-retirees or the self-employed, as mentioned in Section 5.2.

These target groups are reflected in the responses received to the 2014 stocktaking questionnaire and in existing financial education programmes. For example, in Australia information is tailored to a number of specific groups, including young adults, young families, empty nesters (parents whose children have left home) or older single people, over 55s and pre-retirees, and women under 40. Important target groups in the Netherlands include people who are close to retirement (55+) as well as the self-employed, who are not covered by the mandatory occupational pension schemes. In Spain, the national financial education plan targets workers and the elderly, in an attempt to improve knowledge and awareness about pensions. Pre-retirees are also targeted in the Slovak Republic, which aims to reach those aged 50+ with a National Program of Active Ageing.

Latvia will target young people through an annual financial education week on the basis that by inviting schoolchildren to become involved their parents and the general public will be reached. A similar approach is favoured in Brazil, with financial education provided to high-school students, which includes long-term savings topics.

Various initiatives aim at helping women plan for their retirement (OECD, 2013b). For instance, the Tsao Foundation in Singapore develops and delivers a financial education programme for mature women to help them better manage their finances and be financially independent in their older years.

Some countries have also identified more vulnerable segments of the population, who may have particular retirement planning needs. Australia targets Indigenous Australians and others from culturally and linguistically diverse backgrounds, whilst Nigeria targets informal sector workers. Latvia recognises the importance of targeting those at risk of unemployment as well as job seekers in its efforts to increase savings habits.

5.4. Policy guidance and practical tools for financial education for retirement

The OECD Recommendation on Principles and Good Practices for Financial Education and Awareness states that one of the key principles of financial education is to focus on high priority areas and that "The awareness of future retirees about the need to assess the financial adequacy of their current public or private pensions schemes and to take appropriate action when needed should be encouraged" (OECD, 2005c).

In 2008, the OECD Council adopted Good Practices for Financial Education Relating to Private Pensions (OECD, 2008a) to promote financial awareness and education relating to private pensions. In addition, the OECD Roadmap for the Good Design of Defined Contribution Pension Plans identifies the importance of effective communication and the need to address financial illiteracy and lack of awareness as part of a comprehensive public policy (OECD, 2012b).

The analysis contained in this chapter provides background material for the update and refinement of the 2008 Good Practices for Financial Education Relating to Private Pensions, to be carried out within the consolidation of all OECD policy instruments on financial education. Existing OECD policy tools provide useful guidance on recognising the importance of financial awareness and education for retirement planning, but need to be updated to more fully reflect new information about the evolution of pensions systems, the development of new regulatory tools and architecture, the development of national, strategic approaches to financial education,[18] as well as the progress made in recent years in developing financial education initiatives for retirement planning.

Policy guidance

Based on the discussion of financial education initiatives for retirement planning undertaken in this chapter, it is possible to draw some policy guidelines. They aim at complementing recommendations made previously made in the existing Good Practices (OECD, 2008a). They should be applied taking into account national circumstances and the different extent of retirement planning challenges depending on the features of national pension systems and of the financial environment more broadly. The main guidelines include:

Overall framework. Governments and other public authorities should develop national strategies for financial education, to make sure people have ways to acquire general financial skills. National strategies allow policy makers to improve financial literacy for retirement planning within a consistent framework and through a variety of means, even though these means may be not specifically or not only targeted towards retirement issues.

Information and awareness. Governments, other public authorities, private pensions' providers, and other relevant private and not-for-profit stakeholders should make sure that information about pension systems, pension reforms, and private pension schemes is not only available but also clear and not overwhelming for individuals, and that information about features of private pensions (such as costs, performance, quality of service, investment allocation, and level of risk) is comparable and standardised. It is also important to combine in one place the information regarding all pension schemes that an individual has, and to complement pension statements with calculators/simulators in order to maximise the impact of information on retirement outcomes.

Instruction. Considering how important it is not only to have information but also to have the skills to act upon it, governments, employers and other relevant stakeholders should consider expanding the provision of financial literacy training for retirement planning.

Advice. Governments and other public authorities should consider expanding the provision of unbiased advice about retirement planning, including all sources, not only public pensions, in order to guide individuals whenever the system is particularly complex, has been recently reformed, and the provision of information and skills is not enough.

Practical tools

In addition to these guidelines, the chapter also provides practical policy tools for immediate use by policy makers, supporting their efforts to identify financial education needs for retirement and to improve financial education efforts in this area. These tools consist of:

1. A **matrix** of financial education needs and tools to support retirement decision-making, constituted of Figures 5.1 and 5.2 above. It summarises the main needs in terms of financial literacy and possible related ways to address them through different financial education tools. Figure 5.1 offers a starting point to identify financial education needs for retirement given the setup of different pension systems. Then, Figure 5.2 highlights the most relevant financial education tools to address each need. The matrix offers a compact and general tool, but national specificities should be kept in mind when using it, especially accounting for factors such as how long-term savings and investment products are structured, marketed and regulated, and whether there is universal access to such products. They should also take into account regulation and financial consumer protection, as well as aspects of the regulatory architecture such as default mechanisms.
2. A **checklist** on financial education for retirement is available online.[19] The checklist is designed for policy makers intending to complement the regulatory and consumer protection frameworks in relation to pensions with financial education, or wanting to strengthen existing financial education activities to support retirement policies. It can be used in combination with the matrix and is designed to help policy makers to determine the needs of citizens and workers for information, instruction and advice in relation to retirement.

Notes

1. For a description of pension systems, see OECD private pensions glossary (OECD, 2005b), Pensions at a Glance (OECD, 2013a), and OECD Pensions Outlook (OECD, 2012a and 2014). For earlier recommendation and guidance on financial education for private pensions, see Improving Financial Literacy: Analysis of Issues and Policies (OECD, 2005a); Recommendation on Good Practices for Financial Education Relating to Private Pensions (OECD, 2008a); OECD Roadmap for the Good Design of Defined Contribution Pension Plans (OECD, 2012b, 2012c). For an analysis of specific aspects of pensions or retirement planning with implications for financial education, see: annual pension statements (Larsson, Sundén and Settergren, 2008; and Antolín and Harrison, 2012); pensions communication (Antolín and Fuentes, 2012; and Atkinson, et al., 2012), annuities (Brown, 2009); DC plan costs and fees (Ionescu and Robles, 2014); auto-enrolment (OECD 2014 and Paklina, 2014), and private pensions payout options (Stańko and Paklina, 2014).
2. A total of 30 countries and economies responded to the questionnaire, with 28 providing detailed information: Australia; Brazil; Canada; Chile; China (People's Republic of); Colombia; Czech Republic; Denmark; Germany; Hong Kong, China; Hungary; Ireland; Japan; Latvia; Macau, China; Mexico; Netherlands; New Zealand; Nigeria; Norway; Romania; Russian Federation; Serbia; Slovak Republic;

South Africa; Spain; Thailand and Turkey (the Central Bank of Austria and the Banking Superintendency of Guatemala responded to say they did not have the information or programmes in place).

3. The OECD/INFE (2015a) defines financial literacy as "A combination of awareness, knowledge, skill, attitude and behaviour necessary to make sound financial decisions and ultimately achieve individual financial wellbeing". The OECD (2005c) defines financial education as "the process by which financial consumers/investors improve their understanding of financial products, concepts and risks and, through information, instruction and/or objective advice, develop the skills and confidence to become more aware of financial risks and opportunities, to make informed choices, to know where to go for help, and to take other effective actions to improve their financial well-being.
4. While most of the chapter focuses on building and decumulating savings for retirement, it also takes into account that retirement planning and funding decisions influence or are influenced by other important financial decisions over the life cycle. These include the household overall financial situation, any other long-term needs, and potential sources of risk, like health status, labour market status (especially being unemployed or self-employed), any outstanding debts, housing tenure, and so on. For instance, in countries like Canada and the United States, an increasing number of people arrive at the time of retirement with outstanding debts (EBRI, 2015; Marshall, 2011).
5. Actuarial fairness refers to the entire lifetime of a person's contributions and benefits. Actuarial fairness requires that the present value of lifetime contributions equals the present value of lifetime benefits (Queisser and Whitehouse, 2006).
6. The first chapter in this volume discusses DB and DC pensions plans and the shift from DB to DC.
7. In many countries, public pension schemes and rules may differ between employees and self-employed workers, and between private sector and public sector employees: where not specified, pension rules mentioned in this chapter mostly refer to private sector employees.
8. In reading this figure, one has to take into account that not all pension systems cover all elements mentioned in the columns of the table, that there may be national variations with respect to the table, and that financial education needs may also vary according to other national circumstances (level of development, spread of informal economy, access to different saving products and institutions, degree of market regulation and of financial consumer protection, etc.)
9. OECD Roadmap for the Good Design of DC Pensions Plans.
10. Actuarial neutrality refers to the effect of working an additional year on pension benefits. Actuarial neutrality requires that the net present discounted value of retirement benefits is not affected by the decision to retire at a given age or a year later/earlier (Queisser and Whitehouse, 2006).
11. In this chapter, pension schemes are considered mandatory or voluntary from the point of view of employees/individuals.
12. Public pensions are generally DB and they share many features with DB private pensions. The main difference is how they are funded (see Chapter 1 in this volume).
13. The chapter in this volume on annuity products and their guarantees describes to great details the variety and potential complexity of different annuity products.
14. Single annuities pay retirement income to the beneficiaries until they die; on the contrary, joint annuities continue to pay a regular income to the spouse, partner or other chosen beneficiary for the rest of their lives when the primary beneficiary dies.
15. Moreover governments develop financial consumer protection to ensure that long-term saving decisions take place in a safe and appropriate financial environment.
16. Chapter 3 in this volume discusses policy measures to improve the role of financial advice on retirement outcomes.
17. See also the OECD/INFE Guidelines for private and not-for-profit stakeholders in financial education (OECD/INFE, 2014).
18. Taking into account the OECD/INFE High-level Principles on National Strategies for Financial Education developed in 2012 and endorsed by G20 leaders and APEC ministers of finance (OECD/INFE, 2012).
19. See *www.oecd.org/daf/fin/private-pensions/Pensions-Outlook-2016-Ch5-Annex.pdf*.

References

Agnew J., P. Balduzzi and A. Sundén (2003), "Portfolio choice and trading in a large 401(k) Plan", *American Economic Review*, Vol. 93, No. 1, pp. 193-215, *www.aeaweb.org/articles.php?doi=10.1257/000282803321455223*.

Antolín P. and D. Harrison (2012), "Annual DC pension statements and the communications challenge", *OECD Working Papers on Finance, Insurance and Private Pensions*, No. 19, OECD Publishing, *http://dx.doi.org/10.1787/5k97gkd06kth-en*.

Antolín, P. and O. Fuentes (2012), "Communicating pension risk to DC plan members: The Chilean case of a pension risk simulator", *OECD Working Papers on Finance, Insurance and Private Pensions*, No. 28, OECD Publishing, *http://dx.doi.org/10.1787/5k9181hxzmlr-en*.

Atkinson, A. and F. Messy (2012), "Measuring financial literacy: Results of the OECD / International Network on Financial Education (INFE) pilot study", *OECD Working Papers on Finance, Insurance and Private Pensions*, No. 15, OECD Publishing, Paris, *http://dx.doi.org/10.1787/5k9csfs90fr4-en*.

Atkinson A., F-A. Messy, L. Rabinovich and J. Yoong (2015), "Research and literature on financial education for long-term savings and investments" *OECD Working Papers on Finance, Insurance and Private Pensions*, No. 39, OECD Publishing, *http://dx.doi.org/10.1787/5jrtgzfl6g9w-en*.

Atkinson, A., D. Harrison, F.-A. Messy and J. Yermo (2012), "Lessons from national pensions communication campaigns", *OECD Working Papers on Finance, Insurance and Private Pensions*, No. 18, OECD Publishing, *http://dx.doi.org/10.1787/5k98xwz5z09v-en*.

AVIVA (2012), *Tackling the Savings Gap: Engagement and Empowerment. Consumer research into integrated annual pension statements*, London, United Kingdom. *www.aviva.com/data/media-uploads/news/File/RDhub_reports/Tackling%20the%20Savings%20Gap.pdf*.

Banks, J. and Z. Oldfield (2007), "Understanding pensions: Cognitive function, numerical ability and retirement saving", *Fiscal Studies*, Vol. 28, No. 2, pp. 143-170.

Barrett, A., I. Mosca and B.J. Whelan (2013), "(Lack of) pension knowledge", *IZA Discussion Paper*, No. 7596, August 2013, *www.iza.org/en/webcontent/publications/papers/viewAbstract?dp_id=7596*.

Bayer, P.J., B.D. Bernheim and J.K. Scholz (2009), "The effects of financial education in the workplace: Evidence from a survey of employers", *Economic Inquiry*, Vol. 47, No. 4, pp. 605-624.

Benartzi, S. and R. Thaler (2007), "Heuristics and biases in retirement savings behavior", *Journal of Economic Perspectives*, Vol. 21, No. 3, Summer 2007, pp. 81-104.

Bernheim, B.D. and D.M. Garrett (2003), "The effects of financial education in the workplace: evidence from a survey of households", *Journal of Public Economics*, Vol. 87, No. 7, pp. 1487-1519.

Beshears, J., J. Choi, D. Laibson and B.C. Madrian (2013), "Simplification and saving", *Journal of Economic Behavior and Organization*, Vol. 95, pp. 130-145, *www.sciencedirect.com/science/article/pii/S0167268112000583*.

Biggs, A.G. (2010), "Improving the Social Security statement", *Financial Literacy Center Working Paper* No. WR-794-SSA, *www.rand.org/content/dam/rand/pubs/working_papers/2010/RAND_WR794.pdf*.

Brown, J.R. (2009), "Financial education and annuities", *OECD Journal: General Papers*, Vol. 2008/3, *http://dx.doi.org/10.1787/gen_papers-v2008-art20-en*.

Brown, J.R., J.R. Eling, S. Mullainathan and M.V. Wrobel (2008), "Why don't people insure late-life consumption? A framing explanation of the under-annuitization puzzle", *American Economic Review*, Vol. 98, No. 2, pp. 304-309.

Chan, S. and A.H. Stevens (2008), "What you don't know can't help you: pension knowledge and retirement decision-making", *The Review of Economics and Statistics*, Vol. 90, No. 2, pp. 253-266.

Choi, J.J., D. Laibson and B.C. Madrian (2011), "$100 Bills on the sidewalk: Suboptimal investment in 401(k) plans", *The Review of Economics and Statistics*, August 2011, Vol. 93, No. 3, pp. 748-763, *www.mitpressjournals.org/doi/abs/10.1162/REST_a_00100#.VR6T-fmUdHU*.

Choi, J.J., D. Laibson, B.C. Madrian and A. Metrick (2002), "Defined contribution pensions: Plan rules, participant decisions, and the path of least resistance", in J. Poterba (ed.), *Tax Policy and the Economy*, Vol. 16, pp. 67-113, MIT Press, Cambdridge, MA.

Choi, J.J., D. Laibson, B.C. Madrian and A. Metrick (2004), "For better or for worse: Default effects and 401(k) savings behaviour", in D.A. Wise (ed.), *Perspectives on the Economics of Aging*, University of Chicago Press, Chicago, IL, pp. 81-126.

Clark, R.L., and M.B. d'Ambrosio (2003), "Ignorance is not bliss: The importance of financial education", *TIAA-CREF Research Dialogue*, No. 78, pp. 1-14.

Clark, R.L., M.B. d'Ambrosio, A.A. McDermed and K. Sawant (2006), "Retirement plans and saving decisions: the role of information and education", *Journal of Pension Economics and Finance*, Vol. 5, No. 1, pp. 45-67.

Clark, R.L., and M.B. d'Ambrosio (2008), "Adjusting retirement goals and saving behavior: The role of financial education", in A. Lusardi (ed.) *Overcoming the Saving Slump: How to Increase the Effectiveness of Financial Education and Saving Programs*, University of Chicago Press, Chicago, IL.

DiCenzo, J. (2014), *Employees' Retirement Choices, Perceptions and Understanding: A Review of Selected Survey and Empirical Behavioral Decision-Making Research*, Society of Actuaries, March 2014, *www.soa.org/Files/Research/Projects/research-behavioral-dec-retire-report.pdf.*

Dushi, I. and H.M. Iams (2010), "The impact of response error on participation rates and contributions to defined contribution pension plans", *Social Security Bulletin*, Vol. 70, No. 1, *www.socialsecurity.gov/policy/docs/ssb/v70n1/v70n1p45.pdf.*

EBRI (2015), "Debt of the elderly and near elderly, 1992-2013", Employee Benefit Research Institute Notes, January 2015, Vol. 36, No. 1, *www.ebri.org/pdf/notespdf/EBRI_Notes.Jan15.Debt.pdf.*

EBRI and MG&A (Employee Benefit Research Institute and Mathew Greenwald & Associates) (2006), *Retirement Confidence Survey – 2006 Results. www.ebri.org/surveys/rcs/2006/.*

EIOPA (European Insurance and Occupational Pensions Authority) (2013), *Good practices on information provision for DC schemes. Enabling occupational DC scheme members to plan for retirement*, Frankfurt, Germany, *https://eiopa.europa.eu/Publications/Reports/Report_Good_Practices_Info_for_DC_schemes.pdf.*

FCA (Financial Conduct Authority) (2014), *Thematic Review of Annuities*, February 2014, London, UK, *www.fca.org.uk/static/documents/thematic-reviews/tr14-02.pdf.*

Financial Engines (2014), *Claiming Social Security: A Critical & Complex Decision for Retirement Security. Survey Results*, Sunnyvale, CA, *http://corp.financialengines.com/employers/FE_ClaimingSocialSecurity_March2014.pdf.*

Conseil d'Orientation des Retraites (2016), *Les relations entre les assurés et leurs régimes de retraite*. Paris, France, *www.cor-retraites.fr/IMG/pdf/doc-3561.pdf.*

Goda, G.S., C.F. Manchester and A. Sojourner (2012), "What will my account really be worth? An experiment on exponential growth bias and retirement saving", *National Bureau of Economic Research Working Paper*, No. 17927, Cambridge, MA, *www.nber.org/papers/w17927.*

Greenwald, M., A. Kapteyn, O.S. Mitchell and L. Schneider (2010), "What do people know about social security?", *RAND Working Paper* WR-792-SSA, Santa Monica, CA, *www.rand.org/pubs/working_papers/WR792.html.*

Grifoni, A. and F. Messy (2012), "Current status of national strategies for financial education: A comparative analysis and relevant practices", *OECD Working Papers on Finance, Insurance and Private Pensions*, No. 16, OECD Publishing, Paris, *http://dx.doi.org/10.1787/5k9bcwct7xmn-en.*

Gustman, A. and T. Steinmeier (1989), "An analysis of pension benefit formulas, pension wealth and incentives from pensions", *Research in Labor Economics*, Vol. 10, pp. 53-106.

Gustman, A. and T. Steinmeier (2004), "What people don't know about their pensions and social security", in W. Gale, J. Shoven and M. Warshawsky (eds.), *Private Pensions and Public Policies*, Brookings Institution, Washington, DC, pp. 57-125.

Gustman, A., T. Steinmeier and N. Tabatabai (2008), "Do workers know about their pensions? Comparing workers' and employers' pension information," in A. Lusardi (ed.), *Overcoming the Saving Slump: How to Increase the Effectiveness of Financial Education and Saving Programs*, University of Chicago Press, Chicago, IL.

Heinberg A., A.A. Hung, A. Kapteyn, A. Lusardi, A. Savikhin Samek and J. Yoong (2014), "Five steps to planning success. Experimental evidence from U.S. households", *National Bureau of Economic Research Working Paper*, No. 20203, Cambridge, MA, *www.nber.org/papers/w20203.*

Huberman, G. and W. Jiang (2006), "Offering versus choice in 401(k) plans: Equity exposure and number of funds", *Journal of Finance*, Vol. 61, No. 2, pp. 763-801.

Iglesias-Palau, A. (2009), "Pension reform in Chile revisited: What has been learned?", *OECD Social, Employment and Migration Working Papers*, No. 86, OECD Publishing, Paris, *http://dx.doi.org/10.1787/224473276417.*

ILC-UK (2015), *Making the system fit for purpose*. London, UK, *www.ilcuk.org.uk/index.php/publications/publication_details/making_the_system_fit_for_purpose*.

Ionescu L. and E.A. Robles (2014), "Update of IOPS work on fees and charges", *IOPS Working Papers on Effective Pensions Supervision*, No. 20, Paris, *www.iopsweb.org/Working%20Paper%2020%20Update%20on%20IOPS%20Work%20on%20Fees%20and%20Charges%20.pdf*.

IOPS (2011), "Comparative information provided by pension supervisory authorities", *IOPS Working Papers on Effective Pension Supervision*, No. 15, Paris, *www.iopsweb.org/principlesandguidelines/49354396.pdf*.

Iyengar, S.S. and E. Kamenica (2010), "Choice proliferation, simplicity seeking, and asset allocation", *Journal of Public Economics*, Vol. 94, No. 7-8, August 2010, pp. 530-539, *www.sciencedirect.com/science/article/pii/S0047272710000290*.

Iyengar, S.S., G. Huberman and W. Jiang (2004), "How much choice is too much? Contributions to 401(k) retirement plans", in O.S. Mitchell and S.P. Utkus (eds.), *Pension Design and Structure: New Lessons from Behavioral Finance*, Oxford University Press, Oxford, pp. 83-95.

Kahneman, D. and A. Tversky (1979), "Prospect theory: An analysis of decision under risk." *Econometrica*, Vol. 47, No. 2, pp. 263-291.

Knoll, M. (2010), "The role of behavioral economics and behavioral decision-making in Americans' retirement savings decisions", *Social Security Bulletin*, Vol. 70, No. 4.

Laibson, D. (1997), "Golden eggs and hyperbolic discounting", *The Quarterly Journal of Economics*, Vol. 112, No. 2, pp. 443-477.

Larsson, L., A. Sundén and O. Settergren (2008), "Pension information: The annual statement at a glance". *OECD Journal, General papers – Special Issue: Financial education*, Vol. 2008/3, *http://dx.doi.org/10.1787/gen_papers-v2008-art19-en*.

Lewis, S. and F. Messy (2012), "Financial education, savings and investments: An overview", *OECD Working Papers on Finance, Insurance and Private Pensions*, No. 22, OECD Publishing, Paris, *http://dx.doi.org/10.1787/5k94gxrw760v-en*.

Liebman, J.B. and E.F.P. Luttmer (2015), "Would people behave differently if they better understood social security? Evidence from a field experiment", *American Economic Journal: Economic Policy*, Vol. 7, No. 1, pp. 275-99, February.

Lusardi A. and O.S. Mitchell (2011), "Financial literacy and planning: Implications for retirement wellbeing", *National Bureau of Economic Research Working Paper*, No. 17078, Cambridge, MA, *www.nber.org/papers/w17078.pdf*.

Lusardi, A. (2002) "Preparing for retirement: The importance of planning costs", Proceedings of the 95th Annual Conference on Taxation, November 14-16, 2002, Orlando FL, pp. 148-154, National Tax Association, Washington, DC.

Lusardi, A., P.A. Keller and A.M. Keller (2009), "New ways to make people save: A social marketing approach", in Lusardi (ed.), *Overcoming the Saving Slump: How to Increase the Effectiveness of Financial Education and Saving Programs*, University of Chicago Press, Chicago, IL.

Madrian, B.C. and D.F. Shea (2001), "The power of suggestion: Inertia in 401(k) participation and savings behavior", *Quarterly Journal of Economics*, Vol. 116, No. 4, Nov., pp. 1149-1187.

Marshall, K. (2011), "Retiring with debt". *Perspectives on Labour and Income*, Statistics Canada, *www.statcan.gc.ca/pub/75-001-x/2011002/article/11428-eng.htm*.

Mastrobuoni, G. (2011), "The role of information for retirement behavior: Evidence based on the stepwise introduction of the Social Security Statement", *Journal of Public Economics*, Vol. 97, No. 7-8, pp. 913-925.

MBIE (Ministry of Business Innovation and Employment) New Zealand (2015), "Questions and answers: KiwiSaver default scheme providers", *www.mbie.govt.nz/info-services/business/business-law/past-work-older-topics/changes-to-kiwisaver/default-provider-arrangements/documents-image-library/q-and-a.pdf*, accessed online on 18 Jul 2016.

Miranda Pinto, J. (2012) "Proyección de pensión personalizada en Chile: evaluación de su impacto en la decisión de jubilación", Superintendencia de Pensiones, *Documento de Trabajo* No. 53, *www.spensiones.cl/redirect/files/doctrab/DT00053.pdf*.

Mitchell, O. (1988), "Worker knowledge of pensions provisions", *Journal of Labor Economics*, Vol. 6, pp. 21-39.

Money and Pensions Panel (2013), *Basic pension: The default option for labour-market pensions*. Report by the Committee of the Money and Pension Panel, *www.raadtilpenge.dk/~/media/PPP/Pensionsrapport/Basic%20pension_full%20report.ashx*.

O'Connell, A. (2010), "How long do we expect to live? A review of the evidence", *Journal of Population Ageing*, Vol. 4, pp. 185-201, *http://link.springer.com/article/10.1007%2Fs12062-011-9049-1*.

O'Donoghue, T. and M. Rabin (2001), "Choice and procrastination", *The Quarterly Journal of Economics*, Vol. 116, No. 1, pp. 121-160.

O'Donoghue, T. and M. Rabin (1999), "Doing it now or later", *American Economic Review*, Vol. 89, No. 1, pp. 103-124.

OECD (2014), *OECD Pensions Outlook 2014*, OECD Publishing, Paris, *http://dx.doi.org/10.1787/9789264222687-en*.

OECD (2013a), *Pensions at a Glance 2013: OECD and G20 Indicators*, OECD Publishing, Paris, *http://dx.doi.org/10.1787/pension_glance-2013-en*.

OECD (2013b), *Women and Financial Education: Evidence, Policy Responses and Guidance*, OECD Publishing, Paris, *http://dx.doi.org/10.1787/9789264202733-en*.

OECD (2012a), *OECD Pensions Outlook 2012*, OECD Publishing, Paris, *http://dx.doi.org/10.1787/9789264169401-en*.

OECD (2012b), *The OECD Roadmap for the Good Design of Defined Contribution Pension Plans*, *www.oecd.org/daf/fin/private-pensions/50582753.pdf*.

OECD (2012c), "A policy roadmap for defined contribution pension", in OECD, *Pensions Outlook 2012*, Chapter 6, OECD Publishing, Paris, *http://dx.doi.org/10.1787/9789264169401-en*.

OECD (2008a), *Recommendation on Good Practices for Financial Education Relating to Private Pensions*, *www.oecd.org/pensions/private-pensions/40537843.pdf*.

OECD (2008b), *Improving Financial Education and Awareness on Insurance and Private Pensions*, OECD Publishing, Paris, *http://dx.doi.org/10.1787/9789264046399-en*.

OECD (2005), "Improving Financial Literacy: Analysis of Issues and Policies", *Financial Market Trends*, Vol. 2005/2, *http://dx.doi.org/10.1787/fmt-v2005-art11-en*.

OECD (2005), *Private Pensions: OECD Classification and Glossary*, OECD Publishing, Paris, *http://dx.doi.org/10.1787/9789264017009-en-fr*.

OECD (2005c), *Recommendation on Principles and Good Practices for Financial Education and Awareness*, OECD, *www.oecd.org/daf/fin/financial-education/35108560.pdf*.

OECD/INFE (2015a), *2015 OECD/INFE Toolkit to measure financial literacy and financial inclusion*. *www.oecd.org/daf/fin/financial-education/2015_OECD_INFE_Toolkit_Measuring_Financial_Literacy.pdf*.

OECD/INFE (2015b), *National Strategies for Financial Education: OECD/INFE Policy Handbook*, *www.oecd.org/daf/fin/financial-education/national-strategies-for-financial-education-policy-handbook.htm*.

OECD/INFE (2014), *OECD/INFE Guidelines for private and not-for-profit stakeholders in financial education*, *www.oecd.org/daf/fin/financial-education/guidelines-private-not-for-profit-financial-education.pdf*.

OECD/INFE (2012), *High-level Principles on National Strategies for Financial Education*. *www.oecd.org/finance/financial-education/OECD_INFE_High_Level_Principles_National_Strategies_Financial_Education_APEC.pdf*.

Paklina, N. (2014), "Role of pension supervisory authorities in automatic enrolment", *IOPS Working Papers on Effective Pensions Supervision*, No. 22, *www.iopsweb.org/WP_22_Role-Pension-Supervisory-Authorities-Automatic-Enrolment%20.pdf*.

Queisser, M. and E.R. Whitehouse (2006), "Neutral or fair?: Actuarial concepts and pension-system design", *OECD Social, Employment and Migration Working Papers*, No. 40, OECD Publishing, Paris, *http://dx.doi.org/10.1787/351382456457*.

Rinaldi A. and E. Giacomel (2008), "Information to members of DC pension plans: Conceptual framework and international trends", *IOPS Working Paper*, No. 5, *www.iopsweb.org/41269701.pdf*.

SHRM (Society for Human Resources Management) (2014), *2014 SHRM Survey on Financial Wellness and Education*, Alexandria, VA, *www.shrm.org/research/surveyfindings/articles/pages/2014-financial-wellness.aspx*.

Smith, B.A. and K.A. Couch (2014), "How effective is the Social Security Statement? Informing younger workers about social security", *Social Security Bulletin*, Vol. 74, No. 4, 2014.

Song, C. (2012), "Financial illiteracy and pension contributions: A field experiment on compound interest in China", University of California – *Berkeley Working paper*, *https://works.bepress.com/changcheng_song/1/*.

Soto, M. and B.A. Butrica (2009), "Will automatic enrollment reduce employer contributions to 401(k) plans?", Center for Retirement Research at Boston College, *Working paper* No. 2009-33.

Stańko, D. and N. Paklina (2014), "Supervising the distribution of annuities and other forms of pension pay-out", *IOPS Working Papers on Effective Pensions Supervision*, No. 21, *www.iopsweb.org/WP_21_Supervising-Distribution-Annuities-Pension%20Pay-out%20.pdf*.

Swedish Pensions Agency (2011), *Surveys about the Orange Envelope of 2011*, Stockholm, Sweden, *https://secure.pensionsmyndigheten.se/download/18.70e56c27145a7fdc958284a8/1305534269395/The+orange+envelope+surveys+in+2011_2011-04-28_cn.pdf*.

Thaler, R. and S. Benartzi (2004), "Save More Tomorrow: Using behavioral economics to increase employee saving", *Journal of Political Economy*, Vol. 112, No. 1, pp. S164-S187.

Yoong, J. (2011), "Can behavioural economics be used to make financial education more effective?", in OECD, *Improving Financial Education Efficiency: OECD-Bank of Italy Symposium on Financial Literacy*, OECD Publishing, Paris, *http://dx.doi.org/10.1787/9789264108219-6-en*.

OECD Pensions Outlook 2016

Chapter 6

Civil service pensions: Toward a unified system with the private sector*

This chapter examines the pension systems for civil servants in OECD countries, concentrating on those countries that have different rules, or even systems, for civil servants and private sector workers. The chapter starts with a discussion of the history and recent reforms of civil service pension systems including interactions with the private sector. The key parameter values of the civil servant schemes are compared with those for private sector workers, followed by analysis of the future pension promises for workers starting their career today. A discussion of the implications for the ongoing financial commitment for the state for current and future retirees in the public sector follows. The final section summarises key findings and draws policy implications, highlighting the benefits of an integrated framework for all workers.

*The statistical data for Israel are supplied by and under the responsibility of the relevant Israeli authorities. The use of such data by the OECD is without prejudice to the status of the Golan Heights, East Jerusalem and Israeli settlements in the West Bank under the terms of international law.

Historically, civil servants and, more generally, public sector employees were commonly among the first to receive old-age benefits, after the military. While the motivation for the provision of pensions to the general public was primarily to provide at least a minimum income in retirement and to lower poverty levels among the elderly, the reasoning behind civil servant pensions was slightly different. The main objectives of pension provision for government workers were to: secure their independence; make a public sector career more attractive; and shift the cost of remunerating public servants into the future (Palacios and Whitehouse, 2006).

The definition of a civil servant varies by country, as it can include the military, police, teachers, public utility workers, healthcare workers as well as both central and local government workers. For the purpose of this chapter, "civil servant" is defined as a central government worker or a federal government employee. The wider definition including, for example, the military, teachers and local government workers, will be referred to as "public sector".

In most OECD countries, certain categories of workers in the public sector are covered by an independent pension system. This most commonly applies to the military, firefighters and the police. For these groups, which are exposed to increased occupational hazard, retirement ages are set earlier than for private sector workers, even in those countries where all groups fall under the same scheme. Other occupations typically covered in separate schemes include teachers and judges. The largest schemes, however, are those that cover local government employees and civil servants (central or federal government employees). The analysis within this chapter will concentrate on civil servants as defined above.

In many instances, civil service pension schemes remained ring-fenced and were excluded from pension policies and reforms affecting private sector workers. Over the last 20 years, however, many countries closed civil service pension schemes for new entrants and enrolled workers entering the civil service in the main private sector scheme. But a number of OECD countries still maintain a dual system with sometimes large differences in rules and entitlements for civil servants compared to those working in the private sector.

This chapter focuses on those countries that still have separate schemes for civil servants and is structured as follows. Section 6.1 shows how civil service pensions interact with those for private sector workers, particularly whether they are separate or integrated or if civil servants receive a supplement. Section 6.2 highlights the reforms made to civil servant pensions over the last 25 years. Section 6.4 then details the main rules and parameters for civil service pension systems, such as those related to the retirement age, length of service, contributions, indexation and accrual rates and compares these with those for private sector workers. Section 6.4 provides estimates of full-career replacement rates and pension wealth for both civil servants and private sector workers. Section 6.5 discusses the current cost of civil service pensions and how this might evolve in the coming decades based on current employment levels. Finally Section 6.6 draws some policy implications, including why an integrated framework for all workers, public and private, is needed.

6.1. Institutional arrangements

Civil service versus private sector pension arrangement

Like the pension systems covering private sector workers, civil servant pension schemes have been subject to numerous reforms changing their structure and organisation during the past thirty years. Today, only four countries in the OECD have an entirely separate scheme for civil servants: Belgium, France, Germany and Korea, as shown in Table 6.1.

Another ten countries have a top-up component for civil servants above and beyond the mandatory schemes that exist for private sector workers. For example, in the United Kingdom all workers are covered by the new state pension, which is the only mandatory component; civil servants have a mandatory occupational pension as a top-up whereas private sector workers can choose to participate in the new automatic enrolment scheme as occupational pensions are not mandatory.

The remaining 21 OECD countries can be split into two further categories: 17 countries have no special scheme for civil servants, all employees being covered under the same mandatory schemes, at least for new labour market entrants; and the remaining four countries have technically separate schemes for civil servants, but they offer benefits similar to those for private sector workers. In many cases, the only difference is that the pension is managed and granted by a different authority while the actual legislation and parameter values are identical.

Table 6.1. **Institutional arrangements for pensions covering civil servants vs. private sector workers**

Fully integrated	Separate but similar benefits	Fully integrated with top-up	Entirely separate
Chile (1981)	Finland (1995)	Australia	Belgium
Czech Republic	Luxembourg (1999)	Austria (2004, 2009)	France
Estonia	Netherlands	Canada	Germany
Greece (2011)	Sweden	Denmark	Korea
Hungary		Iceland	
Israel (2002)		Ireland (1995)	
Italy (1995/2008)		Mexico (2007)	
Japan (2015)		Norway	
Latvia		United Kingdom	
New Zealand (2007)		United States (1984)	
Poland			
Portugal (2006)			
Slovak Republic			
Slovenia			
Spain (2011)			
Switzerland			
Turkey (2006)			

Note: The years in brackets refer to the date from which newly hired civil servants are no longer covered by an entirely separate scheme, but are rather in the fully integrated private sector scheme or have a top-up. For Italy new civil servants were covered by the private sector scheme from 1995 onwards, while in 2008 future contributions for all civil servants were under the private sector rules. For Austria the pension was fully integrated from 2004 but an additional top-up was introduced in 2009. For Finland the unifying process began in 1995, before which there was more of a top-up element to the system. All countries without a date have been in that particular category for at least the last 35 years.

In many countries, civil servants schemes are in a period of transition: new entrants are covered under the new system while those with many years of service remain in the old scheme. For example, civil servants hired prior to 2011 in Greece are covered under a separate scheme and only those who have been first employed after this date are covered by the mandatory components applicable for private sector workers. The same applies in Chile, Israel, Italy, Japan, Portugal, Spain and Turkey, and technically New Zealand, though all residents are covered by the tax-financed basic scheme with no additional mandatory scheme existing for private sector workers. Austria, Ireland and the United States used to have entirely separate schemes; now the schemes are fully integrated for the mandatory components applicable to private sector workers, but civil servants have an additional occupational scheme which acts as a top-up. Reforms are discussed in more detail in section 6.2 and the full details are provided in the annex.

Vesting periods

Pension arrangements for civil servants might restrain job mobility in an inefficient way. They were designed for a situation when people spent all or most of their career in the civil service from their entry until retirement. Pension schemes can penalise mobile workers through vesting periods, below which no pension entitlement is granted. Half of OECD countries have such vesting periods for civil servants (Figure 6.1). In a further nine countries, although there is a vesting period it is at most one year and in most cases even one contribution is sufficient to be eligible to a future pension.

Figure 6.1. **Vesting periods for civil service pensions**

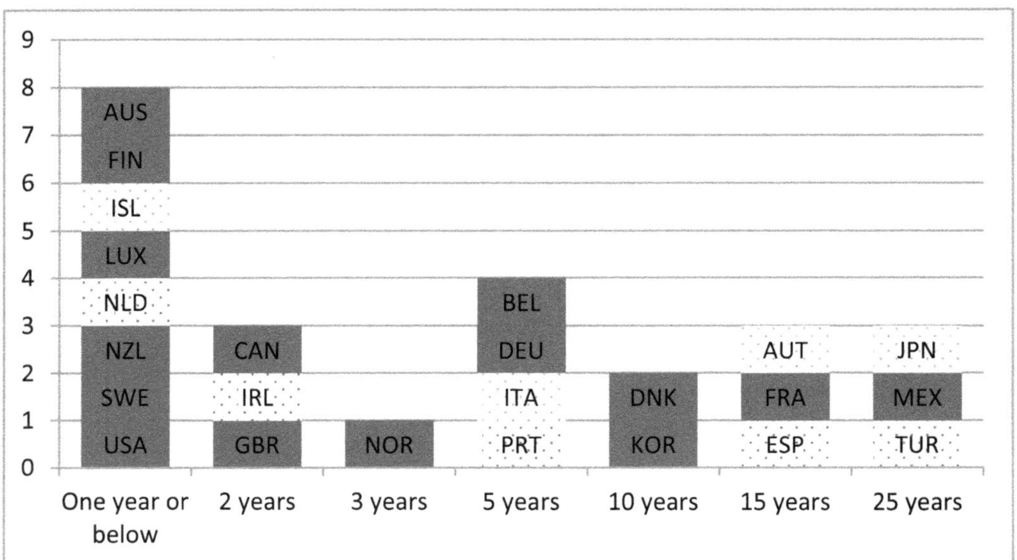

Note: Countries with solid fill reflect rules for new civil servants today. The gradient fill reflects the rules which applied immediately prior to new hires being enrolled in the private sector scheme.

StatLink http://dx.doi.org/10.1787/888933426805

In Austria, 15 years of contribution are required to be eligible, as in Portugal and Spain for those covered by the pre-reform civil service schemes. In Spain, 15 years of contributions are required for any pension, but the contributions can be split between both the civil service and the private sector. An even longer vesting period of 25 years applies in Japan, Mexico and Turkey. The minimum duration in Korea was 20 years prior to the 2015 reform when it was lowered to 10 years; at the same time, the accrual rate was reduced and the maximum number of years that are counted for a pension was increased. In all countries civil servants who have not met the required duration receive a lump-sum at the point of retirement which can be used to generate a stream of pension payments or for other purposes.

Portability

Vesting periods are not the only obstacle to labour mobility. If workers leave the civil service before they are eligible for retirement, for example at mid-career, they may sacrifice some of the benefits they would have been entitled to on the already contributed part had they completed a full career in the civil service. In those countries that fall into the category "separate but similar benefits" (Table 6.1) this is not a concern; the rights gained in the civil service are either transferred to the earnings-related scheme that covers the now private sector worker, or their rights gained are preserved in a vested pension, and their entitlement to the basic or targeted schemes are maintained, as they apply to all.

In the United Kingdom the preserved pension that has been accumulated within the civil service scheme is indexed to prices after the individual moves to the private sector, rather than by wages if they had remained employed in the civil service. Therefore, upon retirement, the pension value related to the contributions made in the public sector is likely to be much lower than if the worker had remained in the civil service, due to real-wage growth in the intervening years. However, in some countries, such as Korea, for example, the benefit is calculated as if the beneficiary had remained in the civil service, using as earnings-base the pay the person received when they left valorised with the civil service pay evolution.

In Germany, some regional or local public servants who leave the civil service prior to retirement have their rights to a public sector pension transferred fully to the national scheme that covers private sector workers, which has a much lower accrual rate than the civil service scheme. There is also a ceiling to contributions under the private sector scheme, equivalent to around 150% of the OECD estimated average earnings, whereas there is no ceiling in the civil service scheme. Rights acquired above the private sector pension ceiling are not credited when the pension is transferred. Therefore, workers at higher earnings levels may lose a substantial part of their pension entitlements as a result of their move to the private sector. This does not apply though to Federal civil servants, or to public sector employees in nearly half of the regional Länders, who have the option of ring-fencing their public sector pensions, rather than transferring, though they need to have served at least seven years in the public sector, with at least five of these years in Federal employment (called "Altersgeld"). At retirement the amount of benefits is based on what they would have received, with the civil servants' old-age pension depending on their last salary and time spent in the public service, minus 15%. Similar rules exist in the regions ("Länder") of Baden-Württemberg, Bremen, Hamburg, Hesse, Lower Saxony and Saxony. Furthermore, these regions do not apply the reduction of 15% and only require 5 instead of 7 years of service. Full details of the penalties applicable to early exit from the civil service are given in Table 6.2.

Table 6.2. **Portability and preservation of pension rights**

Treatment	Country	Details
Full transferability	Finland, Mexico, Netherlands, Sweden	Workers transfer their rights to the private sector mandatory (or quasi-mandatory) occupational plans with similar benefits or rights gained are preserved in a vested pension
Full preservation		Workers' accrued rights are indexed in line with civil service pay between leaving and retirement, so the benefit level is fully maintained
Partial preservation	France United Kingdom	Workers' accrued rights are indexed in line with prices between leaving and retirement, so the value of future benefit will decline relative to earnings
Loss of privilege	Germany	Unless they do not benefit from the rules of "*Altersgeld*", employees lose civil service pension rights but are credited with rights in the national scheme, at a lower rate, with no credit for acquired rights above the private sector ceiling

6.2. Recent reforms

Over the last 20 years the pension rules that apply to workers in the private sector have changed in virtually all OECD countries (OECD, 2007; OECD, 2009; OECD, 2013; and OECD, 2015). Reforms have included measures such as increasing pension eligibility age, increasing contributions or duration of career needed for a full pension or reducing accrual rates. All of these measures were designed to improve the financial sustainability of the pension system. In addition, a number of countries have moved from defined-benefit to defined-contribution schemes, thereby transferring all or part of the risk from the employer or state to the individual, even if ultimately individuals bear the risk of reforming unsustainable defined-benefit schemes.

For civil servants, covered under separate legislation, there have also been a number of reforms. For civil servants the majority of pension schemes remain of defined-benefit type, though their generosity has been reduced in many countries, through either increasing contributions or reducing the associated accrual rates. The reforms made to the pension systems within the civil service can be classified under a number of different headings as shown in Table 6.3.

Table 6.3. **Reforms to civil service pension schemes over the last 25 years**

Reform	Country
Increase in pension age	Australia, Belgium, Canada, Denmark, Finland, France, Germany, Italy, Japan, Korea, Portugal, Spain, Sweden, United Kingdom
Restriction of early retirement	Austria, Australia, Belgium, Canada, Finland, Germany, Italy, Korea, Portugal, Spain, Sweden, United Kingdom
Reduction of pension generosity or increase in career length	Austria, Finland, France, Germany, Greece, Iceland, Korea, Norway, Portugal, Spain, United Kingdom
Increase in contributions	Austria, Canada, Finland, France, Greece, Israel, Italy, Japan, Korea, Netherlands, Portugal, Sweden, United Kingdom
Integration/alignment of civil service with the general state scheme	Austria, Canada, Greece, Israel, Italy, Japan, Luxembourg, New Zealand, Portugal, Spain, Turkey

For example, the 2002 reform to the civil service pension in the United Kingdom increased employee contributions from 1.5% to 3.5% for new entrants. At the same time the accrual rate was increased from 1.25% to 1.67%. Part of the increase in accrual was financed by removing the lump-sum payment of 3.75% of final salary for each year of contribution that existed for those first employed in the civil service prior to October 2002. Therefore, although the future pension benefit increased by around one-third, the cost to the employee more than doubled and the lump-sum payment was also lost. Subsequent reforms have since changed the system further, by again increasing the contribution level and also raising the future retirement age (full details shown in Annex 6.A1). In Korea, the 2015 reform reduced the accrual rate from 1.9% to 1.7% whilst increasing contributions from 7% for both employees and employers to 9%. The full career pension remains at a similar level, as shown later, as the maximum number of contribution years also increased, from 33 years to 36 years.

Increasing contributions or pension age have been the most common reforms over the last 25 years, affecting half of OECD countries that had or still have separate pension schemes for civil servants. For example, in Canada employee contributions were increased initially in 2006 and then again in 2013, with the long-term plan of equalising contributions between employees and those paid by the government to balance the system.

In all countries the long-term retirement ages of civil servants have been brought into line with those of the private sector workers. However, there are long transition periods for civil servants as the increases normally only apply to new hires. Overall, 11 countries have enrolled new civil servant employees into the same system as private sector workers (see the last row of Table 6.3), eliminating the difference between sectors for new employees. For example, in New Zealand all new employees, irrespective of sector, have been automatically enrolled in KiwiSaver since its introduction in 2007, though they can opt out entirely or take contribution holidays. The gradual closure of civil servant specific schemes to new entrants in 2008 (State Sector Retirement Savings Scheme) and 2012 (Individual Retirement Plan) means that all new workers are now under the same rules and over time the old civil service schemes will be less relevant.

Alternatively governments have legislated that new employees in the civil service from a particular date will no longer be enrolled in the separate scheme but will rather be covered by the mandatory private sector system, e.g. from May 2008 for Turkey and January 2011 for Spain. With the future revenues from contributions to the (old) civil servant scheme being diminished as a result, the government will have to finance an increasing proportion of former civil servant pensions from other sources. Those countries with a defined-contribution private sector scheme will face a transitional cost as all contributions from new civil servants are ring-fenced.

6.3. Differences between civil service and private sector rules

Although reforms have led to a closer alignment of the pension systems of civil servants and private sector workers a number of differences remain, even for current new entrants or for those that have only been in the civil service for a relatively short period of time. This section focuses on these differences, particularly for those countries that fall into either the entirely separate or fully integrated with top-up categories. The cases of countries with fully integrated schemes but having only recently aligned their pension systems, such as Portugal and Spain, are also discussed, as many workers will still be covered under the old rules.

The most obvious difference between civil service and private sector schemes is that civil servants have been eligible to retire at an earlier age. However, as many countries have now enrolled new employees in the private sector scheme these differences will be phased out over time. In addition, for those countries that have maintained a partial difference (columns 2 and 3 of Table 6.1) there is normally at least one component of the pension system applicable to all workers, so for a full pension the retirement ages are effectively the same. Even the four countries which still have entirely separate systems are aligning the pension ages. For example, in Korea the age for civil servants is gradually increasing from 60 to 65, dependent on when the individual began contributing to the government employees' pension; in the long term, all workers irrespective of sector will only be able to retire on a full pension at age 65. Similar reforms have been undertaken in Germany, where the pensionable age of civil servants will rise gradually – as in the private sector – from 65 to 67.

The length of contributions required for a full pension may also differ between schemes. For example, in Mexico private sector employees need to contribute for around 24 years (1 250 weeks) before they become eligible to receive a pension, whilst civil servants have to contribute one year longer. In Spain, a full pension is payable at age 65 after 36 years of contributions for private sector workers retiring in 2016 (increasing to 38.5 years by 2027), whereas it is only 35 years for workers who remain in the civil service scheme (employed before 1 January 2011), with retirement at age 60. Differences in retirement age add to the inequities in the level of pension payments.

Accrual rates, i.e. the rates at which the pension accumulates for every year of contribution – a key factor to calculate pension benefits – differ between civil servants and the private sector. Table 6.4 shows that the accrual rates for civil servants are at least equal to those for private sector workers in virtually all countries.

Table 6.4. **Comparison of accrual rates at average earnings between civil servants and private sector workers**

	Civil service accrual rate	Private sector accrual rate
Belgium	1.67	1.03
Canada	1.375	0.64
Denmark	1.54	N/A
Finland	1.5-4.5	1.5-4.5
France	1.40+0.08	0.99+0.29
Germany	1.79	0.83
Greece[1]	1.714	0.8-1.5
Iceland	1.9	1.47
Italy[1]	2.36	1.46
Korea	1.7-1.9	0.87
Luxembourg[1]	1.8-2.08	1.92
Norway	1.5	0.94
Portugal[1]	2	2.3-2
Sweden	0.95	0.95
United Kingdom	2.32	N/A

1. Civil service accrual rates apply to those who started their careers prior to abolition/alignment of separate pension schemes.

Note: For Canada a 2% replacement rate applies before age 65 on all replaced income. At age 65, 2% only applies to the portion of replaced income above the income level subject to the general state scheme. 1.375% is the prevailing replacement rate applied to most income for the longest duration. For Denmark the accrual rate varies from 1.75% per year for the first 16 years, 1.5% between years 17 and 32 and 1% thereafter. In Korea the accrual is being reduced from 1.9 to 1.7 following the 2015 reform. In Luxembourg one-third of salary is given for the first 10 years and 1/60th of salary per year thereafter, but the maximum accrual for a 40-year career has been gradually reduced from 83.33% to 72% from 1999. Private sector accrual rates are sourced from *Pensions at a Glance 2015* (OECD, 2015, p. 129).

StatLink http://dx.doi.org/10.1787/888933426865

The accrual rates for civil servants in both Canada and Norway are both well over twice those of private sector workers, though in Canada in particular many private sector workers will have additional occupational schemes provided by the employer, but these are not mandatory; in France and Germany civil servant accrual rates are just under double the level of those for private sector workers. In Denmark and the United Kingdom, there is no mandatory defined-benefit coverage for private sector workers and therefore there is no associated accrual rate. Denmark has defined-contribution schemes whilst in the United Kingdom there is no mandatory earnings-related scheme.

Beyond the accrual rates, the level of contribution also matters greatly to assess the generosity of pension promises. To simplify somehow (as e.g. wage thresholds for contributions also play a role), a similar generosity, measured by internal rates of return, would imply that if accrual rates are x% larger in one sector (the civil service in that case based on Table 6.4) then contribution rates are x% larger too. However, in most cases, the differences in accrual rates shown in Table 6.4 are not matched by differences in contribution rates paid by employees (Table 6.5); the employer, namely the government, is therefore contributing at a much higher level than many employers in the private sector to maintain financial balances given past commitments.

Table 6.5. **Contribution rates to first and second tier pensions by civil servants and private sector workers at average wage**

	Private sector		Civil service	
	Employee	Employer	Employee	Employer
Australia		9.5		15.4
Austria	10.25	12.55	10.25	13.3
Belgium	7.5	8.86	7.5	
Canada	4.95	4.95	9.05/11.04[1]	
Denmark	0.54	12.82	0.54	
Finland	5.7-7.2	18	5.7-7.2	
France	10.65	14.23	9.54	
Germany	9.5	9.5		
Iceland	4	15.79	4	19.79
Israel	9.25	15.75	**2**	
Italy	9.19	23.81	**10.8**	
Japan	8.56	8.56	**8.285**	
Korea	4.5	4.5	9	
Luxembourg	8	8	8	
Mexico	1.125	5.15	6.125	5.175
Norway	8.2	14.1	8.2	
Portugal	8.527	18.412	**11**	
Spain	4.7	23.6	**4.7**	
Sweden	7	11.4	7	
Turkey	9	11	**9**	

1. 9.05% applies to earnings eligible for replacement under the general state scheme (Canada Pension Plan), 11.04% applies to earnings above this threshold. New entrants as of 1 January 2013 have slightly lower contribution rates to reflect the higher pension age that applies to them.

Note: Figures for employers have only been included where there are specific legislated differences between civil servants and private sector workers.

Countries in **bold** refer to the old civil service systems before alignment.

Source: OECD pension models.

StatLink http://dx.doi.org/10.1787/888933426872

Of the 11 countries that have higher accrual rates for civil servants, whether new entrants or those under the old system, only four have a higher contribution level. Therefore the remaining countries will have a more generous return on the contributions of employees for civil servants than for private sector workers. In fact, in Germany the contribution level is actually lower despite the higher accrual rate as federal civil servants don't make any contribution towards the pension.

Employer contributions are specifically legislated to be higher for civil servants in only three OECD countries, Australia, Iceland and Mexico, with the former having no mandatory employee component. Civil servant contributions tend, across OECD countries, to be at least at the level of their private sector counterparts. Yet, the effective contribution levels of the government as an employer, which is required to finance the generous accrual rates, need to be much higher than those paid by private sector employers. Restoring the balance would thus be achieved by reducing accrual rates applying to civil servants (and therefore replacement rates, see Section 6.4) and/or increasing employees' contribution rates for civil servants (and therefore lowering net wages).

In Korea for current civil servants, and in Portugal for those employed prior to 2006, the employee contribution level is around 4 percentage points above that for private sector workers. Conversely, in Israel (for those employed prior to 2002) the contribution level for civil servants is below one-quarter that of the private sector workers. It is not only defined-benefit schemes that show differences in contributions as in Mexico, the contributions made by civil servants are considerably higher than in the private sector at 6.125% and 1.125% respectively. The contribution levels to the civil service pension in Australia are also much higher than for private sector workers (15.4% and 9.5% respectively [increasing to 12%]), but they are entirely financed through employer contributions.

Only Germany and Turkey index civil service pensions to wages (Table 6.2), with all other countries either indexing solely to prices or to a combination of wages and prices. In Germany private sector workers pensions are also indexed to wages, so there is no difference between sectors. However, although civil servants in Turkey who started their career after 2006 have their pensions indexed to prices as is the case for private sector workers, those civil servants working prior to 2006 still benefit from the more generous wage indexation. Austria, Denmark, Finland, Greece, Japan, Luxembourg, the Netherlands, Norway, Portugal, Spain and Sweden all have a mixed indexation policy for both civil servants and private sector workers (Table 6.2), but the same rules apply to both sectors. Therefore, the relative position of both former civil servants and private sector employees remains constant as people age during retirement.

Table 6.6. **Indexation of current pensions in payment**

	Private sector	Civil Service	Country	Private sector	Civil Service
Australia	Prices	**Prices**	Japan	Mixed	Mixed
Austria	Mixed	**Mixed**	Korea	Prices	**Prices**
Belgium	Prices	**Prices**	Luxembourg	Mixed	Mixed
Canada	Prices	**Prices**	Mexico	Prices	**Prices**
Denmark	Mixed	Mixed	Netherlands	Mixed	**Mixed**
Finland	Mixed	**Mixed**	New Zealand	Prices	Prices
France	Prices	**Prices**	Norway	Mixed	**Mixed**
Germany	Wages	**Wages**	Portugal	Mixed	Mixed
Greece	Mixed	Mixed	Spain	Mixed	Mixed
Iceland	Prices	**Prices**	Sweden	Mixed	**Mixed**
Ireland	Prices	**Prices**	Turkey	Prices	Wages
Israel	Prices	Prices	United Kingdom	Prices	**Prices**
Italy	Prices	Prices	United States	Prices	**Prices**

Note: For Germany the indexation rules refer to civil servants of the federal state only. Countries in **bold** refer to the systems available for new civil servants. For Finland there is no difference in indexation for old or new employees.

Table 6.7 summarises the information given in this section and shows the relative position of civil servants to their private sector counterparts.

6.4. Future theoretical pension entitlements

The value of pension entitlements depends on the individual career trajectory. Theoretical cases based on a full career for private sector workers across the earnings distribution are analysed in the biennial Pensions at a Glance series. Comparing these estimates with estimates of pension entitlements of civil servants helps to quantify the differences that exist across the pension systems, either under the current rules or for those that existed in the old civil service schemes. It is important, however, to keep in mind that focusing on full-career workers undermines the risks of career breaks, which are typically larger in the private sector, and the negative impact of those breaks on pension levels.

As discussed above, the rules differ between the civil service and private sector pension systems in many countries. As a reminder of Table 6.1 there are now only four OECD

Table 6.7. Comparison of pension rules of civil servants relative to private sector workers

	Accrual	Contribution	Indexation		Accrual	Contribution	Indexation
Australia		Same	Same	Japan		Same	Same
Austria		Same	Same	Korea	Higher	Higher	Same
Belgium	Higher	Same	Same	Luxembourg	Higher	Same	Same
Canada	Higher	Higher	Same	Mexico		Higher	Same
Denmark	n.c.	Same	Same	Netherlands			Same
Finland	Same	Same	Same	New Zealand			Same
France	Higher	Higher	Same	Norway	Higher	Same	Same
Germany	Higher	Lower	Same	Portugal	Same	Higher	Same
Greece	Higher		Same	Spain		Same	Same
Iceland	Higher	Same	Same	Sweden	Higher	Same	Same
Ireland			Same	Turkey		Same	Higher
Israel		Lower	Same	United Kingdom	n.c.		Same
Italy	Higher	Higher	Same	United States			Same

Note: Blank cells indicate that the indicator is not applicable to the country; n.c. means not comparable. Both Denmark and the United Kingdom do not have a mandatory defined-benefit scheme for private sector workers so their accrual rates for civil servants are not comparable.

StatLink http://dx.doi.org/10.1787/888933426889

countries that maintain a separate pension system for civil servants; a further ten have at least one separate element, normally in the form of a top-up for civil servants and four more have technically separate schemes that lead to similar benefits. Of the remaining countries eight have aligned their pension systems over the last twenty years and their replacement rates based on the old system will be covered separately, as many current government employees are still covered under these systems.

The modelling results for civil servants cover only the mandatory components of the pension scheme, as data for voluntary civil service pensions is not readily available. Voluntary occupational or personal pensions cover at least 40% of the private sector workforce in a few countries; for these countries the voluntary component is also added for reference. The replacement rates, presented in Figure 6.2, cover workers entering the labour force today in the civil service or private sector and working a full career at average earnings (so workers are compared at the same earnings level across sectors), until the respective retirement age which opens access to a full pension. For all countries in Figure 6.2, the full pension (from all components) is obtained at the same age in the private- and public sector.

The replacement rates for full-career civil servants vary from 41% in Mexico to 106% in the United Kingdom, and the ranking across countries is very different from that obtained for private sector workers. Replacement rates are higher for civil servants in virtually all OECD countries. For mandatory schemes, the average difference across countries is 20 percentage points, with the largest gaps in the United Kingdom and the United States at 84 and 52 percentage points, respectively. Replacement rates for civil servants are less than 4 percentage points higher in Australia and are identical in Finland, Luxembourg, the Netherlands and Sweden. When voluntary schemes are included the average gap is reduced to 12 percentage points, with the largest gap again in the United Kingdom at 55 percentage points while the gap for the United States is then reduced to 19 percentage points; virtually all OECD countries still have higher pensions for civil servants.

In sum, the four countries with entirely separate schemes, Belgium, France, Germany and Korea, have substantially higher replacement rates for civil servants, although to a much lesser extent for France. Many countries with fully integrated schemes with top-up

Figure 6.2. **Long-term gross replacement rates for civil service and private sector average earners, entering at age 20 in 2014, %**

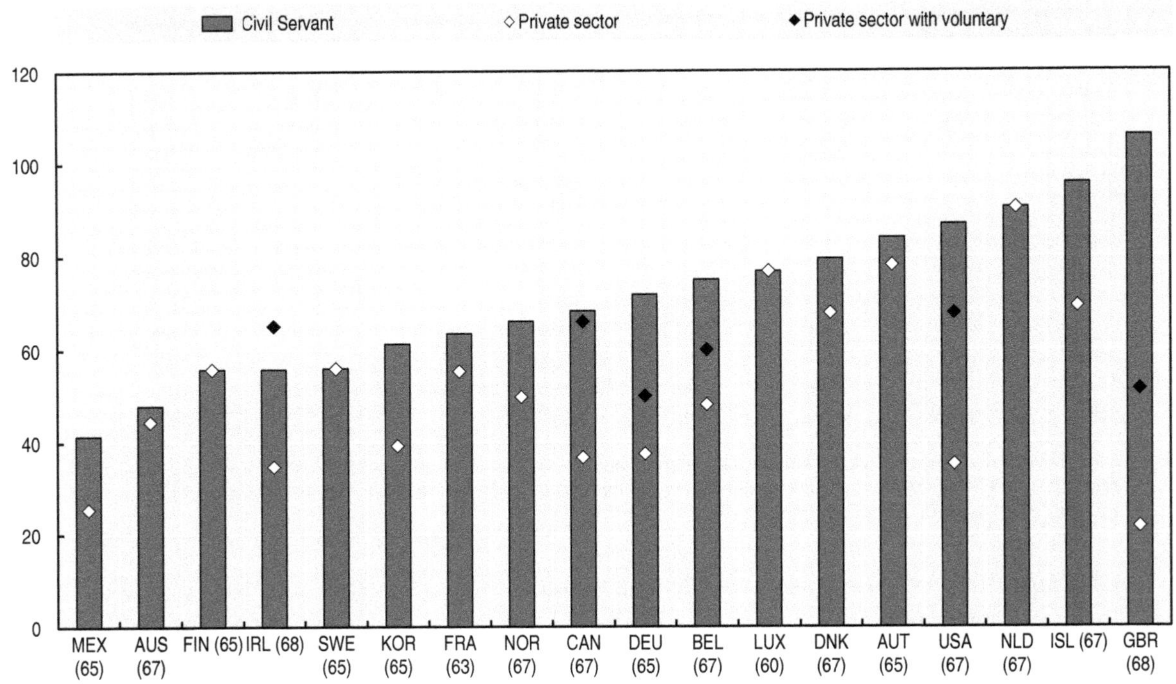

Note: Retirement age (in brackets) is the same for both civil servants and private sector workers.
Source: OECD pension models.

StatLink http://dx.doi.org/10.1787/888933426812

also show huge differences, although there is more heterogeneity within that group. The gap across sectors is large in Iceland, Mexico, Norway, the United Kingdom and the United States, while they are minimal in Australia and Austria.

In Ireland and Canada, the gap even disappears when voluntary components are taken into account. In Ireland, it is even negative although only for those private sector workers who choose to make a voluntary contribution to the defined-contribution pension; otherwise, the replacement rate is 35% for average earners (against 65% including the voluntary component), below that of government workers. Civil servants in Ireland are entitled to a lump-sum payment at the time of retirement, up to a maximum of 150% of the final annual salary; the assumption here is that the lump-sum is annuitised in line with the OECD methodology. In Canada, the voluntary component closes the pension gap from around 30 percentage points without it to 2 percentage points; both civil servants and private sector workers have in that case replacement rates around two-thirds of their previous earnings.

In the United Kingdom, even if private sector workers take up the voluntary component, the civil service replacement rate is still over twice that in the private sector. Without this voluntary component it is nearly five times the level applying to private sector workers (who then rely solely on the basic pension, for which civil servants are also eligible). The United Kingdom has changed the civil service pension scheme more than any other country over the last 20 years, with a total of four different schemes still being applicable to many current workers. The pension has changed from a final salary scheme under both the Classic and Premium schemes to a career average scheme as under Nuvos and Alpha (for details of the four schemes, see Annex 6.A1). The retirement ages have also increased considerably, with members of Classic able to retire with a full pension equivalent to 50% of final salary after 40 years of contribution at age 60 as well as a lump-sum equivalent to 150% of final salary (with the state pension component added when eligible), whereas the newest scheme, Alpha, has the retirement age linked to that of the new State Pension and so will be 68 in the long term, but has a replacement rate of over 100%, as shown in Figure 6.3, for the full 48-year career.

Figure 6.3. **Long-term replacement rates for civil servants and private sector average earners, before the civil service reform**

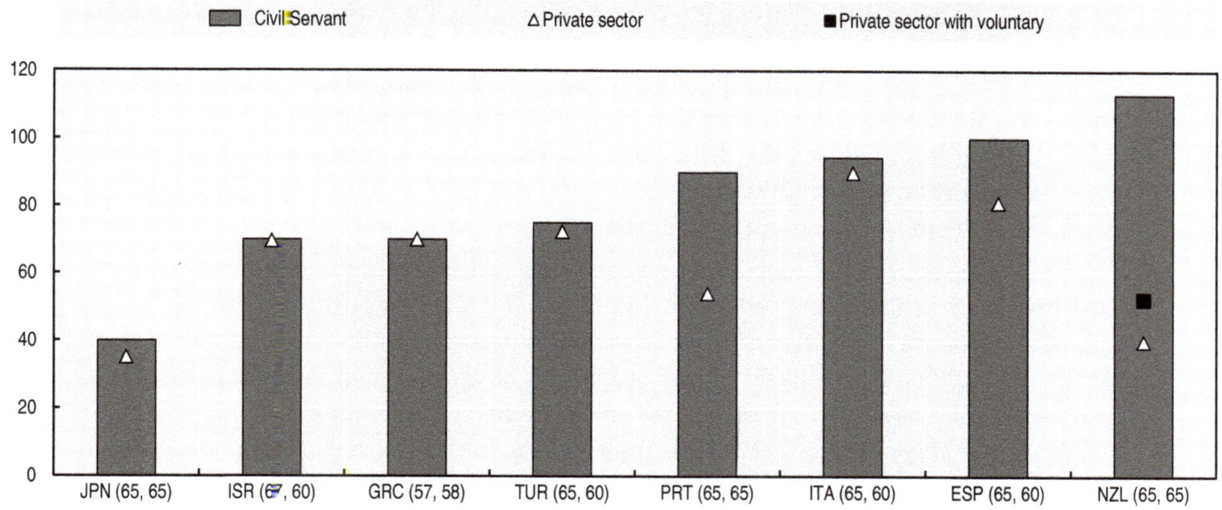

Note: Retirement ages are given in brackets, with private sector first.

StatLink http://dx.doi.org/10.1787/888933426827

Although new entrants into the civil service may no longer be covered by a separate pension scheme, the old system still continues to function as reforms have often only occurred in the last 20 years (first column of Table 6.1). The projected replacement rates for the last cohorts covered by the unreformed system are presented in Figure 6.3. Not all of these reforms have resulted in the closure of the separate civil service scheme, but have rather just modified the rules for new entrants.

The civil service replacement rate is higher than for the private sector in all eight countries except Greece. This reflects the higher accrual rates as in Spain, for example, the replacement rate reaches 100% after only 35 years of contributions (though retirement is only possible from age 60), compared to just over 80% in the private sector with retirement at age 65. In New Zealand it is also possible for civil servants to retire at age 60 with their full occupational pension giving a replacement rate of 60% for a 40-year career. However, they are not eligible for the basic pension until age 65, so by continuing to work for the additional five-year period (with the accrual rate in the civil service scheme increasing benefit by 0.002 percentage points for each additional month), the final replacement rate goes well beyond 100%. Although differences in replacement rates are minimal in Israel, Italy and Turkey, civil servants can retire on full pensions much earlier (5 years in Israel and Italy and 7 years in Turkey) than private sector workers.

Discussion

It is often argued that higher pensions for civil servants represent a form of deferred compensation for lower wages. The relationship between public- and private sector wages is not consistent across countries. According to one recent study (Limo et al, 2011) whilst public sector wages were higher than those in the private sector the gap was reduced during the 1970s and was either eliminated or reversed in the Nordic countries. During the 1980s and early 1990s, the gap remained relatively steady. However, since then there has not been a consistent pattern across the 18 OECD countries included in the study. Whereas wages for private sector workers in Finland and Norway were generally around 20% higher than for public sector workers during the 1990s and early 2000s, the reverse was true for many Southern European countries, where public sector wages were between 30% and 50% higher over the same time period. On average across the Euro area public sector wages were around 25% higher than those in the private sector in the early 2000s. However, outside Europe there is also considerable variation with average public sector wages in Canada and the United States being 90% and 110%, respectively, of those in the private sector. For the United States the differences appear to be more widespread for federal employees (around 40% higher) than for state and local public sector workers (no discernible difference) (Bewerunge and Rosen, 2012).

The studies above only consider the wage levels across the entire sector, without any individual controls distorting the picture as the characteristics of the workforces in the public and private sectors differ. The public sector, for example, employs a disproportionate share of graduates but also has a higher proportion of women than in the private sector. Contrary to the previous figures quoted for Canada, it has been shown that federal employees have wages around 13% higher than those in the private sector, after adjusting for differences in employment mix, age and educational attainment (Mallett, 2015). All other sectors of the public service have higher wage levels in Canada but they are not as high as for federal employees. When accounting for the value of future pensions as well as the more favourable working hours then the benefit for federal employees is now 33%, with most other sectors around 20% higher than their private sector equivalents. Whilst the relative level of public sector wages has decreased over the last few decades they still remain around 10-20% higher in many countries. However, there is evidence that highly educated public sector employees are more likely to be affected by a compressed wage distribution compared to their private sector counterparts (Palacios and Whitehouse, 2006).

More importantly, even if wages were lower in the public sector and higher pensions were to represent compensation in the form of deferred wages, this compensation structure would have serious weaknesses. What could justify the implied opacity and its negative impact on labour mobility? One explanation for the deferred compensation setting is the political temptation arising from such a structure being initially less costly, and thus having short- to medium-term gains offset by long-term costs. Another reason could be to attract workers in the civil service. But if pensions act just as a corrective device for lower wages, this setting can hardly attract anyone. And if higher pensions are meant to be attractive on top of similar wages then: a) why not instead offering higher wages?; and b) why in the first place aiming to attract workers in the public sector by depleting the workforce in the private sector at a cost for the public purse?

OECD (2014b) also shows that some countries need to find a better alignment between public- and private sector pensions. In addition to having different rules to calculate PAYG pension benefits for public- and private sector employees, in some countries, public sector workers tend to have better access to private pension plans. There may therefore be room to reform pension systems in certain OECD countries to allow all workers the same chance to have an adequate retirement income.

6.5. Financial commitment

Government, public agencies and other public sector employers are responsible for the pensions of their workers, irrespective of whether countries have separate systems for civil servants. If the civil service scheme is separate and contributions are heavily sourced from employers rather than from employees, this commitment is more significant. In general these schemes are financed on a pay-as-you-go framework in that the current workers are financing the pensions of current retirees, with the difference being met by the government. As an employer the government may need to raise taxes to finance its share of pension contributions in the face of growing pension liabilities. The size of the government employed workforce is an important parameter in that respect (Figure 6.4). In Germany, for example, the overwhelming majority of civil servants' pensions are paid directly out of the state budget. Only the local and church civil servants, accounting for less than 10% of all German civil servants, are covered by special pension institutions, to which the employers pay contributions.

Figure 6.4. **Public sector employment as a percentage of total employment, 2013**

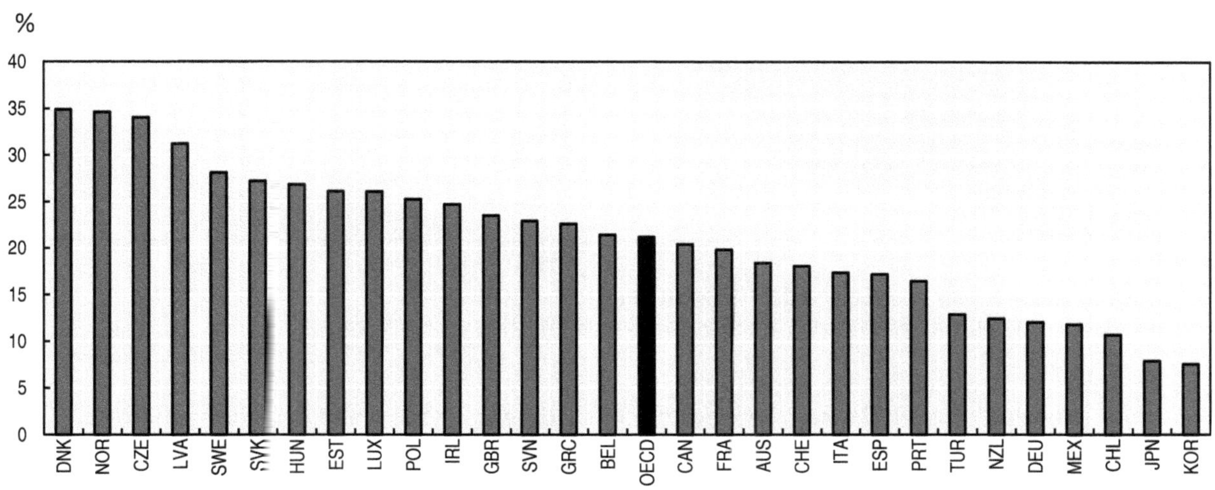

Note: Data for Austria, Finland, Iceland, Israel, Korea, the Netherlands and the United States are not available. Data for Czech Republic and New Zealand are expressed in full-time equivalents (FTEs). Data for Australia, Greece, Hungary, Slovenia and Spain are for 2012. Data for Denmark, Luxembourg, New Zealand and Turkey are for 2011. Data for the Czech Republic is for 2009. Data for Germany is for 2015 and is sourced from "Statistisches Bundesamt: Fachserie 14 Reihe 6".

Public sector employment covers all employment of general government sector as defined in the System of National Accounts (SNA) plus employment of public corporations.

Source: OECD (2015), *Government at a Glance 2015*.

StatLink http://dx.doi.org/10.1787/888933426833

The size of public sector employment, of which civil servants are a subset, varies significantly among OECD countries. Some Nordic countries (Denmark, Norway and Sweden) and Latvia report high public sector employment levels reaching near or over 30% of total employment, though the majority of these employees are not employed in the central government. On the other hand, OECD countries from Asia and Latin America rely less on public sector employees. Only around 8% of Japan's and Korea's total employment is made up of public sector employment, while about one in 10 workers in Chile and Mexico are employed by the public sector.

There has been relatively little change in the share of public sector employment over the last 20 years (OECD, 2009a). Therefore, the considerable variation in government workforces across countries is partly related to that of pension spending (as a % of GDP) associated with former civil servant retirees shown in Figure 6.5. Japan and Korea, having the smallest percentages of government employment also have amongst the lowest expenditure on civil servant pensions, with Korea still maintaining a separate scheme and Japan only unifying the rules for new employees from 2015. Moreover, the particularly low pension spending in Korea reflects the fact that the funded pension scheme was only introduced in 1960 and many retired civil servants have not had sufficient time to contribute for a full pension.

Figure 6.5. **Expenditure on pension schemes specific to civil servants as a % of GDP, 2013**

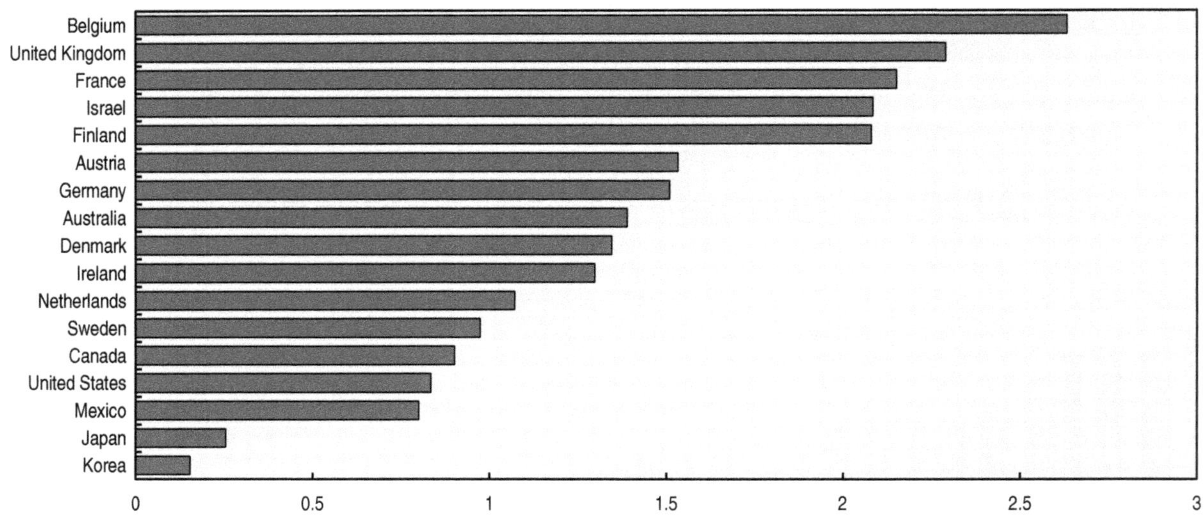

Note: Figures for France include the military and for the Netherlands include teachers
Source: OECD *Social Expenditure Database*; Austria: Budgetbericht 2016; Mexico: National estimates.

StatLink http://dx.doi.org/10.1787/888933426848

However, the relationship between public sector employment and pension spending is not always self-evident. For example, Belgium and Canada have very similar levels of government employment, at 21% and 20% of total employment respectively in 2013, but have considerably different levels of spending. Belgium spends 2.6% of GDP on civil service pensions, whereas Canada only spends 0.9% of GDP. The civil service pension in Belgium is entirely separate, and the benefit can be as high as 75% of previous earnings for a full career worker. In Canada the 0.9% represents only the civil service specific pension, but retired civil servants also receive the mandatory basic components. Similarly, in both Denmark and Sweden the level of benefit that is specific to civil servants is low, while they are covered by the large basic components. Therefore, government expenditure appears as low in Figure 6.6 even though there is a history of high levels of government employment.

Spending is also high in both France and the United Kingdom, at 2.2% and 2.3% of GDP, respectively. As with Belgium the pension system for France is entirely separate from that for private sector workers. In France, to balance the civil servant scheme the employer contribution rate paid by the government increased from the already high level of 49% in the late 1990s to 74% in 2014 (COR, 2015). This high contribution rate might reflect at least in part a legacy of past commitments benefiting current civil servant retirees, as Figure 6.2 above shows that, for central-government employees at least, pension benefit prospects are about 16% more advantageous, which does not justify such a high contribution rate from the employer. In the United Kingdom although the government workforce is eligible to the state pension, the earnings-related component for civil servants differs entirely from that in the private sector. As the civil servant contribution is quite low (4.6%-8.05%), and the accrual rate for current retirees is quite high (1.25-2.32% depending on the scheme), the benefit is primarily financed by government payments as the employer. So a high proportion of the overall financial commitment of 2.3% of GDP has to be financed from general revenues.

A larger share of the public sector workforce is nearer to retirement than in the private sector in many OECD countries (Figure 6.6). The number of civil servant retirees is therefore likely to continue increasing faster over the next few years. With these retirees being replaced by new employees either covered under a different scheme and/or at lower earnings levels given the age structure of public wages, the employee contribution levels might decline, potentially placing more pressure on the government purse.

Figure 6.6. **Share of employees 50 years or older in central government and total labour force (2009)**

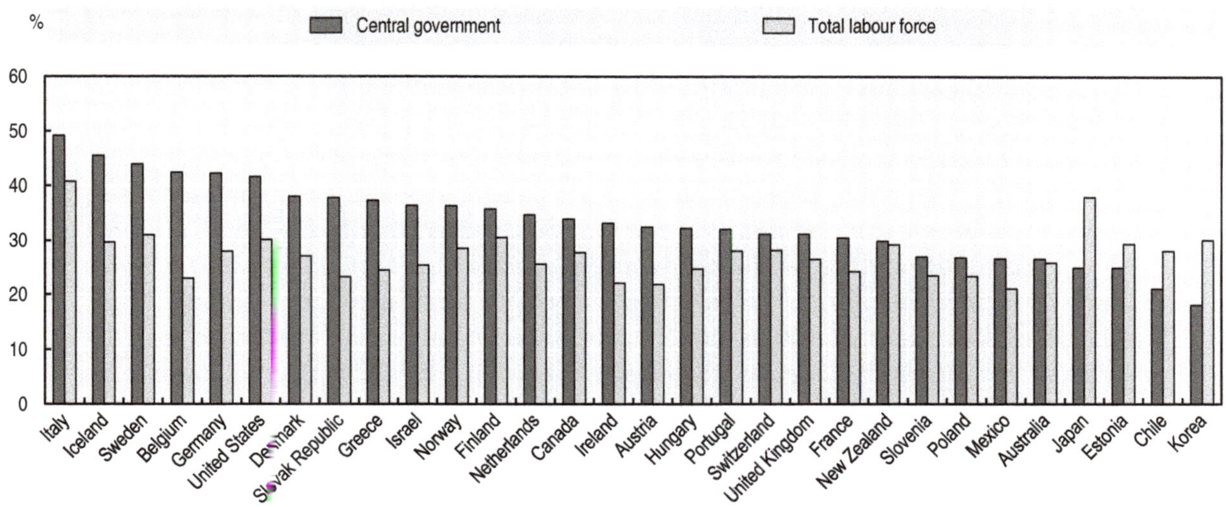

Source: *OECD 2010 Strategic Human Resources Management in Government Survey* and *OECD Labour Force Statistics Database*.

StatLink http://dx.doi.org/10.1787/888933426852

Recent events have affected the employment structure in the public sector in a number of countries beyond what is shown in the chart. Many countries have been heavily affected by the economic crisis at the end of the last decade and have taken action to try and ease the financial burden of government employment, through a number of different measures. Recruitment freezes have been put in place, as in Ireland, which, whilst reducing the overall size of the government workforce because of retirement and natural wastage, will also increase the average age of the workforce, which might create pressure on the pension accounts. In Greece there have not only been substantial pay cuts and reductions in pension entitlements but also a high level of early retirement from the public sector as a whole, removing many of the older workers within a short period, which would reduce the proportion of over 50s.

Of the 30 OECD countries for which data are available, only four have a lower proportion of government workers aged 50 and above in comparison to the total labour force, namely Chile, Estonia, Japan and Korea. Of these Estonia and Japan are both at around 25% with Chile and Korea around 20%, whereas the total workforce is at 38% in

Japan and around 30% in the other countries. By comparison nearly 50% of the central government workforce in Italy is aged at least 50 years, i.e. 8 percentage points higher than for the total labour force. Five OECD countries (Belgium, Germany, Iceland, Italy and Sweden) have a share of 50+ in central government employees above 40%. This represents nearly twice the rate for the total workforce in Belgium, and a higher rate of around 15 percentage points in both Iceland and Germany, suggesting that pension expenditure is likely to remain tilted upward in the foreseeable future. In total the proportion of the central government workforce aged 50 or above is more than 10 percentage points higher than that of the total labour force in 11 countries, whilst the OECD average gap is 6.1 percentage points.

The financial commitments now faced by many governments for public sector pensions as a whole are the result of a legacy of underfunding or an insufficient building up of reserves which has accumulated over time. Beyond France discussed above, several countries including the United Kingdom and the United States face severe financial pressures because of underfunding in both civil-service and more generally public sector pension funds. For example, in the United States about 90 per cent of state and local employee retirement funds would be underfunded, with a total funding gap of roughly USD 1.2 trillion (McKinsey Global Institute, 2016). If investment returns continue to fall this underfunding gap might increase as promises will be difficult to fulfil, unless contributions are raised or pension promises are reduced. Some cities and states might also face shortfalls. In Chicago, for example, to ease the USD 20 billion deficits in public-worker pension plans, future pensions were to be reduced. However this was ruled as illegal by the Illinois Supreme Court in March 2016 and the pension funds are projected to run out of money within 12 years (Chicago Tribune, March 2016). Within Europe many of the funds are financed through taxes, rather than investment returns, as they are pay-as-you-go rather than pre-funded as in the United States. However, there are still substantial pension liabilities that will have to be addressed. For example, in the United Kingdom the unfunded public sector pension schemes have a net liability of GBP 1.37 trillion, according to official figures from the National Audit Office, representing about 75% of GDP. Local government funded DB pension schemes (LGPS) have been classified as unsustainable (Johnson, 2015) and have been estimated to have gross liabilities of around GBP 340 billion (Whole of Government Accounts, 2016), though assets cover around two-thirds of the total. Some countries have however taken steps to help address this issue. For example, in Germany, since 1999, 0.2 percentage points of every salary increase has been diverted to a special pension fund.

6.6. Key findings and policy implications

Key findings

- Recent reforms have brought the pension systems of many public sector workers into line with those of the private sector; only Belgium, France, Germany and Korea maintain entirely separate schemes.
- Twenty years ago, 11 additional OECD countries had separate schemes for civil servants, with Greece, Japan and Spain having only aligned the schemes in the past 5 years. The majority of workers, however, will still be covered under the old schemes in these countries as the new rules for civil servants are applied only gradually, creating a legacy cost that will last for many decades to come. Only nine OECD countries have had one unified pension for all workers over the last 35 years.

- The vesting period for eligibility to a civil service pension range from a high of 25 years in Mexico to at most one year in 10 OECD countries. In 2015, Korea reduced the period from 20 to 10 years while France is at 15 years, all of which can impede mobility between sectors. Mobility in Germany is also restricted, in addition to the five-year vesting period, by a drop in pension rights for many government workers who move to the private sector.
- Future pension promises, measured in terms of replacement rates for mandatory schemes, in the four countries maintaining separate schemes are estimated to average 20 percentage points higher for full-career average earners in the civil service than in the private sector, and are nearly twice as high in Germany for the mandatory components.
- The difference is greater in those countries which make additional top-up payments to civil servants within an otherwise integrated framework, particularly in Canada, the United States and the United Kingdom, with differences of 32, 52 and 84 percentage points, respectively. The gap is also large in Iceland, Ireland, Mexico and Norway. It should be noted, however, that in these countries private sector workers might be covered by voluntary schemes. For those opting for voluntary pensions the gap is reduced to only 2 percentage points for Canada and 19 percentage points for the United States, but remains over 50 percentage points for the United Kingdom, while it becomes even negative in Ireland.
- Retirement ages for new or recently employed civil servants are now in line with those of private sector workers as a result of reforms over the last 20 years. Newly employed civil servants retire at the same age as private sector workers to be eligible for full benefits. However civil servants employed before the reforms can still retire at a much earlier age than their newer colleagues, at five years earlier in Italy, Spain and Turkey and seven years earlier in Israel.

Policy implications

Many of the rationales for the original civil service pension arrangements are less relevant now that national pension systems are in place. Pension schemes were often part of broader reforms of the civil service to ensure professionalism and independence of employees from outside influence. They were also designed to enhance the appeal of working for the civil service, but to be effective such an appeal is, directly or indirectly, costly. A career in the civil service was considered a job for life; in the absence of mobility civil service pensions were therefore best organised in a standalone system.

Moreover, restraining labour mobility across sectors, e.g. through vested periods or limited portability, is inefficient. It introduces rigidities in how individuals can manage their career and restricts their capacity to adapt flexibly to sectoral shifts and new employment opportunities. The evidence on the extent of mobility is somewhat limited, but data from several countries show that despite policy-driven obstacles few retiring public sector workers have spent all or nearly all of their careers in a single scheme (OECD, 2014a). It is therefore important to remove the remaining implied restrictions to labour mobility across the public and private sector.

An integrated framework to cover all workers identically might yield benefits in various dimensions:

- equity
- transparency

- choice of labour mobility
- portability
- administrative costs
- public finance

On the equity side, there is the issue of comparability of benefits between civil service and private sector retirement income provisions. General taxation typically finances much of civil servants pensions, and comparability of pension packages between them is in constant flux. Many national pension schemes which cover private sector workers have seen significant reforms in the past two decades. Furthermore, there has been much change to private pensions for private sector workers in most of the countries where coverage of these is broad. In Canada, Ireland, Sweden, the United Kingdom and the United States, for example, there is a pronounced trend away from DB to DC provision. Granting specific treatment is less suitable today in the world of "revolving doors" between the civil service and the private sector; it is difficult to argue that civil servants, or more widely public sector workers require higher income replacement in retirement (or different consumption smoothing over the lifecycle) than their counterparts in the private sector.

On the efficiency side, administrative issues can be important. There are significant economies of scale in managing unified pension systems: in contribution collection, record-keeping and benefit payment, for example. Dual arrangements can entail significant duplication and wasted administrative expense. Yet, some countries maintain a very fragmented provision between different groups of public sector workers. The complexity of pension arrangements in public and private sectors makes it very difficult for individuals to compare the attractiveness of different jobs. Through greater transparency, a common pension scheme would make such choices easier and facilitate labour mobility.

If a common scheme is not deemed possible in terms of political economy then other possibilities include:

- Improve portability between sectors by shortening vesting periods, whilst eliminating penalties to preserve pension rights if workers leave early.
- Unify indexation procedures so that any discrepancy in pension immediately upon retirement is not exacerbated as the pensioner ages. Indexation differences have been reduced substantially, and still apply in Turkey only.
- As civil servants tend to pay lower personal contributions in relation to the benefit level there is an implied bias in the systems towards them. This is offset by government's contributions via general taxation in a way that often lacks transparency on top of the financial cost. Countries should consider aligning the so-called benefit ratio of employees' contribution to accrual rate to what prevails in the private sector as well as improving transparency on the government contributions.

Despite the steady convergence, there is still considerable disparity in the rules that apply to the different sectors. There is obviously a trade-off between the pace of unifying rules and the overall benefit generated by the measures. While reforms within the private sector typically have a phase-in period, with older workers less affected, the reforms within the public sector often have an overly long transition as current public sector workers usually continue under the old system, with only new employees affected, which could lead to a phase-in period of up to 50 years. The political acceptance of such reforms is facilitated, but its benefits are postponed and diluted. It is therefore important to reach a good compromise between an abrupt change preventing individuals to adapt efficiently their behaviour and a long transition overly diluting its return.

Although not covered in this chapter, many countries have different schemes for specific public sector careers, such as police, firefighters, teachers or local government employees. These schemes not only differ from those of private sector workers but also from that of civil servants. This increases the level of fragmentation, confusion and mistrust within the systems and so at least all public sector workers should be under one unified scheme. To facilitate the change for so-called arduous professions, professional training would need to be provided throughout the career to ensure that workers can find alternative employment when they are deemed unfit to continue in their previous occupation.

References

Bewerunge, P. and H.S. Rosen (2012), "Wages, Pensions, and Public-Private Sector Compensation Differentials", *Griswold Center for Economic Policy Studies Working Paper* No. 227.

Chicago Tribune (2016), *Illinois Supreme Court ruling forces city to find new fix for 2 pension funds.*

Johnson, M. (2015), *The LGPS: Unsustainable, Pointmaker*, Centre for Policy Studies.

La lettre du COR N° 12 – septembre 2015.

Lamo, A., J.J. Pérez and L. Schuknecht (2012), "Public or Private Sector Wage Leadership? An International Perspective*", *The Scandinavian Journal of Economics*, 114: 228-244, *http://dx.doi.org/10.1111/j.1467-9442.2011.01665.x.*

Mallet, T. (2015), *Wage Watch – A Comparison of Public sector and Private sector Salaries and Benefits*, Canadian Federation of Independent Business.

McKinsey Global Institute (2016), *Diminishing Returns: Why investors may need to lower their expectations.*

OECD (2007), *Pensions at a Glance 2007: Public Policies across OECD Countries*, OECD Publishing, Paris, *http://dx.doi.org/10.1787/pension_glance-2007-en.*

OECD (2009), *Pensions at a Glance 2009: Retirement-Income Systems in OECD Countries*, OECD Publishing, Paris, *http://dx.doi.org/10.1787/pension_glance-2009-en.*

OECD (2013), *Pensions at a Glance 2013: OECD and G20 Indicators*, OECD Publishing, *http://dx.doi.org/10.1787/pension_glance-2013-en.*

OECD (2014a), *OECD Reviews of Pensions Systems: Ireland*, OECD Publishing, *http://dx.doi.org/10.1787/9789264208834-en.*

OECD (2014b), OECD Pensions Outlook 2014, OECD Publishing, *http://dx.doi.org/10.1787/9789264222687-en.*

OECD (2015), *Pensions at a Glance 2015: OECD and G20 indicators*, OECD Publishing, Paris, *http://dx.doi.org/10.1787/pension_glance-2015-en.*

Rauh, J.D. (2016), *Hidden Debt, Hidden Deficits: How Pension Promises are Consuming State and Local Budgets*, Hoover Institution Essay.

Whole of Government Accounts (2016), year ended 31 March 2015, HM Treasury.

ANNEX 6.A1

Civil service pension rules

Australia	Current position	Australian Government employees receive their superannuation benefits under defined benefit schemes or accumulation (defined contribution) schemes, depending on the employer and the rules of the fund. The majority of defined benefit schemes are closed to new members. There are several separate defined contribution schemes established for Australian Government employees. Employer contributions made to these schemes (both defined benefit and accumulation schemes) meet the employers' obligations for the superannuation guarantee where the rate contributed is at least the current minimum SG rate of 9.5% of salaries. Public sector funds include superannuation schemes established by a Commonwealth, State or Territory law (known as exempt public sector superannuation schemes).While some of the public sector (or civil service) schemes are sovereign guaranteed, they can still choose to register with the regulator, the Australian Prudential Regulation Authority (APRA), and many schemes are registered. This does not make them part of APRA's regulated population. Note that a number of APRA-regulated funds are former public sector funds that chose to bring themselves within APRA's regulatory framework.Public sector schemes, including exempt public sector superannuation schemes, often have complex benefit structures and are publicly accountable for their administrative effectiveness and efficacy and performance. They are controlled by legislative and other arrangements. Superannuation funds run by the States and Territories are controlled by legislative and other arrangements under the relevant State and Territory law and, even if not directly regulated by APRA, are subject to substantial prudential controls imposed by the States and Territories.
	Recent reforms	The Commonwealth Superannuation Scheme (CSS) was closed to new members in 1990. It was a partially funded hybrid defined benefit (DB) and defined contribution (DC) scheme with member contributions of 0% or 5% of superannuation salary for the DB part. No ceiling applied to the DC contributions. The CPI indexed retirement pension is based on age at retirement, final superannuation salary and length of contributory membership. The Public Sector Superannuation Scheme (PSS) started in 1990. It is a partially funded DB scheme. Employees can make member contributions of between 2% and 10% of superannuation salary or choose not to contribute at all. Employer contributions accrue depending on the level of individual member contributions. The retirement benefit is based on an accrued benefit multiple times final average superannuation salary. The benefit can be taken as a lump sum, a CPI indexed pension or combination of lump sum and CPI indexed pension. The accrued benefit multiple reflects the member's rate of member contributions and years of contributory membership. Final average salary is the average of the last three years of superannuation salaries. The PSS was closed to new members in 2005. The Public Sector Superannuation accumulation plan (PSSap) commenced in 2005. New Commonwealth Government employees have a choice of funds with PSSap being the default where they do not make a choice. PSSap is a fully funded DC or accumulation scheme with employer contributions of 15.4% of superannuation salary, much higher than the Superannuation Guarantee at 9.5%. Member contributions are optional. Retirement benefits take the form of a lump sum. State and Territory schemes may be either defined benefit or accumulation schemes depending on the employer and the rules of the fund. In general, in Australia there has been a movement away from defined benefit schemes to accumulation schemes due to the costs associated with defined benefit schemes.
Austria	Current position	Covered by the earnings-related scheme for private sector employees with an additional supplementary defined contribution scheme. The so-called "second pillar of pension" was introduced in 2009 and is in transition so the benefits are currently very low. It is estimated that in future about 5-10% of total pension income will come from the funded system. The employer pays 0.75% of gross wages into the system. Employee contributions are voluntary but cannot exceed EUR 1000 annually.
	Recent reforms	Civil servants had a separate system until 2004, since when new employees were fully enrolled in the earnings-related scheme for private sector employees. Civil servants given tenured status as from 1 January 2005 or born on or after 1 January 1976 are also fully covered under the private sector scheme whilst those aged 50 or under in January 2005 are covered by transitional rules.

Belgium	Current position	Civil servants have their own separate system. There are no personal contributions for the old-age retirement pension; however civil servants pay 7.5% of earnings for survivors' pensions. The retirement pension is calculated as: the average wage over the last 10 years of the career x (number of career years (max 45) / 60). The pension cannot amount to over 75% of the wage which has served as a basis of the calculation.
	Recent reforms	Alignment of the early retirement conditions to those of the private sector, with a gradual elimination of the "diploma bonification"for those civil servants where it was applicable (functions for which a specific degree condition is applicable). This means that for the calculation of the seniority condition for those applying for early retirement, the assimilation of the study period to years worked will be gradually abolished (by 6 months a year starting in 2016). (By 2029 this "bonification" will be fully abolished for all durations of studies). Early retirement conditions (age and seniority) are increasing in the same way as for the private sector by 2019 to age 63, with 42 years of seniority (or 61 with 43 years of seniority or 60 with 44 years of seniority). Legal retirement age will increase to 66 by 2025 and 67 by 2030 (as for private sector). This remains in principle a system of mandatory retirement.
Canada	Current position	Covered by national schemes (the universal basic pension, means-tested "guaranteed income supplement" and the earnings-related "Canada Pension Plan/Québec Pension Plan"). Nearly 100% of public sector employees are members of an occupational plan; benefits are integrated with CPP/QPP by offering a lower accrual rate on pay up to CPP/QPP ceiling.
	Recent reforms	Public Service Pension Fund created 1 April 2000. Employee contributions are no longer tied to Canada Pension Plan (CPP) and Quebec Pension Plan (QPP). 2005: Treasury announced increases in employee contributions starting January 2006. In 2006, the employee contribution rate was increased to 4.3 per cent on salary up to the year's maximum pensionable earnings (YMPE) under the CPP or QPP and 7.8 per cent on salary over the YMPE, up from 4.0 per cent and 7.5 per cent respectively in 2005. 2012: Contribution rates for all active and future civil service pension plan members were increased in January 2013 with the objective of reaching a more balanced cost-sharing ratio for employer/employee contribution of 50:50 over time. Contributions increased to 9.05% below, and 11.04% above the maximum covered by the CPP/QPP in 2016. For new employees the rates are 7.86% and 9.39%. The age at which a new employee who began participating in the public-service pension plan on or after 1 January 2013 can receive an unreduced pension benefit was increased from age 60 to 65 with at least 2 years of service and from 55 to 60 with 30 years.
Chile	Current position	Covered by the national schemes.
	Recent reforms	Public sector workers had a separate scheme until 1981.
Czech Republic	Current position	The national system has always covered all workers from both the public and private sectors.
	Recent reforms	
Denmark	Current position	Covered by the basic and ATP pensions as well as the means-tested component but with a separate occupational scheme for public sector employees. This scheme has a replacement rate of 57% with at least 37 years of contribution, with retirement at age 62.
	Recent reforms	
Estonia	Current position	The national system has always covered all workers from both the public and private sectors.
	Recent reforms	
Finland	Current position	From the beginning of 2017 the benefit rules of all public sector employees (including the Evangelical Lutheran Church of Finland) are covered by the same occupational pension scheme (JuEL). However, from the financing perspective, the schemes remain separate for the central government, the local government and the church employees and employers. The benefit rules are effectively the same as for mandatory occupational pensions for private sector workers (provided by four separate schemes for different sectors).
	Recent reforms	Public sector employees who started before 1992 have an effective accrual rate of 2.2% and maximum replacement rate of 66%. From the beginning of 2005 new accruing pension rights have effectively been the same for all mandatory occupational pension schemes, public sector or private sector. At the moment yearly accrual is calculated from indexed annual earnings at an accrual rate of 1.5% for ages less than 53, 1.9% for ages between 53 and 62, and 4.5% thereafter. From the beginning of 2017, the accrual rate is 1.5% for all ages except for those between 53 and 62, for whom the accrual rate will be 1.7% until the end of 2025. The normal pensionable age will start to rise from 63 in 2017 to 65 in 2025, and thereafter the normal pensionable age is linked to life expectancy development. Those who delay their retirement after the normal pensionable age receive an increase of 0.4% to their pension for every month of deferred retirement. This replaces the so called super accrual rate of 4.5% for ages 63 and up which was effective between 2005 and 2016.

France	Current position	The civil service pension has two components: a base component (the SRE for civil servants employed by the central government and the CNRACL for civil servants employed by local authorities) and an additional one (the RAFP).The base pension is computed as 75% of the last civil servant salary without taking into account bonuses (on average bonuses are equivalent to 20% of the total remuneration). The RAFP is a points system. Points are accumulated only on the part of the salary not eligible for the base component (bonuses). Civil servants cannot retire before 62 years old (some of them can have derogations – long contribution period, specific employment categories, etc.). To get a full pension a civil servant needs to justify a contribution period which depends on their generation (43 years for those born after 1973). The pension rate is reduced by 1.25% for each missing quarter (or 5% for each missing year). In all cases, at the age of 67 a civil servant can receive a full pension. Some public sector employees (contractuels) are in the national scheme.
	Recent reforms	The contribution period required to get a full pension was increased in 2014 for future generations. Moreover contributions were increased. Employee contributions are set to increase to reach 11.1% as of 1 January 2020 in both SRE and CNRACL (as against 9.54% in 2015). The employer contributions for civil servants affiliated to the CNRACL scheme (civil servants not employed directly by the government but by local authorities) are set to increase to reach 30.65% as of 1 January 2017 (as against 30.50% in 2015).
Germany	Current position	Civil servants' pensions are covered by an entirely separate system. Due to the German federalism each public employer is responsible for the payment of the pensions to their civil servants. The federal civil servants' pension scheme (which includes federal judges and military servants) and the civil servants' pension schemes of other public employers – such as the Länder – are based on the same system. Certain benefits may differ. The federal civil servants' pensions not only cover the first pillar (i.e. the statutory pension scheme) but also cover the second pillar, i.e. the supplementary occupational pensions. By contrast, the general public pensions only cover the first pillar. The benefits of the supplementary occupational pensions in the private sector vary significantly depending on the employer and the chosen scheme. According to the federal civil servants' pensions scheme retirement benefits are calculated by multiplying the pensionable remuneration by the pension rate. The amount of the pensionable remuneration depends on the remuneration level in the two years preceding retirement excluding bonuses and allowances. The pension rate depends on the length of service; the maximum rate is 71.75% after 40 years in the federal civil, judicial or military service. The pension rate increases by 1.79375% with each year of service. The average pension rate is 68% at the federal level.
	Recent reforms	The pension age is increasing from 65 to 67 by 2029, in line with the changes in the private sector. To partly capitalise the obligations, since 1999, 0.2 percentage points of every salary increase have been injected into a special pension fund managed by the federal bank (Deutsche Bundesbank). According to current draft legislation the financial means of the fund will be used to cover parts of the federal government's pension expenditures, starting in 2032. In addition, in 2007 a second pension fund has been established for all federal civil servants, federal judges and military servants hired since 1 January 2007. This fund is also managed by the federal bank (Bundesbank). Starting in 2020, the pensions for this group of civil servants will to a considerable extent be provided from the fund's resources. For this purpose, their employers regularly transfer money (a certain percentage of their pensionable remunerations) to the fund, reflecting the future costs of the pensions for those servants and judges. Additionally, some German regions (the Länder of Baden-Württemberg, Bremen, Hamburg, Hessen, Niedersachsen and Sachsen) as well as the Federal State have introduced a so-called "Altersgeld". "Altersgeld" means that in spite of a job-change into the private sector, the civil servant maintains their (special) pension claims and hence do not suffer any inconvenience due to the job-change.
Greece	Current position	Covered by the national schemes as for private sector workers.
	Recent reforms	Prior to 2011 civil servants were covered by a separate system, since when new employees are covered by the national schemes. Civil servants employed prior to 1992 could retire at age 58 after 35 years of contributions and receive a pension equivalent to 80% of final salary. After this the replacement rate was reduced to 70%.
Hungary	Current position	The national system has always covered all workers from both the public and private sectors.
	Recent reforms	
Iceland	Current position	Covered by the national scheme (basic pension and means-tested supplementary pension) with top-up defined contribution occupational scheme for public sector workers. The public sector component has a higher contribution from employers, normally 12% rather than 8% in the private sector.
	Recent reforms	Prior to the 1998 reform, pensions accrued at 2% of final salary per year and civil servants could retire at either age 65 or from age 60 under the so-called 95 year rule (age of member + total years of contribution). The 1998 reform eliminated the 95-year rule and reduced the accrual to 1.9% of full salary at time of payment. It also established an independent funded pension fund for new civil servants (defined contribution) to run parallel to the old underfunded system.

Ireland	Current position	Covered by the national scheme (universal basic pension); top-up defined-benefit occupational scheme for public sector workers. The new single scheme was introduced from 1 January 2013, with an accrual of 0.58% below 3.74 times the State Pension contributory (SPC) level and 1.25% above with a lump sum accrual of 3.75%.
	Recent reforms	Prior to 6th April 1995 public sector workers had an entirely separate system. The pension accrued at 1.25% per year to a maximum of 50% (40 years) with a gratuity of 3.75% of final salary per year to a maximum of 1.5 times final salary. The pension entitlement (but not the gratuity) of those who joined the public service after 6th April 1995 is integrated with their State Pension entitlement so that their total pension is made up partly by a public-service pension and the balance by their State Pension. The integration is accomplished by providing a lower rate of pension accrual, 1/200th instead of 1/80th, for each year of reckonable service, for that part of pensionable remuneration which falls below 3.333333 x the maximum annual rate of State Pension (Contributory) payable to a single person without dependants. Employees recruited before 1st April 2004 generally have a minimum retirement age of 60 and a maximum of 65; those recruited after 1st April 2004 generally have a minimum retirement age of 65 but no maximum.
Israel	Current position	Covered by the national scheme (universal insurance) and by the mandatory defined contribution scheme as with private sector workers.
	Recent reforms	Separate scheme covering all public sector workers was closed to new members in 2002. The accrual rate was 2% up to a maximum replacement rate of 70%. Prior to 2005 employees did not pay contributions, since when they have paid 2%.
Italy	Current position	Covered by the national scheme (notional defined contribution).
	Recent reforms	Separate scheme covering civil servants was closed to new members from 1995 and merged for old employees from 2008. The old system had a replacement rate of 94.4% for 40 years of contribution.
Japan	Current position	Covered by the national scheme (universal flat-rate and earnings-related scheme).
	Recent reforms	Before October 2015 there was an additional lump-sum retirement allowance within the earnings-related pension. This meant that government employees received 20% more than those in the private sector. However in October 2015 the government employees system was merged into that of the private sector. From 1986 the civil service pension was changed from final salary to the same calculation process as for the private sector.
Korea	Current position	Covered by the defined benefit government employees' pension scheme.
	Recent reforms	1995: Increase in employee and employer contributions from 3.6% to 4.2%. Legislate retirement at age 60 for new entrants. 2000: Further increase in contributions to 5.5%. Increase in retirement age for those hired prior to 1996 from 50 in 2001 to age 60 by 2021. Pensions are now calculated using final 3 years' salary rather than final salary. Indexation changed from wages to mixture of CPI and wages. 2009: Increase contributions to 7%. Accrual rate falls from 2.1% to 1.9%. Retirement age increases to 65 for new hires. Pension calculated on career average salary. Indexation set to CPI with transition period. 2015: Pensions in payment frozen from 2016 to 2020. Contributions increasing from 7% to 9% within 5 years whilst accrual rate decreases from 1.9% to 1.7% over 20 years. Retirement age will increase to 65 for all, with an 11 year transition period. Minimum service falls from 20 years to 10 years, whilst maximum number increases from 33 years to 36 years.
Latvia	Current position	The national system has always covered all workers from both the public and private sectors.
	Recent reforms	
Luxembourg	Current position	Separate pension scheme for public sector workers. Since 1999 the public sector pension scheme is (almost) identical to the general pension scheme for private sector workers. Special transitory measures apply to public sector workers in service or retired prior to 1999. The public sector pension regime is financed by employee contribution (8%) and state budget.
	Recent reforms	The 2013 reform of the general pension scheme for the private sector also applies to public sector pensions. The old system had a maximum pension of 83.33% of final salary after 40 years of contribution.
Mexico	Current position	Public sector workers have their own separate system. Post 2007 reform new employees are covered by a defined contribution scheme, contributing 6.125% of their salary, with the government contributing 5.175% up to 10 times the minimum wage. They are also covered by the social fee, though at a different rate to private sector workers.
	Recent reforms	Prior to the 2007 reform public sector workers were covered by a defined benefit scheme, paying 50% of final salary for 15 years of contribution, increasing by 2.5 percentage points for each of the next 10 years reaching 75% after 25 years. Each subsequent year earns 5 percentage points for men reaching a maximum of 100% after 30 years. For women, years 26 and 27 gain 5 percentage points whilst 100% of final salary is paid with 28 years of contribution. Retirement ages for men and women are both increasing from 55 to 60 for those with at least 15 years of contribution but not full careers. The retirement ages for full career workers are increasing by 10 years but women can still retire earlier than men at 58 years and 60 years respectively. Those covered under the old-system were given 6-months to choose to remain or move to the new DC scheme.
Netherlands	Current position	Quasi-mandatory occupational pensions imposed by collective agreements have same rules for public- and private sector workers but formally separate schemes; All Dutch residents are covered by the national basic (first pillar) pension.
	Recent reforms	
New Zealand	Current position	Covered by the national scheme (flat-rate, universal) and by the auto-enrolment KiwiSaver plan as with private sector workers.
	Recent reforms	Government Superannuation Fund (GSF) covering all public sector workers was closed to new members in 1992 and was replaced by the Individual Retirement Plan (IRP), which subsequently closed in December 2012. The State Sector Retirement Savings Scheme (SSRSS), launched in July 2004, was a voluntary retirement savings scheme that was designed for State sector employees. Since 1 April 2008, the SSRSS has been closed to new members. KiwiSaver: Since 1 July 2007 all public sector employees have been auto-enrolled into KiwiSaver as in the private sector.

Norway	Current position	Covered by the national scheme (mix of income-tested, flat-rate and earnings-related plans) with top-up occupational pension arrangement. The retirement age is 67 with a maximum replacement rate of 66%, before adjustment for life expectancy increases, after 30 years of contributions, for those born prior to 1958. The rules for those born after 1958 have yet to be announced. As with private sector workers there are early retirement schemes (AFP) to enable retirement between age 62 and age 66.
	Recent reforms	
Poland	Current position	The national system has always covered all workers from both the public and private sectors.
	Recent reforms	
Portugal	Current position	Covered by the same national earnings-related scheme as private sector workers.
	Recent reforms	Public sector workers had a separate scheme until 2005, since when new employees are in the national scheme. Contributions are 11% (8% for retirement and 3% for survivors) for employees and 23.75% for employers. Workers can retire at age 66 years and 2 months in 2016 (as in the private sector) with at least 15 years of contributions, or age 70 with at least 5 years. The pension is the sum of 2 slices: the 1st is calculated upon the old rules (The calculation method depends on age and duration of contributions at the end of 2005, but can be up to 80% of 2005 – salary) and the 2nd is calculated according to the private workers' pension scheme rules.
Slovak Republic	Current position	The national system has always covered all workers from both the public and private sectors.
	Recent reforms	
Slovenia	Current position	The national system has always covered all workers from both the public and private sectors.
	Recent reforms	
Spain	Current position	Covered by the national scheme (earnings-related pension).
	Recent reforms	Previously covered by the national scheme (earnings-related pension) with top-up scheme for the public sector, but fully covered in the national scheme for new employees from 1 January 2011. The old system pays 100% of theoretical salary base by professional group with 35 years of contributions.
Sweden	Current position (until 31/12/2015)	Covered by the national scheme (income-tested "guarantee pension", earnings-related "income pension" and mandatory personal pensions) with a top-up scheme PA 03. Under PA 03 defined contribution credits for the two separate defined-contribution portions start accumulating at age 23, with contribution rates of 2.3 (up to 30 income base amounts) and 2.0 per cent respectively. For those with a pension basis larger than 7.5 income base amounts per year there is also a defined-benefit portion, calculated on the average of the pensionable wages in the last five years prior to retirement above 7.5 income base amounts, up to 30 income base amounts. The full benefit is available after 30 years of covered work, with proportional amounts for shorter careers. Credit toward this pension is earned starting at age 28.
	Recent reforms	The occupational pension agreement PA 03 has recently been replaced with the new occupational pension agreement PA 16. The PA 16 entered into force on 1 January 2016. The agreement is divided into two sections. Section II For employees born 1987 or earlier the conditions of PA 03 were (almost entirely) transferred into PA 16 section II. Section I For employees born in 1988 or later, the PA 16 scheme conditions imply that the retirement pension is entirely financed by defined contributions. On the part of the pensionable income that is below 7.5 income base amounts three separate defined-contribution portions exists. The contribution rates are 2.5 per cent, 2.0 per cent and 1.5 per cent respectively. On the part of the pensionable income that exceeds 7.5 income base amounts the contribution rates are 20.0 per cent, 10.0 per cent and 1.5 per cent. There is no longer a minimum age that needs to be passed in order for the accumulation of the defined contribution retirement pension to start (in PA 03 accumulation started at age 23).
Switzerland	Current position	Covered by national scheme (means-tested 'supplementary benefits', earnings-related public scheme) and the general occupational pension scheme, applicable to both the private and the public sectors.
	Recent reforms	
Turkey	Current position	Covered by the same national earnings-related scheme as in the private sector.
	Recent reforms	Public sector workers had a separate scheme until May 2008. Retirement age depends on initial service date. It ranges from 40-58 for women and 44-60 for men. Contributions rate were 16% for employees and 20% for employers (public). Income replacement rate was 75% of final salary. Additionally the replacement rate was decreased by one point if the worker's service years are less than 25 (women can retire with 20 years of service if they entered the system before 8 September 1999) and increased by one point if it is greater than 25. Contributions were paid on partial salary while benefits were paid based on the full salary. These rules are still valid for those who entered the system before 1 May 2008.

United Kingdom	Current position	Covered by the national scheme (new state pension); top-up defined-benefit occupational scheme for public sector workers.
	Recent reforms	Principal Civil Service Pension Scheme (PCSPS renamed Classic in September 2002): Retirement at age 60. Employee contribution of 1.5%. Accrual rate of 1.25%, with lump-sum of 3.75%. Not covered by private sector second tier pension (S2P). Closed to new members from 30 September 2002. Premium: Introduced 1 October 2002 to new members. Employee contribution of 3.5%. Accrual rate of 1.67%. Those opting to move from classic were credited with 0.92 years of premium for every year in classic. Maximum of 40 years of contribution up to 1 March 2008, then increased to 45 years. Scheme was closed to new member from 30 July 2007. Classic Plus: For those not opting to transfer to Premium their rights under Classic were frozen, with contributions from 1 October 2002 going to premium. Upon retirement an additional lump-sum can be taken from the premium component, but annual pension will be reduced by GBP 1 for every GBP 12 of lump-sum. Was not available to new employees. Nuvos: Introduced from 30 July 2007 to new employees with no option to move for current employees. Normal pension age is 65. Contribution remained at 3.5%. Pension based on career average earnings rather than final salary with annual accrual of 2.3% with contributions uprated in line with cost of living. Maximum replacement rate is 75% of highest salary in last 10 years uprated with cost of living. Can take a lump-sum at retirement up to 30/7 times annual pension, but pension is reduced by GBP 1 for every GBP 12 of lump-sum. Closed to new entrants from 31 March 2015. 2012 reform: Contribution rates in all schemes were increased over 3 years from 2012 to 2014. Final contributions are dependent on earnings but range from 1.5% to 6.85% for classic members and from 3.5% to 8.85% for premium, classic plus and Nuvos members for those earning under GBP 15 000 per year and those earning over GBP 60 000 per year respectively. Alpha: Started 1 April 2015 for new employees and all those at least 10 years from retirement. Previous entitlements under other schemes are preserved. Contribution rates are harmonised for all and will range from 4.6% for earnings under GBP 15 000 to 8.05% for earnings over GBP 150 000 from 2017 onwards. Retirement age will increase in line with state pension age. Annual accrual is 2.32%. Contributions are uprated annually in line with cost of living (can be negative).
United States	Current position	Covered by national scheme (earnings-related "social security") but with top-up defined contribution arrangement ("Thrift Savings Plan").
	Recent reforms	The Civil Service Retirement System (CSRS) had a contribution of 7% and was entirely separate from the basic pension but was closed to new members in 1984. Since then new employees are covered by the Federal Employees' Retirement System (FERS).

ORGANISATION FOR ECONOMIC CO-OPERATION AND DEVELOPMENT

The OECD is a unique forum where governments work together to address the economic, social and environmental challenges of globalisation. The OECD is also at the forefront of efforts to understand and to help governments respond to new developments and concerns, such as corporate governance, the information economy and the challenges of an ageing population. The Organisation provides a setting where governments can compare policy experiences, seek answers to common problems, identify good practice and work to co-ordinate domestic and international policies.

The OECD member countries are: Australia, Austria, Belgium, Canada, Chile, the Czech Republic, Denmark, Estonia, Finland, France, Germany, Greece, Hungary, Iceland, Ireland, Israel, Italy, Japan, Korea, Latvia, Luxembourg, Mexico, the Netherlands, New Zealand, Norway, Poland, Portugal, the Slovak Republic, Slovenia, Spain, Sweden, Switzerland, Turkey, the United Kingdom and the United States. The European Union takes part in the work of the OECD.

OECD Publishing disseminates widely the results of the Organisation's statistics gathering and research on economic, social and environmental issues, as well as the conventions, guidelines and standards agreed by its members.

OECD PUBLISHING, 2, rue André-Pascal, 75775 PARIS CEDEX 16
(21 2016 04 1 P) ISBN 978-92-64-26519-6 – 2016

www.ingramcontent.com/pod-product-compliance
Ingram Content Group UK Ltd.
Pitfield, Milton Keynes, MK11 3LW, UK
UKHW051502290926
15471UKWH00008B/1362

9 789264 265196